欢迎：中学汉语课本

HUANYING
An Invitation to Chinese

JIAYING HOWARD AND LANTING XU

VOLUME
3

Cheng & Tsui Company
Boston

2nd Printing, 2016

22 21 20 19 18 17 16   2 3 4 5 6 7 8 9 10

Published by
Cheng & Tsui Company, Inc.
25 West Street
Boston, MA 02111-1213 USA
Fax (617) 426-3669
www.cheng-tsui.com
"Bringing Asia to the World"™

Hardcover edition:
ISBN 978-0-88727-740-5

Paperback edition:
ISBN 978-0-88727-739-9

Library of Congress Cataloging-in-Publication Data

Howard, Jiaying.
    Huanying : an invitation to Chinese = [Huan ying : Zhong xue Han yu ke ben] / by Jiaying Howard and Lanting Xu.
        p. cm.
    Chinese and English.
    Includes index.
    Parallel title in Chinese characters.
    ISBN 978-0-88727-662-0 (v. 1) — ISBN 978-0-88727-615-6 (v. 1 : pbk.) 1. Chinese language—Textbooks for foreign
speakers—English. I. Xu, Lanting, 1963 Jan. 28- II. Title. III. Title: An invitation to Chinese. IV. Title: Huan ying :
Zhong xue Han yu ke ben.

    PL1129.E5H67 2008
    495.1'82421—dc22

                                    2008062314

Illustrations: Murray Thomas, Landong Xu, Qiguang Xu, and Augustine Liu
Photos: Peizhi Bai, Junye Bai, Lanting Xu, Jiaying Howard, Yun Zhuang, Chuan Zhuang, Xuexue Zhuang, and Jing Chai
Textbook design: Linda Robertson
Chinese text editing: Jing Wu

PUBLISHER'S NOTE

Demand for Chinese curricular materials at the secondary school level has never been greater. In response, Cheng & Tsui is pleased to offer *Huanying*—the first comprehensive secondary-school series written by experienced Chinese teachers in North American schools and based on ACTFL National Content Standards for Foreign Language Learning. Designed specifically for the North American classroom, *Huanying* offers a learner-centered communicative approach, a great variety of engaging activities, contemporary topics that appeal to secondary school students, a full-color textbook design, and additional resources that will reduce teacher preparation time and allow teachers to focus on teaching.

The Cheng & Tsui Chinese Language Series is designed to publish and widely distribute quality language learning materials created by leading instructors from around the world. We welcome readers' comments and suggestions concerning the publications in this series. Please contact the following members of our Editorial Board, in care of our Editorial Department (e-mail: **editor@cheng-tsui.com**).

- Professor Shou-hsin Teng, *Chief Editor*
  Graduate Institute of Teaching Chinese as a Second Language
  National Taiwan Normal University

- Professor Dana Scott Bourgerie
  Department of Asian and Near Eastern Languages
  Brigham Young University

- Professor Samuel Cheung
  Department of Chinese
  Chinese University of Hong Kong

- Professor Ying-che Li
  Department of East Asian Languages and Literatures
  University of Hawaii

- Professor Hong Gang Jin
  Department of East Asian Languages and Literatures
  Hamilton College

ONLINE RESOURCES

Audio Downloads

Users of this textbook have access to free, downloadable audio files that correspond to both the textbook and workbook for *Huanying* Volume 3. The sections in your textbook and workbook that have corresponding audio files are marked with an audio CD icon: ⊙. To download the audio files, you simply need to enter your product key on our website.

Instructions for Downloading Audio Files:

1. Visit the Cheng & Tsui Download Center at

   http://www.cheng-tsui.com/downloads/Huanying

2. Enter your product key.

3. Download the audio files.

4. For technical support, please contact support@cheng-tsui.com or call 1-800-554-1963.

Textbook Audio Content:

- Dialogues
- New Words

Workbook Audio Content:

- Listening Practice

COMPANIONS FOR HUANYING

The Way of Chinese Characters, 2nd Edition
The Origins of 670 Essential Words
By Jianhsin Wu, Illustrated by Chen Zheng, Chen Tian
Learn characters through a holistic approach.

Tales and Traditions, 2nd Edition *Volume 1: Fables, Myths, and Historical Figures*
Compiled by Yun Xiao, et al.
Read level-appropriate excerpts and adaptations from the Chinese folk and literary canon.

Cheng & Tsui Chinese Measure Word Dictionary
A Chinese-English / English-Chinese Usage Guide
Compiled by Jiqing Fang, Michael Connelly
Speak and write polished Chinese using this must-have reference.

Visit www.cheng-tsui.com to view samples, place orders, and browse other language-learning materials.

CONTENTS

UNIT 4   学校生活   School Life

PREFACE

Huanying: An Invitation to Chinese (欢迎：中学汉语课本) is a series designed for secondary school students who are non-native speakers of Chinese with minimal or no background in Mandarin Chinese. Following the *Standards for Foreign Language Learning* developed by the American Council on the Teaching of Foreign Languages (ACTFL), *Huanying* will offer four volumes covering four years of study at the secondary school level and taking students to an intermediate-high level of language proficiency, or the equivalent of two years of college Chinese.

Huanying is organized around thematic units that are essential to everyday communication. All material in each unit—vocabulary, grammar, idiomatic expressions, and culture—is carefully developed with learners' interests and real-life uses in mind. *Huanying* intends to develop language proficiency by taking students gradually from their immediate surroundings to the bigger world. The topic domain is similar throughout the series—self, family, school, daily life, and the larger community—with each subsequent volume building more complexity and depth into the themes and calling for more complex language use. Throughout the series, students learn vocabulary related to each theme, grammar and idiomatic expressions needed to communicate about the theme, and cultural information that helps to contextualize the language use. Language practice focuses on authentic communicative tasks that integrate several modalities of language skills and are intellectually engaging. Individual, pair, and group activities are rooted in meaningful contexts that appeal to students' interests and allow them to present, interpret, and negotiate meanings through active communication.

Each volume of *Huanying* is designed for an entire school year, based on one instructional hour (50 minutes) of language class per day. With language use gaining more depth and complexity, the length of material grows as well. Volumes 1 and 2 are comprised of six units, Volumes 3 and 4 are comprised of four units. Each unit includes five lessons and one unit review lesson. Teachers may plan to use a week to study one lesson. After the unit review lesson, a unit test can be given to students to assess their learning; pre-prepared unit tests appear in the *Huanying Teacher's Book*.

What Is the Pedagogical Philosophy Behind *Huanying*?

Our Goal: Communication and Self-Awareness

Huanying was developed based on a belief that the purpose of learning Chinese is not only to communicate in Chinese accurately and appropriately, but also to develop competence in shaping the content of interactions by understanding speakers of other languages. *Huanying* is designed to help students achieve this goal through monitored language input via sequenced and organized instruction; vigorous language practice via performance-based communicative tasks and constant reinforcement of language skills; systematic evaluation via quizzes, unit tests, and student self-assessment; and in-depth experience of the rich and varied social and cultural contexts in which language practice is embedded. All of the above serve the purpose of helping students communicate in Chinese from the very first day of class and gradually develop the knowledge and ability not only to understand but also to reflect.

Our Content: Incorporating the "5 C's"

Huanying reflects the philosophy outlined by the *Standards for Foreign Language Learning* developed by the American Council on the Teaching of Foreign Languages (ACTFL). Incorporating the principles of "5 C's" (Communication, Culture, Connections, Comparisons, Communities), it strives to provide students with the necessary knowledge and skills that will enable them to be "linguistically and culturally equipped to communicate successfully in a pluralistic American society and abroad." *Huanying*'s primary focus is on meaningfulness, which is the core of communication. By embedding language input and output in communicative tasks set in a broader socio-cultural context, *Huanying* requires students to draw from other academic disciplines and the knowledge of their own cultures to facilitate their understanding of Chinese language and culture. *Huanying* also provides students with opportunities to extend their knowledge in Chinese by exploring the Chinese-speaking communities around them. The ultimate goal of *Huanying* is for students to become more aware of themselves, as well as their own language and culture, through the study of Chinese.

Our Approach: Teaching for Understanding

Huanying differs from traditional Chinese language instructional approaches by adopting an integrated approach that promotes teaching for understanding. Instead of teaching discrete bits and pieces of language (vocabulary, sentence structures, and idiomatic expressions) through repetitive drills without any meaningful context, *Huanying* takes real-life communication tasks as its starting point. This holistic approach allows *Huanying* to teach vocabulary, grammar, and cultural information not in isolation, but rather in context. In order to enhance accuracy in language use, language points are practiced in context. Practice of form, meaning, and function are always interwoven in the communication tasks. Through varied forms of learning tasks, students learn to comprehend, use, and analyze the Chinese language. In brief, *Huanying*'s approach affords students opportunities to construct their own understanding of new concepts and, therefore, to become more effective learners. Based on our belief in teaching for understanding, *Huanying* pays particular attention to topics and situations that are both authentic and appealing to students. Authenticity and relevance are motivational tools that produce life-long learners.

Our Strategy for Success: Negotiate Meaning in Context

Successful language learners know how to negotiate meaning by relying on their previous knowledge and by analyzing and discovering cues from the communicative context. To help students become successful language learners, the activities in *Huanying* are designed to stimulate students' schemata, or schemes of how one perceives the world, to aid students in comprehension—understanding both the main ideas and specific information—and to guide students step-by-step through challenging tasks. *Huanying* also tries to convey the idea that language proficiency cannot be achieved from word-by-word translation. Effective learners approach language learning by looking at context and structure, not by putting together dictionary definitions.

Huanying involves students in every step of the learning process. Students not only actively participate in learning activities, but also make decisions about using appropriate strategies to accomplish tasks. To help students build a tolerance for some ambiguity and risk as they explore a new language, we have purposefully made certain pedagogical decisions: 1) We do not provide English translations for dialogues and texts in the textbook and workbook, 2) In the texts and activities we include some new words that are not glossed yet do not interfere with students' overall comprehension of the text/task, 3) We gradually decrease the use of pinyin as learning progresses, 4) Starting from Volume 3, we gradually increase the use of Chinese in language explanation and culture information, and 5) We ask students to periodically assess their own learning.

How Is *Huanying* Structured?

The structure of *Huanying* can be best described by using the "3 P's" (Presentation, Practice, Production) language instruction model as an analogy. The textbook focuses on presentation, and the student workbook focuses on practice and production.

As many teachers still rely on textbooks as the starting point for class organization and planning, we want to assist teachers to achieve success in their teaching. The textbook and workbook are derived from a carefully planned communicative curriculum, with corresponding goals and tasks. The teacher's book is intended to make lesson preparation more efficient for busy teachers; it contains workbook activities, answer keys, suggestions on how to facilitate a learner-centered classroom, plus quizzes and unit tests.

Textbook

Volume 3 of *Huanying* includes four units, each focusing on one theme. There are five lessons and a review lesson in each unit, so that two units are typically covered per semester. Learning goals are clearly stated at the beginning of each unit, and students can check their progress by taking a self-assessment questionnaire at the end of the unit. A typical lesson consists of two dialogues or texts (with new vocabulary highlighted in color), a new word list (with simplified and traditional characters, pinyin, parts of speech, and English explanations), language notes, some knowledge-related language activities ("Extend Your Knowledge"), and information about Chinese proverbs, idioms, stories, and culture.

At the end of the textbook four indexes are provided: vocabulary (Chinese-English and English-Chinese), proper nouns, and language notes. There is also an appendix of dialogues and texts in traditional characters, designed for students who would like to learn traditional Chinese characters alongside simplified ones.

Workbooks

The workbook component contains a wealth of communicative, ready-to-use language activities and is divided into two parts: Volume 3 Part 1 for the first semester, and Volume 3 Part 2 for the second semester. For each lesson, the workbook has three types of language practice: Listening Practice, Integrated Language Practice, and Writing Practice. Listening Practice involves two or more skills—usually listening/reading, listening/writing, listening/speaking, etc. It is distinct from Integrated Language Practice because students will need the accompanying audio files to complete these activities. Integrated Language Practice includes a variety of communicative activities such as interviews, bingo, board games, role-play, email correspondence, oral reports, and more. Students will benefit from this hands-on format that lets them use different language skills simultaneously (for example, interviewing a classmate while taking notes and filling out a chart in the workbook). Teachers will benefit because all of the activities are presented in a convenient, ready-to-use format—students can do all activities directly in their workbooks and photocopying other materials is not necessary.

Writing Practice (in place of Chinese Character Practice in Volumes 1 and 2) focuses on helping students master the new words and sentence structures while improving language accuracy. It can also be used for homework assignments.

Audio Files

Huanying's accompanying audio files contain recordings of the dialogues, texts, and vocabulary in the textbook, along with audio clips to be used for Listening Practice in the workbook. Audio files can be downloaded free of charge from the publisher's website http://www.cheng-tsui.com/downloads/huanying.

Teacher's Books

The teachers' book includes copies of all student workbook activities with answer keys, together with "Notes to the Teacher" (in both simplified Chinese and English) that help teachers effectively conduct the activities and facilitate a communicative classroom environment. Additional information at the front of the book includes general tips on lesson planning and classroom management, and an overview chart of content covered in the course. The appendix contains quizzes and unit tests, with answer keys. Two quizzes are provided for every lesson: one is a vocabulary quiz that can be given at the beginning of the lesson or after the vocabulary is learned, and the other is a general quiz that can be given at the end of the lesson. Preparing for quizzes and tests is made simple for teachers—just a matter of photocopying.

Acknowledgments

First of all, we would like to thank Ron and Ken for their support and understanding when we spent more time with *Huanying* than with them. Without them, *Huanying* would be impossible.

We wish to thank our illustrators Dr. Murray R. Thomas, Qiguang Xu, Landong Xu, and Augustine Liu for creating wonderful line art to suit our special instructional needs. Many thanks also go to Chuan Zhuang, Jing Chai, Xuexue Zhuang, Yun Zhuang and Peizhi Bai for giving us permission to use their photographs. We would also like to thank the foreign language teachers at Bellarmine College Preparatory for sharing their best practices over the years, and many Chinese language teachers whom we met at professional conferences and workshops. Their professional support and encouragement are invaluable to the compilation of this textbook series. Our gratitude also goes to the Chinese language students at

Bellarmine College Preparatory and La Jolla Country Day School. Their unique perspectives and insightful comments serve as a constant reminder that this textbook series is designed for them and that the successful implementation of the curriculum relies, by and large, on their involvement.

Last, but not least, we would like to thank the editors at Cheng & Tsui for their meticulous reading of our manuscripts and their suggestions and comments to make *Huanying* a better series.

We hope that *Huanying* will introduce secondary school students to Chinese language and culture in a practical and engaging way. Learning a foreign language opens up a new world for exploration, and the new world welcomes (*huanying*) young adventurers.

ABBREVIATIONS OF PARTS OF SPEECH

Abbreviation	Part of Speech
abbr.	abbreviation
adj.	adjective
adv.	adverb
aux.w.	auxiliary word
conj.	conjunction
excl.	exclamation
m.w.	measure word
n.	noun
num.	number
o.v.	optative verb
part.	particle word
p.n.	proper noun
prep.	preposition
pron.	pronoun
s.p.	set phrase
v.	verb
v.c.	verb plus complement
v.o.	verb plus object

第一单元: 新学期

UNIT 1   A New Semester

By the end of this unit, you will learn how to:

- Give detailed personal information about family, work, study and hobbies
- Describe, in some detail, personal experiences
- Describe personalities
- Describe, in some detail, academic courses
- Describe, in some detail, student clubs
- Narrate, in some detail, past events
- Narrate, in some detail, present events
- Narrate, in some detail, future events
- Make and respond to compliments
- Give procedural instructions

1.1 新同学
A New Student

🔘 对话一

汤姆：你好，我叫汤姆。你是新来的吧？我好像没见过你。

明英：你好！我叫明英。很高兴认识你。我是这个学期转学来上海国际学校的。

汤姆：你以前在哪个学校？

明英：北京第四中学。

汤姆：哇噻，那么厉害啊？北京第四中学是有名的好学校，能进北京四中可不容易。能认识你这么聪明的人，非常幸运，也非常高兴。

明英：别开玩笑了。

汤姆：你是怎么考进北京四中的？

明英：是这样的，我父母都是美国大学的教授，去年在北京做研究，所以我就在北京四中借读了一年。

汤姆：那你怎么又到上海来了呢？

明英：今年我父母来上海历史博物馆做研究，我们就把家搬到上海来了。你呢？你一直在这个国际学校上学吗？

汤姆：对。我是在美国旧金山出生的。四年前，我爸爸到上海来工作，我就跟父母来中国了。来上海以后，我一直在这儿上学，因为我父母觉得上国际学校可以让我一边学英语一边学汉语，不会影响我将来回美国上大学。你也是美国人吧?

明英: 对。可是我是在中国出生的,两岁的时候跟父母去了美国。我是在美国上的小学和初中,所以现在我的中文没有英文好。去年我父母带我来中国,就是希望我能好好地学习中文。你的中文好还是英文好?

汤姆: 我的英文比较好。可是这两年,我的中文也进步很快。对了,将来你打算回美国上大学吗?

明英: 这个我还没决定。我很喜欢北京。要是有机会,我可能会报名上北京大学。你呢?

汤姆: 我也挺喜欢中国的,我的朋友又都在中国。和你一样,我也可能会在中国上大学。

上海华东政法大学
East China University of Political Science and Law in Shanghai

对话二

汤姆：凯丽，来，我给你介绍一下，这是新来的同学，明英。

凯丽：你好，我叫凯丽。欢迎你来我们学校。

明英：你好，认识你很高兴。

汤姆：凯丽是我的好朋友，特别理解我。她可聪明了，今年暑假，她上了一个准备高考的暑期学校，现在是我们班的数学天才。

凯丽：好了，汤姆，别甜言蜜语了。有什么事，你就说吧。

汤姆：你看，我说你最理解我了嘛。你能把《数学高考题分析》借给我看看吗？

凯丽：当然可以。明英，你看，我知道汤姆说我好是为了借书。

明英：也不完全是吧。可能汤姆真的觉得你非常聪明。

汤姆：谢谢你，明英，我又找到了一个特别理解我的人。

凯丽：我明天可以把书带来给你。

明英：那本书很不错，我把里边的题都做了一遍。

凯丽：是吗？你用多长时间做完的？

明英：两三个星期吧。因为我喜欢数学，一有空儿就做。

汤姆：真的？我多么幸运啊！两个数学天才都是我的朋友。

明英：又开玩笑了。我们互相学习吧。

20   **14**   9   71

61    $$\frac{-b \pm \sqrt{b^2 - 4ac}}{2a}$$ 58

32   **41**   6   18

生词

	Simplified	Traditional	Pinyin	Part of Speech	English
1.	转学	轉學	zhuǎnxué	v.o.	transfer to another school
2.	幸运	幸運	xìngyùn	adj./n.	fortunate, lucky; fortune, luck
3.	开玩笑	開玩笑	kāiwánxiào	v.o.	joke, make a joke
4.	教授		jiàoshòu	n.	professor
5.	研究		yánjiū	n./v.	research; do research
6.	借读	借讀	jièdú	v.	study at a school on a temporary basis
7.	把		bǎ	part.	a structural particle word
8.	搬家		bānjiā	v.o.	move, move house
9.	一直		yīzhí	adv.	always, continuously
10.	出生		chūshēng	v.	to be born
11.	将来	將來	jiānglái	adv./n.	in the future; future
12.	希望		xīwàng	n./v.	hope; hope
13.	进步	進步	jìnbù	n./v.	progress; advance
14.	甜言蜜语	甜言蜜語	tiányán mìyǔ	s.p.	sweet words, speak sweet words

15. 遍		biàn	*m.w.*	*time (frequency) of taking an action*
16. 多么	多麼	duōme	*adv.*	such, how, what
17. 互相		hùxiāng	*adv.*	mutually, each other

专名

18. 明英	Míngyīng		a personal name

语言注释

1. 又 (again, in addition)

We learned in Lesson 2.5 of *Huanying*, Volume 2 that 又 can mean "again," as in the sentence: 我又找到一个理解我的朋友。(I have again found a friend who understands me.)

又 can have another meaning of "in addition, moreover."

我挺喜欢中国的，我的朋友又都在中国，我可能会在中国上大学。

I like China. Besides, my friends are in China. I will probably go to college in China.

他一直很喜欢数学。这个学期又有一位很好的数学老师。他的数学一定会进步得很快。

He has always liked math. Moreover, he has a great math teacher this semester. His math will definitely progress quickly.

2. The 把 construction

把 is a common structure in Chinese, in which the Object is moved to the front of a verb. In contrast to the normal "Subject + Verb + Object" (SVO) sentence order, the 把 construction looks like this: "Subject + 把 Object + Verb + other elements."

It is important to note that the 把 construction requires some "other elements" after the verb, because in meaning the structure indicates "something has happened to the Object" or "the Object has been changed from one position/state to another."

Subject	把 Object	(Adverb) Verb	Other elements	English meaning
我	把题	(都)做	了。	I did (all) the exercises (changed the state of exercises).
谁	把咖啡	(都)喝	完了？	Who drank (all) the coffee (changed the quantity of coffee)?
她	把手机	摔	坏了。	She broke the cell phone (changed the cell phone's conditions).
你	把书	借	给我。	Lend your book to me (changed the book's location).
我	把光盘	带	来给你。	I will bring the CD to you (changed the CD's location).
我们	把家	搬	到上海来了	We moved to Shanghai (changed the family's location).

The negative form of the 把 construction is:

Subject + Negative + 把 Object + Verb + other elements

Since the 把 construction indicates the Object has changed from one state to another, its negative indicates the change of the state has not been achieved. Therefore, the negative for the 把 construction is usually 没（有）or 别.

别把门开着。
Don't leave the door open.

他没有把作业做完。
He didn't finish doing his homework.

3. Using 遍 to indicate the number of times an action is made

In Lesson 2.5 of *Huanying* Volume 2, we learned the word 次. Both 次 and 遍 can be used to indicate the number of times an action is made. The difference between the two words lies in a slight difference in meaning. 遍 means "once through," stressing the entire process from beginning to end, while 次 means "one time, once." For example:

这个电影我看了三次。

I have seen this movie three times (could be part of it, not necessarily the entire movie).

这个电影我看了三遍。

I have seen this movie three times (from beginning to end).

明英把《数学高考题分析》里的题都做了一遍。

Mingying did every exercise in the Analyzing Math Test Items on the College Entrance Examination once.

请你再说一遍，好吗？

Can you please repeat it (everything you've said)?

请你再去一次，好吗？

Can you go there one more time?

4. 多么···啊！ (How...!/What a...!) in an exclamation sentence

To exclaim about the high degree of something, we can place 多（么） before an adjective or a verb of certain types (such as 爱、喜欢、希望、想···).

我多么幸运啊！	How fortunate I am!
多么聪明的学生啊！	What a brilliant student!
他们多么爱你啊！	They love you so much.
我多么想去旅游啊！	I want to travel so much.

5. 互相 (mutually, each other)

Because 互相 is an adverb, it usually goes before a verb.

我们应该互相帮助。

We should help each other.

大家可以互相学习。

Everyone can learn from one another.

学无止境 EXTEND YOUR KNOWLEDGE

Now you have learned some words about attending school. The following words describe educational institutions at different levels in China.

教育	英文大意	年龄
大学	university or college	18–23 岁
大专 (dàzhuān)	junior college	18–22 岁
高中	senior high school	15/16–18 岁
技校 (jìxiào)	vocational school	15/16–18 岁
初中 (chūzhōng)	junior middle school	12–15/16 岁
小学	primary school	6/7–12/13 岁
幼儿园	pre-school	3–6 岁

YOUR TURN:

回答下面的问题：
1. 在你的国家，孩子几岁上幼儿园？
2. 在你的国家，小学要上几年？
3. 在你的国家，中学要上几年？
4. 你的国家有没有技校？技校一般要上几年？上些什么课？
5. 在你的国家，上大学的人多还是上大专的人多？为什么？

中国文化一瞥 A Glimpse into Chinese Culture

Chinese proverbs and idioms

Apart from 甜言蜜语, there are many proverbs and common sayings about "words." Here are a few examples:

1. yán xíng yī zhì
   言 行 一 致
   match words with actions

2. yán xíng bù yī
   言 行 不 一
   words are not matched by actions; contradiction between words and actions

3. kǒu mì fù jiàn
   口 蜜 腹 剑
   honey-mouthed and dagger-hearted—play a double game; a cruel heart under the cover of sweet words

4. kuài rén kuài yǔ
   快 人 快 语
   straightforward person with straightforward words—straight talk from an honest person

IN USE:

小对话一

小平：你怎么不高兴？

明远：我妈妈说，要是我考试考得好，她就给我买一台新电脑。上次我考了100分，两个月过去了，她还没给我买电脑。真是言行不一。

小平：我父母可是言行一致。他们说如果我一个月打100条以上的短信，他们就不让我用手机了。上个月我才打了101条短信，这个月我就不能用手机了。

Xiaoping: Why are you unhappy?

Mingyuan: My mother said if I did well on a test, she would buy me a new computer. I scored 100% on the last test. Two months have passed and she still hasn't bought me a computer. What she said and what she did do not match.

Xiaoping: My parents always match their words with actions. They said if I sent more than 100 text messages a month, they wouldn't let me use my cell phone any more. Last month, I only sent 101 text messages, and this month I can no longer use the cell phone.

小对话二

英丽：   我爷爷说，以前他有一个邻居。那个邻居常常带着微笑说我爷爷的狗又聪明又漂亮。可是有一天我爷爷不在家的时候，那个邻居把狗带到很远的地方扔 (rēng, throw away) 了。好在我爷爷的狗很聪明，自己找回家来了。

红红：   真的？这个邻居口蜜腹剑，不是个好人。那你爷爷怎么知道是他把狗扔了？

英丽：   他告诉了他女儿。他女儿快人快语，就把这件事告诉了我爷爷。

红红：   听上去他女儿还不错。

英丽：   是啊，她后来成了我奶奶。

Yingli: My grandfather said he had a neighbor in the past. When the neighbor saw him, he would smile and praise his dog for being smart and handsome. But one day when my grandfather was not home, the neighbor took the dog to a remote place and left it there. Fortunately my grandfather's dog was clever and found its way home.

Honghong: Really? This neighbor was playing a double game. He was not a good man. How did your grandfather know that it was he who had thrown away the dog?

Yingli: He told his daughter. His daughter was an honest and straightforward girl. She told my grandfather about it.

Honghong: Sounds like the daughter was a pretty good person.

Yingli: You are right. Later she became my grandmother.

YOUR TURN:

Based on the two mini-dialogues, answer the following questions:

1. 为什么小平说他的父母言行一致？
2. 为什么明远说他的父母言行不一？
3. 为什么说英丽爷爷的邻居口蜜腹剑？
4. 为什么说英丽的奶奶快人快语？

The origin of 口蜜腹剑

李林甫 (Lǐ Línfú) 是唐玄宗 (Xuánzōng, 公元 712–756) 的宰相 (zǎixiàng, prime minister)。他没有能力，也没有道德 (dàodé, morals)。在他当宰相的十九年里，除了让唐玄宗高兴以外，他什么都没做。虽然他看上去很客气也很友好，总是用甜言蜜语说别人好，但是他常常在背后害 (hài, harm) 别人，特别是那些有能力有道德的官员 (guānyuán, official)。大家慢慢地都知道李林甫是什么人了。他们说他"口有蜜，腹有剑。"后来"口蜜腹剑"这个成语就被用来形容 (xíngróng, describe) 那些伪君子 (wěijūnzi, hypocrite) 和两面派 (liǎngmiànpài, double-dealer)。

Li Linfu was the prime minister for Emperor Xuanzong (AD 712–756) in the Tang Dynasty. He was an incompetent and immoral man. Throughout the nineteen years that Li was the prime minister, he did nothing but find ways to please the emperor. Although he appeared to be gentle and friendly, always using sweet words to praise others, he was very good at stabbing people in the back, particularly those officials who were honest and capable. After a while, people started to see through Li. They described him as "having honey in his mouth and having a dagger in his heart." Later the phrase was used to describe hypocrites and double-dealers.

Lyrics of a folk song

小二郎上学
小呀么小二郎，
背着书包上学堂。
不怕太阳晒，
不怕风雨狂，
只怕先生骂我懒，
没有学问，无颜见爹娘。

生词	意思	生词	意思
小二郎 (láng)	一个小男孩的名字	学堂	学校
太阳晒 (shài)	太阳很大很热	风雨狂 (kuáng)	大风大雨
先生	老师	骂 (mà)	批评
懒 (lǎn)	不努力	学问	知识
无颜 (wúyán)	不好意思	爹娘 (diēniáng)	父母

YOUR TURN:

1. Translate the lyrics into English.
2. Write lyrics for a song: **XXX（你的名字）上学**

你知道吗？

中国有两种高中："普通高中"(pǔtōng gāozhōng, average high schools) 和"重点高中"(zhòngdiǎn gāozhōng, key high schools)。一个学校是"普通高中"还是"重点高中"要看这个学校有多少学生能考进大学，特别是考进中国最好的大学。"重点高中"又分成"省(shěng, province)重点"、"市重点"、和"区重点"、"县 (xiàn, county)重点"。重点中学除了有比较多的学生上大学以外，还常常得到比较多的政府资金(zījīn, funding).

　　许多中国父母觉得，如果孩子能考进重点高中，特别是省重点或者市重点，他考进大学的可能就比较大。上海中学和北京第四中学（北京四中）都是有名的市重点高中。要考进这两个高中，非常不容易。

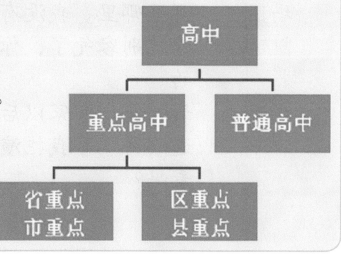

1.2 竞选班长
Running for Class President

对话

凯丽： 要选新班长了，我觉得你当班长挺合适的。
你想参加竞选吗？

玛丽娅： 我得好好想想。当班长需要跟同学老师打交
道，需要为大家服务，是一个学习为人处事
的好机会。

凯丽： 我觉得你又聪明又能干，学习好，喜欢运
动，还常常帮助别人。你应该参加竞选。

玛丽娅： 我有的优点你都有，你怎么不参加竞选呢？

凯丽： 当班长第一得愿意听大家说话，不能着急。
第二要能领导大家一起工作。第三做事要做
得又快又好。可是我有时候一听别人说的跟
我想的不一样，我就会着急。再说，有时候
我做事做得挺慢的。所以我当班长不合适。
你比我能干多了。

玛丽娅： 哪里哪里。我没有你说的那么能干。

凯丽： 你就别客气了，你一定能好好领导我们班
的。

玛丽娅： 好吧，我回家以后，先准备一下，写一个竞
选演讲。等我把演讲写好了，你能帮我看一
看吗？

凯丽：　　当然可以。大卫和汤姆也能帮你。我们还会发电邮给大家，让大家选你。对了，我们还应该做几个"玛丽娅，加油！"的牌子，把这些牌子挂在教室和学生餐厅里。有我们当你的竞选助手，你一定能竞选成功。

玛丽娅：真的吗？太谢谢你了。

加油， 玛丽娅！	玛丽娅，加油！ Go, Maria!	玛丽娅， 加油！加油！

 课文

同学们，老师们：

你们好！我叫玛丽娅罗西尼。我在竞选当班长。班长是很重要的工作。如果有了一个好班长，一个班就能进步得比较快。大家常常说，我努力、聪明、能干、爱帮助别人。这些优点能让我好好地为大家服务。

我们上海国际学校是一个特别的学校，因为大家是从许多不同国家来的，有不同的文化。我是在意大利出生的，因为父母的工作，我在很多国家住过：美国、英国、法国、韩国、巴西、南非。五年以前，我们又搬家来到上海这个国际大城市。因为我去过很多国家，跟不同国家的人打过交道，看到过许多不同的文化，我特别能理解国际学生的需要。我觉得一个班长只有理解了班里的同学才能领导一个班。

　　大家都知道，我不但自己的学习成绩很好，而且还常常帮助别的同学。我当了班长以后，会把大家的学习需要告诉老师，让我们的学习进步得更快。

　　除了学习以外，我还参加许多体育和娱乐活动。我当了班长以后，会组织更多的体育和文化活动，让大家来参加。只有身体健康，我们才能更努力地学习。

高中生

　　在过去的两年中，我做过义工，也打过工。我当了班长以后，会领导大家更好地为社区服务，把我们的世界变得更美好。

　　当然，大家一定知道我还有一个优点—我组织的晚会是学校里最受欢迎的。你们都还记得高三同学的毕业招待会，和在我家开过的晚会吧？要是我当了班

长，那么下一次我们班的晚会一定会是你参加过的最
难忘的晚会。

　　同学们，请投我一票，谢谢大家！

投票箱

A ballot box

💿 生词

	Simplified	Traditional	Pinyin	Part of Speech	English
1.	选	選	xuǎn	v.	elect, select
2.	班长	班長	bānzhǎng	n.	class president
3.	当	當	dāng	v.	serve as, work as
4.	竞选	競選	jìngxuǎn	v.	campaign for, run for
5.	打交道		dǎjiāodào	v.o.	interact with
6.	为人处事	為人處世	wéirénchǔshì	s.p.	the way to conduct oneself and deal with others
7.	能干	能幹	nénggàn	adj.	capable, competent
8.	优点	優點	yōudiǎn	n.	merit, strong point, virtue
9.	领导	領導	lǐngdǎo	n./v.	leader, leadership; lead

10.	演讲	演講	yǎnjiǎng	n./v.	speech, lecture; give a speech
11.	加油		jiāyóu	v.o.	add fuel, come on, make a greater effort
12.	成功		chénggōng	n./v.	success; succeed
13.	重要		zhòngyào	adj.	important, essential
14.	努力		nǔlì	adj./v.	hard-working; work hard
15.	只有…才…		zhǐyǒu…cái…	conj.	only…then…
16.	社区	社區	shèqū	n.	community
17.	变得	變得	biàndé	v.c.	change into
18.	受		shòu	v.	receive, bear, endure
19.	难忘	難忘	nánwàng	adj.	unforgettable
20.	投（票）		tóu (piào)	v.	cast (a vote)

专名

21.	意大利	義大利*	Yìdàlì		Italy
22.	巴西		Bāxī		Brazil
23.	南非		Nánfēi		South Africa

语言注释

1. 当 (serve as, work as)

When one takes an occupation or serves in a certain capacity, the verb 当 is used.

我将来要当老师。

I would like to be a teacher in the future.

玛丽娅想当班长。

Maria would like to serve as the class president.

* 意大利 is used in mainland China and 義大利 in Taiwan. The Simplified form of 義 is 义.

他大学毕业以后当了工程师。
He became an engineer after graduating from college.

你是什么时候当经理的？
When did you become a manager?

2. 跟…打交道 (deal with…)

他的工作是跟人打交道。
His job is to deal with people.

我们每天都跟电脑打交道。
Every day, we deal with computers.

3. 只有…才… (only…then…)

只有 introduces a condition and the adverb 才 indicates the result.

只有理解了大家，才能为大家服务。
Only when you understand everyone can you serve everyone.

只有去了那儿，你才会知道那儿有多么美丽。
Only when you go there will you know how beautiful it is.

4. The 把 construction *(continued)*

We learned in Lesson 1.1 that the 把 construction requires some "other elements" after a verb, because in meaning it indicates "something has happened to the Object" or "the Object has been changed from one position/state to another." Here are some examples of 把 used with 得 (indicating a complement of degree) and with the prepositions 在 and 到 (indicating a change of location/position).

Subject	把 Object	(Adverb) Verb	Other elements	English meaning
我们	要把世界	变得	更美好。	We will change the world into a more beautiful place (change the quality of the world).

你	可以把字		写得	大一点儿。	You can write the words a little bigger (change the size of the characters).

我们	可以把牌子	挂在	教室里。	We can hang the signs in the classroom (change the location of the signs).

她	把车	停在	停车场了。	She parked the car in the parking lot (change the location of the car).

你	把书	拿到	楼上去。	Take the book upstairs (change the location of the book).

5. Responding to compliments

By now, we know that the Chinese way of expressing politeness is not the same as that in Western cultures. A typical response to compliment in the West is "Thank you." A Chinese person, however, considers this response conceited and immodest, because you are acknowledging that you are as good as the compliment. Therefore, a typical Chinese response to a compliment is almost always negative, in order to show modesty, such as "I have a long way to go, I am not as good as you say, I still need to work hard…" 哪里哪里 is a set phrase that you can use to respond to compliment in a polite way.

A: 你比我能干多了。

A: You are so much more capable than I.

B: 哪里哪里。

B: Not really.

A: 你儿子非常聪明。

A: Your son is really smart.

B: 哪里哪里，
（马马虎虎吧）。

B: Oh, no, he is average.

A: 你说英语说得
很好。

A: You speak English very well.

A: 你的外衣很漂亮。

A: Your jacket is beautiful.

B: 哪里哪里，
（我还说得不太好）。

B: I still don't speak it well.

B: 哪里哪里，
（这件衣服很便宜）。

B: It is inexpensive.

学无止境 EXTEND YOUR KNOWLEDGE

Here are some words for describing positive characteristics.

rènzhēn 认真 *conscientious*	fùzé 负责 *responsible*	yǒuhǎo 友好 *friendly*	dàfāng 大方 *generous*
chéngshí 诚实 *honest*	zìxìn 自信 *self-confident*	zhèngzhí 正直 *honest, fair and just*	kāimíng 开明 *open-minded*
rèxīn 热心 *warmhearted*	rèqíng 热情 *warm*	zhíshuǎng 直爽 *candid, straightforward*	línghuó 灵活 *flexible, quick*
yōumò 幽默 *humorous*	kèqì 客气 *polite, courteous*	yǒnggǎn 勇敢 *brave*	suíhé 随和 *amiable, easygoing*

中国文化一瞥 A Glimpse into Chinese Culture

Chinese proverbs and idioms

Some animals possess admirable traits. The following proverbs portray these traits.

1. mǎ   bù   tíng   tí

马   不   停   蹄

the horse gallops on without pause—continuously; push on with one's journey without stopping

IN USE:

你给他一件事去做，他就会马不停蹄地工作。

If you give him a task to do, he will work at it continuously.

为了让毕业典礼开得成功，我们马不停蹄地准备了一个星期。

For the success of the graduation ceremony, we made preparations continuously for a week.

YOUR TURN:

1. 你做什么事情会马不停蹄？
2. 每天你马不停蹄地忙来忙去，在忙什么呢？

2. mǎ   yǐ   bān   tài   shān

蚂   蚁   搬   泰   山

ants move Mount Taishan—the united efforts of the masses can accomplish mighty projects

IN USE:

上个周末，有五百多人来我们学校参观。要为这么多人准备午饭不很容易。好在我们班的同学老师都来当义工。大家蚂蚁搬泰山，就把午饭都准备好了。

Last weekend, more than five hundred people visited our school. It was not easy to prepare lunch for so many people. Fortunately the students and teachers from our class all came to volunteer. Everyone pitched in his or her effort and prepared lunch for all.

YOUR TURN:

Can you use 蚂蚁搬泰山 to describe the following situations?

	可以	不可以
1. 数学对我来说很难，但是我可以每天学习，慢慢地我的数学会进步。		
2. 我们公司现在很有名，那是大家一年一年努力的结果。		
3. 这个教授一个人就写了十本书。		
4. 那个班的每个同学都很努力地练习，最后他们班在汉语演讲比赛中得了第一名。		

3. lóng téng hǔ yuè

龙 腾 虎 跃

dragons rising and tigers leaping—a scene of bustling activity;

a scene with a lot of positive energy

IN USE:

每次学校开运动会，师生们就龙腾虎跃的。

Every time there is a sports event at school, both the students and teachers give off a lot of positive energy.

如果你去那个新公司看一下，就会注意到那里龙腾虎跃。

If you visit that new company, you will notice a lot of bustling activity.

高中生在运动

YOUR TURN:

Are you likely to see 龙腾虎跃 in the following situations?

	可能	不可能
1. 参观历史博物馆		
2. 帮助老人院打扫卫生		
3. 篮球训练		
4. 听校长演讲		
5. 准备中秋节晚会		
6. 参加欢迎新同学招待会		

Joke: "哪里哪里"

中国人都知道"哪里哪里"是为了表示 (biǎoshì, express) 客气。有一位外国先生刚学了一点儿汉语，有一天，他去参加一个朋友的婚礼 (hūnlǐ, wedding ceremony)。他看到朋友的太太很漂亮，就对朋友说："你太太真漂亮。"他朋友回答："哪里哪里。"外国先生想，他朋友不知道他太太哪里漂亮吗？他就对朋友说："头发、眉毛、眼睛、鼻子、耳朵、嘴都很漂亮。"

Chinese use the phrase "nǎlinǎli" to express courtesy. A foreigner had learned a little Chinese language. One day, he went to his friend's wedding. He complimented the beautiful bride to his friend, "Your wife is really beautiful." The friend answered, "Nǎlinǎli." The foreigner thought it was strange that his friend didn't know where his wife looked beautiful, so he told the husband, "Her hair, eyebrows, eyes, nose, ears, and mouth are all beautiful."

你知道吗？

中国文化和西方文化不一样。西方人听到别人夸奖 (kuājiǎng, compliment, praise) 自己的时候，常常会说："谢谢！"意思是谢谢你看到了我的优点，也谢谢你夸奖我。中国人觉得，一个人要进步，就需要知道自己哪儿做得不够好。只有知道了自己的短处 (shortcomings)，一个人才能进步。在中国，如果一个人听到别人夸奖他以后，只说谢谢，别人会觉得他自高自大 (conceited, have a high opinion of oneself)。再说，这样回答别人的夸奖也不客气。所以，中国人在听到别人夸奖他以后，常常会告诉夸奖他的人，自己还有许多地方不够好，还需要努力。常用的回答有：我还差得远呢(I have a long way to go)；我做得还不够(I haven't done enough)；我还不够好 (I am not that good)。"哪里哪里"是一个常用的回答。意思是"你太客气了，我没有你说得那么好。"

1.3 选课
Course Selection

对话一

凯丽：明英，这学期的课你都选好了吧？

明英：是的，我选了英语、数学、化学、物理、历史和体育。可是我不是很喜欢历史课，想换一门。你知道怎么换课吗？

凯丽：你需要填写一张退课加课表。你先写上要退什么课，然后再写上你要加的课、上课的时间和老师的姓名就可以了。今天好像是可以退课加课的最后一天，你知道去哪儿拿表吗？

明英：在教务处吗？

凯丽：对，图书馆和电脑房也有退课加课表。

明英：谢谢。我们是不是一个学期要上四门必修课和两门选修课？

凯丽：是的。

明英：在我们学校，除了外语课以外，还有哪些是选修课？

凯丽：还有美术、音乐、健康教育、地理什么的。

明英：地理课听上去很有意思。

凯丽：是啊。教地理课的张老师上课上得非常好。每个学期都有很多学生要上他的课，常常是学期还没有开始，他的课已经满了。

明英：是吗？如果我上不了张老师的地理课，那我就
　　　选经济学。教经济学的老师怎么样？

凯丽：不太清楚，因为我没有上过经济学。你可以问
　　　问大卫，他上过。

🔘 对话二

玛丽娅：大卫你好，这个学期你上几门课？

大卫：　七门。

玛丽娅：那么多啊？除了必修课以外，你上哪些选修课？

大卫：　我上地理和电脑。

玛丽娅：这么多课里，你最喜欢哪门课？

大卫：　我的课都不错，可是我最喜欢地理课。教地理课
　　　　的是张老师。他教地理教了二十多年了。上课的
　　　　时候，他常常讲故事。他不但告诉我们一个地方
　　　　的地理环境，还告诉我们那儿的历史。那门课的
　　　　作业挺多的，我们每个星期都需要上网做研究，

了解地理环境怎么影响了一个地区的经济和文化。你呢？你最喜欢什么课？

玛丽娅：除了历史课以外，别的课我都喜欢。

大卫：这个学期谁教历史？

玛丽娅：是那个新来的白老师。她讲课的时候，从来不看着学生，也不注意我们听得懂听不懂，就看着书说啊说啊。同学们就自己做自己的事，有人用手机发短信，有人画画儿，有人做作业，还有人睡觉。

大卫：是吗？上这门课听上去跟玩儿一样，是不是很容易？

玛丽娅：不容易。每天白老师给我们很多作业，让我们看书背书。每次考试都很长，有五十个问题。要是你不背书，就回答不了。这门课开学的时候有二十五个学生，现在不少人已经退课了，只有十四个人了。

大卫：那你怎么还不退课呢？

玛丽娅：我也想过要退课，可是有一天白老师对我们说，她大学刚毕业，还在学习怎么教书，希望我们能帮助她，给她一个学习的机会。你想，老师都这么说了，我还好意思退课吗？

大卫：是啊。那你跟她说过她上课的问题了吗？

玛丽娅：说过了，可是白老师好像理解不了我们的学习需要。她常说，在大学的时候，她的老师也是每天让她背书。要是她背得了，我们也一定背得了。

大卫：我看，你现在可真是进退两难啊。

 生词

	Simplified	Traditional	Pinyin	Part of Speech	English
1.	填写	填寫	tiánxiě	*v.*	fill in (a form)
2.	退课	退課	tuìkè	*v.o.*	drop a class
3.	加课	加課	jiākè	*v.o.*	add a class
4.	表		biǎo	*n.*	form
5.	教务处	教務處	jiàowùchù	*n.*	academic affairs office
6.	必修课	必修課	bìxiūkè	*n.*	required course
7.	选修课	選修課	xuǎnxiūkè	*n.*	elective course
8.	地理		dìlǐ	*n.*	geography
9.	满	滿	mǎn	*adj.*	full
10.	了		liǎo	*part.*	*used in potential complements*
11.	讲	講	jiǎng	*v.*	tell
12.	环境	環境	huánjìng	*n.*	environment
13.	了解		liǎojiě	*n./v.*	understanding; understand
14.	地区	地區	dìqū	*n.*	region, area
15.	从来	從來	cónglái	*adv.*	always, all along
16.	背书	背書	bèishū	*v.o.*	recite a lesson from memory
17.	刚	剛	gāng	*adv.*	just, just now, just about to
18.	进退两难	進退兩難	jìntuìliǎngnán	*s.p.*	be in a dilemma, difficult to proceed or to draw back

语言注释

1. Potential complement

To indicate whether it is possible or impossible for an action to reach a goal or achieve a result, we can insert a particle (得 or 不) between a verb (the action) and its complement (such as a result or a direction complement). In pronunciation, the particle is always unstressed.

Positive Form		*Negative Form*	
Verb + 得 + Complement		*Verb + 不 + Complement*	
听得懂	can understand	听不懂	can't understand
找得到	can find	找不到	can't find
去得了	can go	去不了	can't go
进得来	can come in	进不来	can't come in
上得去	can go up	上不去	can't go up

了 (pronounced liǎo) is often used in a potential complement, with the meaning of "able to."

我明天去不了。
I can't go tomorrow.

你一个人吃得了那么多菜吗？
Can you finish so many dishes by yourself?

这间小房间放不了三个桌子。
This small room can't hold three tables.

我觉得玛丽娅当得了班长。
I feel Maria has the ability to be the class president.

2. 从来（不，没）(never)

从来 is an adverb with the meaning of "always, all along." It is usually used in a negative sentence. When it goes before adverbs such as 不 and 没, it has the meaning of "never."

他从来就不喜欢打冰球。

He has never liked to play hockey.

他考试从来没有得过100分。

He has never gotten a perfect score on any test.

3. V 啊 V 啊 (keep on doing something, do something continuously)

To indicate that someone keeps doing something, we can repeat a verb and add 啊 to each verb.

他一见到我，就说啊说啊。

As soon as he saw me, he kept on talking.

我们找啊找啊，还是没找到。

We kept looking but haven't found it.

他吃啊吃啊，一口气吃了三个汉堡。

He kept eating, and ate three hamburgers without a break.

我做啊做啊，做到十一点才把作业做完。

I kept on working and didn't finish my homework until eleven o'clock.

4. 刚 (just, only a short while ago)

白老师刚来我们学校工作。

Teacher Bai came to our school a short while ago.

他刚出去，不在家。

He just went out and is not home.

5. 都 (already)

In addition to its meaning of "all," 都 can also mean "already."

我们快走吧，都三点了。

Let's go. It is already three o'clock.

丁老师都批评过他了。

Teacher Ding has already criticized him.

学无止境 EXTEND YOUR KNOWLEDGE

In addition to the words we have learned about adding and dropping a course, here are some more words related to taking courses at a school or university.

zhùcè 注册 *registration; register for a class*	zhùcèbiǎo 注册表 *registration form*	xuéshēng fǔdǎoyuán 学生辅导员 *academic counselor* *(in secondary schools)*
dǎoshī 导师 *academic adviser (in colleges)*	zhuānyè 专业 *major, major field of study*	zhǔxiū 主修 *major, major field of study*
fùxiū 副修 *minor, secondary field of study*	cìxiū 次修 *minor, secondary field of study*	rèménkè 热门课 *popular class, a class in popular demand*
lěngménkè 冷门课 *unpopular class, a class not in popular demand*	xuéfēn 学分 *units of credit*	kèshí 课时 *class/course meeting hours*
qiānmíng 签名 *signature; sign*	qǔxiāo 取消 *cancellation; cancel*	hòubǔrén míngdān 候补人名单 *waiting list*

中国文化一瞥 A Glimpse into Chinese Culture

Chinese proverbs and idioms

Many Chinese sayings are about teacher-student relations. Here are some:

1. yán shī chū gāo tú
严 师 出 高 徒

a strict teacher produces outstanding students; a strict master trains capable pupils

IN USE:

这个滑冰运动员的比赛成绩很好。她说这都是因为她的教练很严格 (yángé, strict)。严师出高徒嘛。

The figure skater did well in a competition. She said it was because she had a strict coach. Obviously a strict coach can produce outstanding athletes.

YOUR TURN:

1. 你觉得"严师出高徒"的说法对吗？为什么对？为什么不对？
2. 你比较喜欢严格的老师还是不严格的老师？
3. 严格的老师对你的学习有什么帮助？
4. 不严格的老师对你的学习有什么帮助？

2. qīng chū yú lán, ér shèng yú lán
青 出 于 蓝，而 胜 于 蓝

indigo blue is extracted from the indigo plant but is bluer than the plant—
a student excels his/her teacher; a student surpasses the teacher

IN USE:

这种新电脑可以说是青出于蓝而胜于蓝。比原来的电脑更好更快。

This new computer excels its predecessor. It is better and faster than the older model.

王老师在中学教了三十年数学。他常说他的学生是青出于蓝而胜于蓝，因为他的不少学生现在是工程师和科学家。

Teacher Wang has taught math in a middle school for thirty years. He often says that his students have surpassed him, because quite a few of his students are now engineers and scientists.

YOUR TURN:

Can you use 青出于蓝而胜于蓝 to describe the following situations?

		可以	不可以
1.	李老师在大学教汉语。他的一个学生现在是作家，已经写了十多本小说。		
2.	他爸爸开了一个饭店，是那个饭店的经理。现在他爸爸退休了，他当了这个饭店的经理。		
3.	他的老师非常会教书，现在他也很会教书。		
4.	她妈妈是体育老师。小时候，妈妈教她怎么游泳。现在她是游泳运动员。		

3. bān　mén　nòng　fǔ

班　门　弄　斧

show off one's proficiency with the axe before the master carpenter Lu Ban (鲁班, Lǔ Bān)
— display one's slight skill before an expert; show off before a superior man; teach fish to swim
(To show modesty, this phrase is often used as an opening remark before making a
presentation to professional peers.)

IN USE:

你刚学了几天中国历史，就打算批评中国历史学家。我看你就不要班门弄斧了。

You have only studied Chinese history for a few days and have decided to criticize
Chinese historians. I don't think you should show off before experts.

今天我是班门弄斧，向大家介绍一下我写的书，请大家多批评。

Today I am going to tell you about my book. It is like showing off before experts.
Please feel free to criticize my work.

YOUR TURN:

Do you think the following are examples of 班门弄斧?

	是	不是
1. 他刚学会开车，现在他在教他弟弟开车，因为他弟弟还没有学过开车。		
2. 那个学生学了两个星期的日文。他对日文老师说："我的日文可好了，是我们学校最好的。"		

The legend of 鲁班

传说鲁班 (Lǔ Bān) 生在中国的北方。没有人知道他的生日是几月几日。也没有人知道他是哪一年生的。有人说是在公元前（公元前770年到476年）。听说鲁班非常聪明，会用木头 (mùtóu, wood) 做很多东西。他做过一只很大的木鸟，就像现在人们用的滑翔机 (huáxiángjī, hang glider) 一样。这只木鸟做好以后，在天上飞啊飞啊，飞了三天。传说鲁班有时候坐着木鸟从一个地方飞到另外一个地方。

两千多年过去了，鲁班的木鸟不知道飞到哪儿去了，可是中国人都还记得鲁班，因为他是中国历史上最有名的木匠 (mùjiàng, carpenter)。

According to legend, Lu Ban was from northern China. No one knows his exact birth date. Some say he was born sometime between 770 – 476 BC. Lu Ban is said to have been extremely clever. He was able to make many things with wood. He once made a large wooden bird, somewhat like the present-day hang glider. After the wooden bird was made, it flew in the sky for three days. The legend also said that Lu Ban would ride the wooden bird to travel from one place to another.

More than 2000 years have passed. No one knows where the wooden bird is, but the Chinese still remember Lu Ban, because he was the most famous carpenter in Chinese history.

上海的鲁班路

A Shanghai street named after Lu Ban

你知道吗？

跟美国高中不一样，在许多中国高中，学生不用选课。一个学生进了学校以后，就被分到一个班里。一个班有三十个左右的学生。每个班都有自己的教室。每个学期学生应该上哪些课都是学校决定的。中国高中生和美国高中生上的课差不多一样，有数学、物理、化学、历史、地理、体育、外语什么的。中国的高中生每天上六七节课。下课以后，有些学校还让他们在学校做作业。

高中三年，一个班的学生天天在一起。上课的时候，学生不用换教室，不同的老师会来给他们上课。上汉语课的时候，汉语老师来；上数学课的时候，数学老师来。

高中生在教室里

不少中国人说，他们最好的朋友常常是在高中的时候认识的。因为那时候，大家从早到晚在一起，有同样的学校生活，同样的兴趣，同样的爱好，和同样的烦恼 (fánnǎo, worries)。

1.4 学生社团
Student Clubs

🔘 对话一

大卫：今天下午，各个学生社团要向大家介绍情况。
　　　你去吗？

凯丽：当然去。这个学期你参加了几个社团？

大卫：我还没决定参加哪一个呢。你有什么好建议
　　　吗？

凯丽：你那么喜欢运动，为什么不参加一个运动队
　　　呢？

大卫：参加了运动队，就得每个星期去训练。我喜欢
　　　的运动太多了，又比较喜欢自由，所以还是不
　　　参加运动队的好。这样我有空的时候，可以喜
　　　欢玩什么就玩什么。

凯丽：那参加戏剧社吧。你比较外向，
　　　又对戏剧有兴趣。

大卫：不行，不行。我唱歌唱不好，
　　　跳舞跳不好，哪能当演员呢？

凯丽：不会唱歌跳舞没关系，你可以
　　　演话剧。比方说，你可以在话
　　　剧里演一个侦探。你又高又瘦，
　　　穿上一件长大衣，再戴上一顶
　　　帽子，一定很像那个有名的
　　　英国侦探。

大卫： 好了好了，别开玩笑了。

凯丽： 对了，你不是也很喜欢电脑吗？
怎么不参加电脑兴趣小组呢？
听说电脑小组正在计划做一个
机器人。

大卫： 是吗？今天下午我一定要去听
一听电脑小组的介绍。

 对话二

凯丽： 汤姆，这个学期你还参加数学兴趣小组吗？

汤姆： 对。数学小组对我的学习挺有帮助的。我们
每次活动，都会有一位数学老师来参加。这
位老师会给我们分析一些比较难的数学题，
然后让我们做。做完了以后，老师会检查我
们做得对不对。每次活动，我都能学到一些
新知识。

凯丽： 听上去很有意思。

汤姆： 你不是也很喜欢数学吗？为什么不来参加
数学兴趣小组呢？

凯丽： 这学期不行，我已经参加了学校的乐队。

汤姆： 乐队不是一个星期活动一次吗？这不会影响
你参加数学兴趣小组的。

凯丽： 可是我还参加了棒球队。棒球队一个星期要
训练两个下午。你呢？这个学期还在学校的
网球队打网球吗？

汤姆： 我已经退出网球队了。网球队
来了一位新教练，以前是国家队
的网球运动员。他觉得我们的
训练时间太少，要我们每天训
练两个小时。你想，我们又不
是运动员，哪有那么多时间训
练？特别是现在，每天有许多
作业，还常常要考试，所以我
退出了。

凯丽： 那你除了数学兴趣小组以外，不参加别的社
团了吗？

汤姆： 我还参加了美国学生俱乐部。俱乐部里都是
美国来的学生，我们每个月活动两次，都是
很轻松的活动，比方说，看电影、听音乐、
去美国餐厅吃饭、开晚会什么的。又轻松又
好玩。

 生词

	Simplified	Traditional	Pinyin	Part of Speech	English
1.	社团	社團	shètuán	*n.*	club, organization
2.	各		gè	*adj.*	various, each, every
3.	自由		zìyóu	*adj./n.*	free; freedom
4.	外向		wàixiàng	*adj.*	extroverted
5.	戏剧	戲劇	xìjù	*n.*	drama, theater, play
6.	社		shè	*n.*	organization
7.	演员	演員	yǎnyuán	*n.*	actor (in a play/movie)
8.	演		yǎn	*v.*	act (in a play/movie)
9.	话剧	話劇	huàjù	*n.*	modern drama, stage play
10.	比方说	比方說	bǐfāngshuō	*s.p.*	for example, for instance
11.	小组	小組	xiǎozǔ	*n.*	small group
12.	机器人	機器人	jīqìrén	*n.*	robot
13.	听上去	聽上去	tīngshàngqu	*s.p.*	sound, sound like
14.	退出		tuìchū	*v.c.*	withdraw (from)
15.	国家队	國家隊	guójiāduì	*n.*	national (athletic) team
16.	运动员	運動員	yùndòngyuán	*n.*	athlete
17.	俱乐部	俱樂部	jùlèbù	*n.*	club
18.	轻松	輕鬆	qīngsōng	*adj.*	relaxing, relaxed, light

语言注释

1. 哪 + Verb (there is no way…, can't, don't)

We have learned how to use 哪 in a question, such as 你是哪国人？ (What country are you from?) and 哪个电脑最贵？ (Which computer is the most expensive?). In these two examples, 哪 is used as a pronoun, with the meaning of "which." When 哪 is used as an adverb before a verb in a question, it has the different meaning of "there is no way…" See the examples below:

我哪能当演员？

There is no way I can be an actor.

我们哪有时间每天训练两个小时？

There is no way we have the time to train two hours a day.

她哪会教书？

She doesn't know how to teach.

他哪有那么多钱买车？

He doesn't have that much money to buy a car.

2. 比方说 (for example)

When giving an example, we can use 比方说 before the example. 比方说 is usually used in spoken Chinese.

北京有很多旅游点，比方说天安门、长城、北海公园。

There are many tourist sites in Beijing, such as Tiananmen, the Great Wall, and Beihai Park.

你需要多练习汉语。比方说，你可以多看看中国电影，也可以多跟中国人说说话。

You need to practice Chinese more. For example, you can watch more Chinese movies and speak more to Chinese people.

3. 听上去 (sound like)

听上去 is a set phrase. We learned a similar phrase, 看上去 (seem, look like), in *Huanying* Volume 2. Both phrases are used as verbs.

那个电影听上去很有意思。

The movie sounds very interesting.

听上去那门课很轻松。

It sounds like the course is relaxed.

4. 又⋯又⋯ (both...and...)

又⋯又⋯ can be used to combine two verbs or two adjectives.

那个俱乐部的活动又好玩又轻松。

The club's activities are both fun and relaxing.

凯丽又喜欢音乐又喜欢运动。

Kelly likes both music and sports.

学无止境 EXTEND YOUR KNOWLEDGE

In Chinese, 兴趣小组、社、团、队、俱乐部 all refer to "clubs." Generally speaking, 兴趣小组 refers to academic clubs, 社 to literary clubs, 团 to performing arts clubs, 队 to clubs that engage in competitive sports and activities, and 俱乐部 to clubs that have a lot of fun, but there are always exceptions. Here are some common student clubs:

kēxué xìngqù xiǎozǔ 科学兴趣小组 *science club*	wénxué shè 文学社 *literary arts club*	shīgē shè 诗歌社 *poetry club*
héchàng tuán 合唱团 *choir*	juéshì yuèduì 爵士乐队 *jazz band*	biànlùn duì 辩论队 *debate club*
lālāduì 啦啦队 *cheerleading squad*	shèyǐng xìngqù xiǎozǔ 摄影兴趣小组 *photography club*	guójì xuéshēng jùlèbù 国际学生俱乐部 *international students club*
měishù shè 美术社 *fine arts club*	xuéshēng bàoshè 学生报社 *student newspaper*	Hànyǔ jùlèbù 汉语俱乐部 *Chinese club*

中国文化一瞥 A Glimpse into Chinese Culture

Chinese proverbs and idioms

Many Chinese sayings are about how to acquire a skill. Here are a few:

1. shú néng shēngqiǎo

熟 能 生 巧

skill comes from practice; practice makes perfect

IN USE:

王老师说，要记住汉字，就应该把一个汉字写很多遍。这样熟能生巧，以后就能很快很好地写那个汉字了。

According to Teacher Wang, for us to remember a Chinese character, we should write it many times. Practice makes perfect. In the future, we will be able to write that character quickly and correctly.

YOUR TURN:

Do you think 熟能生巧 can work for the following learning situations?

	能	不能
学习怎么打武术		
学习数学		
学习说汉语		
学习怎么更好地为社区的老人服务		
学习中国历史		
学习怎么开车		

2. zhǐ yào gōng fū shēn, tiě bàng mó chéng zhēn

只　要　功　夫　深，铁　棒　磨　成　针

as long as one keeps working at it, an iron rod can be ground into a needle.

This saying has the same meaning as the proverb 铁杵磨针 (tiě chǔ mó zhēn).

IN USE:

小弟：　　　数学太难学了，我学不会。

大哥：　　　世界上哪有学不会的东西？只要功夫深，
　　　　　　铁棒磨成针。

Younger brother:　　Math is too difficult, and I will never learn it.

Older brother:　　There is nothing in the world that can't be learned. If you keep

　　　　　　working at it, even an iron rod can be ground into a needle.

YOUR TURN:

Can you use 只要功夫深，铁棒磨成针 to encourage the following people?

You hear	*Your encouragement*
汉字太难写了，我记不住。	
弹钢琴怎么那么难？我要什么时候才能学会？	
今天有那么多作业，我做到明天也做不完。	
听说学法语要很多年才能学好，你觉得我能学好吗？	

The story behind 铁杵磨针

中国历史上有名的诗人 (shīrén, poet) 李白 (公元 701-762)，小时候不喜欢学习，只喜欢玩儿。有一天李白去逛街，走到一条小巷 (xiàng, alley) 里。他看到有一位老奶奶，手里拿着一根 (gēn, *measure word for long object*) 铁棒，正坐在一个房子的前面，很努力地磨着。

李白觉得很奇怪，就问："老奶奶，您在做什么呢？"老奶奶说："我要把这根铁棒磨成一根针。"李白想，这怎么可能呢？他对老奶奶说："您的铁棒这么大，您要磨到哪一年，才能磨成针啊？"老奶奶回答："一定会磨成的。我天天努力地磨，怎么会磨不成呢？"李白听了以后，非常感动 (gǎndòng, moved)。他决定自己也应该每天都好好学习。

Li Bai (AD 701–762) was a famous poet in Chinese history. When he was a child, he liked playing instead of studying. One day when wandering on the street, he went into a small alley. In the alley, he saw an old lady sitting in front of a house, grinding away at an iron bar. He was curious and asked, "Granny, what are you doing?" The old lady replied, "I am grinding this iron bar into a needle." Li thought it was impossible. He said to the old lady, "The iron bar is so big. How many years will it take for you to finish grinding?" The old woman answered, "Of course I will finish it, as long as I keep grinding away every day." The old woman's words impressed Li Bai. He decided that he should study diligently every day as well.

你知道吗？

中国的高中和美国的一样，也有一些学生社团。比方说，每个高中都有运动队，还有一些兴趣小组和俱乐部。常见 (common) 的运动队有篮球队、足球队、排球 (páiqiú, volleyball) 队、田径 (tiánjìng, track and field) 队。兴趣小组常常跟学习有关系 (have something to do with studies)。比方说，科学兴趣小组、数学兴趣小组、电脑兴趣小组、外语兴趣小组什么的。还有一些跟艺术 (yìshù, arts) 有关系，比方说，戏剧社、美术社、乐队、合唱团。学生社团一般是一个星期活动一两次。每次活动都会有一位指导老师 (faculty advisor) 来参加。

有些中国父母觉得，上高中就是为了准备高考。高中生应该只注意学习，别的都不那么重要。所以他们常常只让孩子参加那些跟学习有关系的社团。如果一个社团的活动听上去又好玩又轻松，这些父母一般不会让孩子去参加。

1.5 开班会
Holding a Class Meeting

🔘 对话一

玛丽娅： 谢谢大家选我当班长。今天开班会我们要讨论两件事：第一件是关于作业的问题，有些同学觉得现在的作业太多了，也有同学觉得不多不少。第二件是关于中国文化讲座活动。好，请大家说吧。

同学一： 现在学习压力挺大的，每门课的老师都给我们很多作业。有时候，我从下课以后就开始做作业，一直要做到晚上十二点钟。除了上课以外，我每天做作业就要做六七个小时。能不能请老师少给我们一些作业？

汤姆： 你说得对。作业越少越好。

玛丽娅： 你也要花六七个小时做作业吗？

汤姆： 不，我每天两三个小时就能把作业做完。不过，要是没有作业，我不就可以多参加一些别的活动了吗？

凯丽： 你两三个小时就能做完作业，还抱怨什么呀。

玛丽娅： 请问大家一般每天要花多少时间做作业？

同学一： 六七个小时。

凯丽： 我一般要花三四个小时。

大卫： 我也只要三四个小时。

同学一： 为什么我花的时间比你们多呢？

汤姆：　　　是不是因为你做作业的时候特别认真，做好
　　　　　　了还要检查三四遍？

同学一：　　不检查怎么行呢？我得不到100分，就会玩
　　　　　　不好，睡不好。

玛丽娅：　　好吧，听上去大家的学习方法不太一样，不
　　　　　　一定是作业太多的问题。

汤姆：　　　玛丽娅，你可真是一言中的。

🔘 **对话二**

玛丽娅：　　现在我们请大卫给我们介绍这个学期中国文
　　　　　　化讲座的情况。

大卫：　　　大家好。这个学期我们班打算组织四次讲
　　　　　　座。讲座的时间是每个月第一个星期一的下
　　　　　　午四点半。

汤姆：　　　这些讲座是关于什么的？

大卫：　　　这个学期的四个话题是：一.中国的电影历
　　　　　　史；二.饮食文化；三.现代画；四.太极拳和
　　　　　　健康。大家觉得这几个话题怎么样？

中国点心

汤姆：　第四个话题好像是给老年人准备的。打太极拳是老年人的运动。不信，你早上到公园去看看，在那儿打太极拳的都是老人。

打太极拳

老人在公园运动

凯丽：　　我觉得汤姆说得对。能不能换个话题？

大卫：　　当然可以，大家有什么建议吗？

明英：　　能不能请人来给我们谈谈在中国上大学的情况？

玛丽娅：我的邻居是个大学生，我可以把他请来。

大卫：　　你的邻居是法国人吧？他的汉语说得怎么样？

玛丽娅：他是在法国出生的，可是三岁就离开了法国，跟父母到中国来了。他是在北京上的小学和中学，汉语讲得非常好，听上去跟中国人一样。

汤姆：　　我也可以请我的邻居，她是中国人，现在是音乐学院的学生。她好像在学习钢琴，我常常听到她在家一边弹钢琴一边唱歌。下课以后，她在一个俱乐部打工，可能是在那儿弹钢琴，也可能是在那儿唱歌。我不太清楚。

大卫：　　没关系，如果你邻居来了，她可以告诉我们她在做什么。

生词

	Simplified	Traditional	Pinyin	Part of Speech	English
1.	班会	班會	bānhuì	*n.*	class meeting
2.	讨论	討論	tǎolùn	*n./v.*	discussion; discuss
3.	关于	關於	guānyú	*prep.*	about, with regard to
4.	讲座	講座	jiǎngzuò	*n.*	lecture
5.	压力	壓力	yālì	*n.*	pressure, stress
6.	越···越		yuè	*adv.*	the more...the more

7.	花		huā	*v.*	spend
8.	不过	不過	bùguò	*conj.*	but (*informal*)
9.	抱怨		bàoyuàn	*n./v.*	complaint; complain
10.	呀		ya	*aux.w.*	a variant of 啊
11.	认真	認眞	rènzhēn	*adj./adv.*	conscientious(ly), serious(ly)
12.	方法		fāngfǎ	*n.*	method, means
13.	一言中的		yī yán zhòng dì	*s.p.*	right on target, right to the point
14.	话题	話題	huàtí	*n.*	topic
15.	信		xìn	*v.*	believe
16.	谈	談	tán	*v.*	speak, talk, discuss

专名

17.	太极拳	太極拳	*Tàijíquán*	*n.*	Taiji boxing (Chinese exercise)

语言注释

1. 越…越… (the more...the more...)

This is a set phrase. 越 is an adverb, and it is followed by a verb or an adjective.

我觉得作业越少越好。

I feel the less homework we have the better.

她越说越高兴。

The more she spoke, the happier she was.

今天的雨越下越大。

Today, the rain is getting heavier as it falls.

2. 不过 (but)

不过 has the same meaning as 可是 and 但是, but it is often used in informal speech.

我奶奶喜欢看电视，不过不喜欢看烹调节目。

My grandmother likes to watch TV, but doesn't like to watch cooking shows.

我以前好像看过那本书，不过记不得书上说了什么了。

I have probably read the book before, but I can't remember what it says.

3. 不就可以…了吗？ (be able to...)

This phrase is a variation of 就可以, which is generally used in a suggestion or in a prediction. Instead of making a direct statement, you can express the same meaning in the form of a question. This makes your suggestion or prediction milder and more tactful.

要是你现在就把作业做完，晚上不就可以去看电影了吗？

(要是你现在就把作业做完，晚上就可以去看电影了。)

If you finish your homework now, wouldn't you be able to go to the movie tonight?

(If you finish your homework now, you can go to the movie tonight.)

如果你去云南，不就可以看到雪山了吗？

(如果你去云南，就可以看到雪山了。)

If you go to Yunnan, wouldn't you be able to see snow-covered mountains?

(If you go to Yunnan, you can see snow-covered mountains.)

4. 呀 (a variant of 啊)

呀, like 啊，can be added to the end of a sentence to express different moods, such as surprise, happiness, doubt, emphasis, etc.

这个问题真让我头疼呀。

This problem really makes my head ache.

那个饭店很大的呀，怎么会没有座位呢？

That restaurant is really big. How come there are no vacant seats?

5. 关于 (about, regarding)

关于选课的问题，你最好问问王老师。

With regard to course selection, you'd better ask Teacher Wang.

你看过那个关于熊猫的电影吗？

Have you seen the film about the panda?

学无止境 EXTEND YOUR KNOWLEDGE

Here are some Chinese words related to class councils.

bānwěi 班委 *class council*	xuéxí wěiyuán 学习委员 *academic chair*	wàilián wěiyuán 外联委员 *public relations chair*
wényù wěiyuán 文娱委员 *recreational activities chair*	tǐyù wěiyuán 体育委员 *sports chair*	wèishēng wěiyuán 卫生委员 *health chair*
cáiwù wěiyuán 财务委员 *treasurer*	shēnghuó wěiyuán 生活委员 *logistics chair (collecting lunch money, arranging transportation, etc.)*	láodòng wěiyuán 劳动委员 *work/project chair*

中国文化一瞥 A Glimpse into Chinese Culture

Chinese proverbs and idioms

We have learned 一言中的 in this lesson. Since it is important for communication to be "right to the point," there are several other Chinese proverbs that have the same meaning as 一言中的. The following proverbs can be used interchangeably.

1. yī yǔ zhòng dì
一 语 中 的

come to the point in a single sentence— right on target, hit the nail on the head

2. yī yǔ pò dì
一 语 破 的

hit the target with one remark— hit the nail on the head, come to the point,

3. yī zhēn jiàn xiě
一 针 见 血

draw blood with one prick—go straight to the heart of the matter, hit the nail on the head, pinpoint

IN USE:

"要成功，就必须努力。"这句话真是一语中的。
"One has to work hard to achieve success." This saying is right to the point.

丁老师一针见血地批评汤姆，"在图书馆前边玩滑板非常不安全。"
Teacher Ding criticized Tom with a single sentence, "It is not safe to skateboard in front of the library."

张校长一语破的地说："我们什么时候都应该注意安全。"
Principle Zhang hit the target with one sentence, "We should pay attention to safety at all times."

YOUR TURN:

How would you give a "straight to the point" (一语中的，一针见血，一语破的) type response to these complaints/explanations?

1. 昨天晚上我刚想做作业，小明就给我打电话，她在电话上说啊说啊，说了两个半小时。后来我的猫又要跟我玩儿。我哪有时间做作业？

   Your response: _____

2. 我昨天上午见到你的时候，你正在看书，我不想打扰你，就没有把这件事告诉你。下课以后，我想告诉你，可是你正在和大卫说话，所以我又没有告诉你。不过，你知道，我是想把这件事告诉你的。

   Your response: _____

3. 我看到你的短信就要给你打电话，可是我邻居的狗一直在叫，我怕你听不清楚我说什么，就没有给你打电话。

   Your response: _____

4. 我的邻居都很奇怪。住在我左边的邻居每天在家唱歌。他唱歌唱得特别难听，可是很喜欢唱。住在右边的邻居特别爱说话。她养了三只猫，一看见我就说她的猫，说啊说啊，可以一口气说半个小时。

   Your response: _____

你知道吗？

中国的小学、中学和大学都有班委。班委是学生选出来的。一般来说 (generally speaking)，班委有五六个人：有班长，副班长 (fùbānzhǎng, class vice-president)，还有几个委员 (wěiyuán, council members)。常见的委员有学习委员、文娱委员、体育委员、财务委员、生活委员、卫生委员或劳动委员。学习委员负责学习。文娱委员和体育委员负责课外活动、体育活动、娱乐活动、晚会、运动会什么的。如果课外活动不太多，有的班就只选一个"文体委员"，把这两个委员的工作放在一起，让一个人做。财务委员负责钱。生活委员要注意教室的安全，同学们的吃、住、交通。一般的学校都有卫生委员或者劳动委员。跟美国学校不同，在中国，教室是学生打扫的。每个学生都要轮流值日 (lúnliú zhírì, take turns to be on duty for the day)。值日生的工作是下课以后把教室打扫干净 (gānjìng, clean)。每个月学校还有大扫除 (general cleaning)。卫生委员或劳动委员不但要决定每天的值日生，而且要组织班里的同学参加大扫除。

1.6 第一单元复习
Unit 1 Review

 课文

（这是汤姆给爷爷奶奶写的电子邮件。）

New	Reply	Reply All	Forward	Delete	Print

爷爷奶奶：你们好！

奶奶的电子邮件收到了。奶奶说爷爷正在学习电脑打字，学会了就给我们写电邮。爷爷学得怎么样了？

学校九月一日开学了。这个学期，我比以前更忙了。因为再过两年我们就要参加高考，所以老师们非常注意我们的学习，每天给我们很多作业。我们班有的同学每天要花六七个小时做作业。我做作业做得很快，但是每天还要花三四个小时。

这个学期我上了六门课，四门是必修课，两门是选修课。我最喜欢的是数学课。教我们数学的王老师以前在两个重点中学教过书，听说他的不少学生现在成了大学的数学教授。王老师的教学方法非常好。他能把一个很难的问题一下子就讲清楚。讲完了以后，他就让我们马上练习做题。跟有些老师不一样，他给的作业不太多。可是数学作业不容易，需要我花时间去想，去做。

除了上课以外，我还参加了学校的数学兴趣小组和美国学生俱乐部。每个月有一个周末，我去"老人爱，爱老人"组织做半天义工。暑假的时候，我在那个组织做过义工，认识了几位老人，跟他们成了好朋友，他们希望我能常常去看看他们，所以现在我每个月去看他们一次。

杰米说，他要给你们写电子邮件，把他的秘密告诉你们。我不知道他的秘密是什么，因为他还没有告诉我。

爸爸妈妈都很好，也很忙。他们让我问你们好！

汤姆

对话

大卫： 张爷爷，请您看一下这张图片，你认识这个人吗？

张爷爷：这个人是谁啊？我看不太清楚，我的眼镜呢？

玛丽娅：您的眼镜在这儿呢。

张爷爷：人老了，看近的东西，没有眼镜就看不清楚了。哦，这个人有点儿像小高，可是小高比这张图片上的人好看多了。

玛丽娅：张爷爷，这是我一边听看门师傅说一边画的，我画得不太好。这个小高是谁？

张奶奶：小高啊，他是我们老邻居的孩子。他出生以后，身体不太好，常常因为生病不能去幼儿园，他父母工作又非常忙，所以我常常照顾他。他就跟我自己的孩子一样。

大卫： 他常常来看你们吗？

张奶奶：对，以前他每个星期都要来一两次。怎么了？你们认识小高吗？

玛丽娅：哦，是这样的，我们很想知道张爷爷丢了优盘的那一天，有没有人来过你们家。看门师傅说，小高来过，可是因为你们在睡觉，他就走了。

张爷爷：对，对。那天小高是要来跟我们说再见的。他那天下午就要坐飞机去加拿大，因为我们在睡觉，就没见到他。他现在正在加拿大学习呢。上个星期，他还给我来了电邮，说他马上要高中毕业了，想到美国去上大学。

张奶奶：　玛丽娅，等小高回来，你可以见见小高。小高画画儿画得可好了。你看，这张画儿是他画的。

玛丽娅：　这只猫很可爱。

张奶奶：　这是我们楼下邻居养的猫，叫"黄黄"。黄黄很友好。从一楼到九楼，它哪儿都去过。只要你家的门开着，它就会进去。夏天的时候，我常常把大门开着，所以它常常来我们家。

黄黄和它的朋友

张爷爷：　黄黄还喜欢把这家的东西带到那家去，把那家的东西带到这家来。要是我们家多了什么东西，我们就知道是黄黄带来的。它带来的东西可多了，有袜子啊、糖啊、饼干啊、小玩具啊什么的，有一次它还带来了半条鱼。

大卫：　哎，张爷爷，你的优盘会不会是黄黄拿走的呢？

张奶奶：　对啊，我们怎么没想到呢？我们应该一家一家地去问问。

生词

	Simplified	Traditional	Pinyin	Part of Speech	English
1.	开学	開學	kāixué	*v.o.*	semester begins
2.	秘密		mìmì	*n.*	secret
3.	图片	圖片	túpiàn	*n.*	picture
4.	眼镜	眼鏡	yǎnjìng	*n.*	eyeglasses, spectacles
5.	照顾	照顧	zhàogù	*v.*	care for, look after
6.	丢		diū	*v.*	lose, be missing
7.	友好		yǒuhǎo	*adj.*	friendly

生词扩充 EXPAND YOUR WORD POWER

Many Chinese words are formed by combining two or more characters. If you know the characters in a word, you can often guess the meaning of that word. See if you understand the meaning of the following words.

图画		出生地	
打拳		退步	
笑话		满座	
甜蜜		研究生	
填表		太阳眼镜	
借住		队友	

SELF-ASSESSMENT

In Unit 1, you have learned to talk about personal experiences and characteristics. You have also learned to describe academic courses and student clubs. Have you achieved the learning goals of Unit 1? After completing the exercises for Unit 1 in your Workbook, fill out the following self-assessment sheet.

Yes/No	Can you say and write these things in Chinese?
	Describe, in some detail, personal experiences
	Describe personalities
	Describe, in some detail, academic courses
	Describe, in some detail, student clubs
	Narrate, in some detail, a past event
	Narrate, in some detail, a present event
	Narrate, in some detail, a future event
	Make a compliment
	Respond to a compliment
	Give procedural instructions

9–10   yes   excellent
6–8   yes   good
1–5   yes   need some work

第二单元： 我的家人和亲戚

UNIT 2 My Family and Relatives

By the end of this unit, you will learn how to:

• Talk about dating and marriage

• Describe, in some detail, your family members

• Talk in some detail about your personal history

• Use Chinese terms to address your close relatives

• Use Chinese terms to address members of a non-traditional family

• Talk about the "one child" practice in China

• Briefly discuss the advantages and disadvantages of being an only child

• Talk about a typical Chinese family in the past and in the present

• Talk about cultural diversity in a family setting

• Describe various types of families

2.1 姥姥和姥爷
Grandma and Grandpa

🔘 对话一

（星期一玛丽娅在学校见到了汤姆。）

玛丽娅： 星期天我给你发短信，请你去看电影，你怎
么没回？

汤姆： 哦，我把手机忘在家里了。昨天为了庆祝我
姥姥和姥爷结婚四十周年，我们一家都去美
心酒家参加酒席了。

玛丽娅： 你姥姥姥爷不是住在
北京吗？

汤姆： 是的。不过他们上个星
期来上海看亲戚朋友了。
我姥姥姥爷都是上海人，
后来因为工作，才把家
搬到北京去的。所以他们
的很多亲戚朋友还住在上海。

玛丽娅： 有多少人去参加酒席？

汤姆： 一百多人。多数是亲戚，还有一些是姥姥姥
爷在上海的朋友。

玛丽娅： 那么多人一定很热闹吧？

汤姆： 当然热闹了。我姥姥有四个兄弟姐妹，我姥
爷有六个兄弟姐妹，住在上海的都来了。他
们的子女，只要是在上海的，也都来参加
了。

玛丽娅：你妈妈有兄弟姐妹吗？

汤姆：她有一个妹妹，两个弟弟。星期日的酒席就是他们四个人组织的。

玛丽娅：他们都住在上海吗？

汤姆：不，我妈妈的两个弟弟住在上海，妹妹住在北京。

玛丽娅：听上去，以前的中国家庭，孩子都不少。

汤姆：是啊，可是现在不一样了。一般的中国家庭只有一个孩子。星期六的时候，来的老人比孩子多。

玛丽娅：这么多亲戚，你都认识吗？

汤姆：有一半以上我都不认识。

玛丽娅：那么多亲戚朋友来参加酒席，你姥姥姥爷一定很高兴吧？

汤姆：对。我姥爷特别喜欢唱歌。昨天他高兴得不得了，一下子唱了五首歌。我把他的表演都录了像。下次你来我家，我给你看录像。

玛丽娅：好。

对话二

汤姆： 妈妈，星期天我听姥姥说，她跟姥爷是中学同学。

妈妈： 对，那时候，他们不在一个班，可是都参加了学校的合唱团，后来就成了好朋友。

汤姆： 他们在中学就结婚了吗？

妈妈： 在中国不能那么早就结婚。中国的结婚年龄是：男的二十二岁以上，女的二十岁以上。

汤姆： 你和爸爸不是常常说，我们在中学最好不要谈恋爱，要一心一意学习吗？怎么姥姥姥爷在中学就谈恋爱了呢？

妈妈： 他们是中学毕业以后开始谈的。那时候，姥姥在上海的一个幼儿园当老师，姥爷去北京上大学了，他们俩就互相写信。越写越有话说，慢慢地就谈恋爱了。

汤姆： 他们不打电话吗？

妈妈： 四十多年以前，一般的中国家庭都没有电话。

汤姆： 那他们是什么时候结婚的呢？

妈妈： 姥爷大学毕业以后又过了两年，他们才结婚。因为姥爷的工作在北京，所以姥姥就搬到北京去了。

汤姆： 那你是在北京出生的吗？

妈妈： 是的，我和你舅舅阿姨都是在北京出生的，我们的小学、中学也都是在北京上的。

汤姆： 那两个舅舅怎么都搬到上海来了呢？

妈妈：大舅舅是在上海上的大学，毕业以后就在上海
　　　工作。小舅舅前几年在上海找到了他喜欢的工
　　　作，就把家搬过来了。

汤姆：哦，是这样。

上海幼儿园

A Shanghai kindergarten

 生词

	Simplified	Traditional	Pinyin	Part of Speech	English
1.	姥爷	姥爺	lǎoyé	n.	maternal grandfather
2.	结婚	結婚	jiéhūn	v.	marry, get married
3.	周年	週年	zhōunián	n.	anniversary
4.	酒席		jiǔxí	n.	banquet
5.	亲戚	親戚	qīnqi	n.	relatives
6.	多数	多數	duōshù	n./adj.	majority; most
7.	热闹	熱鬧	rènao	adj.	lively, full of noise and excitement
8.	不得了		bùdéliǎo	adv.	Extremely
9.	首		shǒu	m.w.	for songs and poems
10.	录像	錄像	lùxiàng	n./v.	video; record on video
11.	合唱团	合唱團	héchàngtuán	n.	chorus
12.	年龄		niánlíng	n.	age
13.	谈恋爱	談戀愛	tán liàn'ài	v.o.	date
14.	一心一意		yī xīn yī yì	s.p.	wholeheartedly, devote wholly to
15.	信		xìn	n.	letter
16.	这样	這樣	zhèyàng	adv.	in this way, like this
17.	舅舅		jiùjiù	n.	uncle (mother's brother)
18.	阿姨		āyí	n.	aunt (mother's sister), *way to address an adult woman*

语言注释

1. 只要 (as long as, provided)

只要常常运动，注意饮食，你就会比较健康。

As long as (you) exercise often and pay attention to your diet, you will be quite healthy.

明天只要有时间，我一定去。

As long as (I) have time tomorrow, I will definitely go.

2. Complex directional complement

In a complex directional complement, two indicators of direction appear in a verb phrase. The first indicator of direction is usually one of these seven words: 上、下、进、出、回、过、起. The final indicator is always 来 or 去.

In Lesson 1.2 of *Huanying* Volume 2, we showed you that 来 or 去 can be added to the six verbs 上、下、进、出、回 or 过. The addition of 来 or 去 is to indicate whether an action happens towards or away from the speaker. The six words described in Volume 2, plus 起, can also be used as directional words. Together with 来 or 去, they form a complex directional complement. Here is a list of possible complex directional complements:

Verb +	上来	下来	进来	出来	回来	过来	起来
	上去	下去	进去	出去	回去	过去	

A complex directional complement is added to a verb to show whether the action takes place in the direction of or away from the speaker.

他们把家搬过来了。

They moved their family here.

小猫跑出去了。

The kitten ran out.

请你把报纸拿上去给张爷爷。

Please take the newspaper upstairs to Grandpa Zhang.

你可以把车开回去吗？

Can you drive the car back there?

Complex directional complements can be also used in potential complements (whether or not something can or will happen).

这个桌子你们搬得进去吗?

Will you be able to move the table in?

这件事你想得起来吗?

Can you recall this matter?

3. Using 后来 and 以后

后来 can only be used to describe past events. 以后 can be used to describe both past and future events.

他是在北京出生的, 后来/以后又在北京上了
小学。

He was born in Beijing and later attended elementary school there.

昨天晚上我们先去看了电影, 后来/以后又去逛了
商店。

Last night, we went to a movie first and then went window shopping.

今年暑假我先去上海旅游, 以后要去南京大学
学习。

This summer vacation, I will first travel to Shanghai, and afterwards study at Nanjing University.

以后我会常常给你打电话的。

I will call you regularly in the future.

学无止境 EXTEND YOUR KNOWLEDGE

Now you have learned some words about dating and marriage. Here are several additional words related to both topics. Since you know most of the characters in the following words already, pinyin is provided only for new characters.

男朋友 *boyfriend*	女朋友 *girlfriend*	介绍人 *matchmaker*
约 (yuē) 会 *meeting, date*	爱情 *love (between lovers)*	订婚 *engaged, engagement*
婚礼 *wedding*	未 (wèi) 婚 *unmarried, single*	已婚 *married*

中国文化一瞥 A Glimpse into Chinese Culture

Chinese proverbs and idioms

Many proverbs and idioms describe love. Here are a few:

1. yī   jiàn   zhōng qíng

一   见   钟   情

fall in love at first sight

IN USE:

很多年以前，姥爷在篮球队训练的时候见到了姥姥，他们俩一见钟情。

Many years ago, grandpa met grandma during basketball training. They fell in love at first sight.

他那么不客气，怎么可能有人会对他一见钟情呢？

He is quite rude. How could anyone fall in love with him at first sight?

YOUR TURN:

你觉得"一见钟情"是一件好事还是一件坏事？为什么？

2. xīn   xīn   xiāng   yìn
心   心   相   印

hearts linked together in perfect harmony — mutual understanding and attraction

IN USE:

姥姥姥爷结婚四十年了，他们俩心心相印。

(My) grandparents have been married for 40 years. They have been in perfect harmony.

YOUR TURN:

1. 有没有人跟你心心相印？
2. 你觉得什么样的人可能跟你心心相印？

The legendary love story of 梁山伯和祝英台

"梁山伯 (Liáng Shānbó) 和祝英台 (Zhù Yīngtái)" 是中国一个有名的爱情传说，一般的中国人都知道。

传说一千七百多年以前，中国的浙江省 (Zhèjiāng province) 住着一家姓祝的人家，家里有一个女儿，叫祝英台。祝英台很想去杭州上学，可是因为那时候学校只收男学生，所以她就女扮男装 (nǚ bàn nán zhuāng, a woman dressing in men's clothes) 到杭州去。在路上，她遇到 (yùdào, met) 了一位男同学，叫梁山伯，也要去杭州的那个学校上学。他们俩就一起去杭州，在路上成了好朋友。到了学校以后，他们又在一起学习了三年。虽然梁山伯和祝英台心心相印，但是梁山伯一直不知道祝英台是女的。

三年以后，祝英台离开学校回家了。梁山伯非常想她，有一天，他去祝英台家看她，才知道他的好朋友是女的，而且非常美丽。梁山伯觉得他应该跟祝英台结婚，可是那时候，祝英台已经跟别人订婚了。梁山伯知道以后非常伤心，因为太伤心，过了几年他还很年轻就死 (sǐ, die) 了。

祝英台结婚的那一天，经过 (jīngguò, pass) 梁山伯的坟墓 (fénmù, tomb)，她就去祭拜 (jìbài, pay tribute) 他。这时候，突然刮起了大风，梁山伯的坟墓裂 (liè, split) 开了，祝英台跳进了坟墓。后来，大家就看到有两只漂亮的蝴蝶 (húdié, butterfly) 从坟墓里飞了出来，双双飞去。

The legendary love story "Liang Shanbo and Zhu Yingtai" is well known in China. Over 1700 years ago, Chinese schools only admitted boys. Miss Zhu Yingtai, a young woman from the present-day Zhejiang Province, wanted to attend school so much that she decided to dress up as a young man. On her way to a school in Hangzhou, she met Mr. Liang Shanbo, who was admitted to the same school. They traveled together and became friends. For three years, the two studied together, helped each other, and became best friends, but Mr. Liang Shanbo never knew that Miss Zhu was a woman.

Eventually, Miss Zhu left school and returned home. Mr. Liang missed his friend so much that he paid her a visit at her house. He was very surprised to see that his best friend was a beautiful young woman. Mr. Liang wanted very much to marry her but was told that Miss Zhu was already engaged to another man. He felt so sad that he died of a broken heart soon after.

On the day when Miss Zhu was taken to the wedding ceremony, the bride's party passed by Mr. Liang's tomb. Miss Zhu left to pay tribute to her lost love. When she got to Mr. Liang's tomb, a strong wind came and the tomb suddenly opened. Miss Zhu jumped into the tomb.

Soon afterwards, a pair of beautiful butterflies flew out. They flew side by side, higher and higher into the sky.

YOUR TURN:
1. 你知道别的有名的爱情传说吗？请你用中文说一说。
2. 上网去找一找，有没有关于"梁山伯和祝英台"的音乐、电视剧、电影、书、光盘、和戏剧。

你知道吗？

汉语里有许多特别的词，是用来称呼(chēnghū, address)家里人的。我们可以用一个英文词 sister 来称呼姐姐和妹妹，可是在汉语中，就一定要用两个不同的词"姐姐"和"妹妹"。同样，英文的 uncle 可以是爸爸的兄弟，也可以是妈妈的兄弟。可是在汉语中，爸爸的哥哥是"伯伯(bóbo)"，爸爸的弟弟是"叔叔"，妈妈的兄弟是"舅舅"。我们还知道，英文的 grandparents 可以是爸爸的父母，也可以是妈妈的父母。可是在汉语中，爸爸的父母是"爷爷奶奶"，妈妈的父母是"姥爷姥姥"。

要知道怎么用汉语称呼亲戚不是很容易，许多中国孩子也常常称呼错，所以中国父母一有机会就教孩子。如果叔叔来了，父母会说："你看，叔叔来了，快叫叔叔。"如果见到了舅妈（舅舅的太太），父母就告诉孩子："这是舅妈，说舅妈好。"这样练习了很多很多次，最后中国孩子就知道应该怎么称呼每个亲戚了。

2.2 独生子女
The Only Child

🔘 对话一

（星期六，凯丽去林叔叔家做客。）

凯丽： 林叔叔林阿姨好！

林叔叔：凯丽，快进来，请坐。我给你去拿饮料。

凯丽： 谢谢林叔叔。林东呢？他出去了吗？

林阿姨：他还在睡觉呢。

林叔叔：什么？都十点了，他还没起床？

林阿姨：他啊，昨天晚上做作业做到半夜。我让他做完作业就睡觉，可是他不听，一直在网上跟朋友聊天，到两三点钟才睡觉。反正今天他不用去上学，晚一点起床也没有关系。

林叔叔：林东这个孩子啊，就是不懂事。我常说，要是林东能像凯丽那样独立，能把自己照顾好就好了。林东到现在还像个小孩，吃饭要我们帮他做，房间要我们帮他打扫，衣服要我们帮他洗，买东西要我们帮他买，出门要我们告诉他坐什么车。

凯丽： 你们可以教林东怎么做。我父母总是让我自己先试着做，要是我做不好，他们才帮我。这样练习了几次，我就会做了。

林叔叔：凯丽说得对。我们不能怪林东不独立，是我们自己不放心，做什么事都怕他做不了，做不好。

林阿姨： 对啊，还有爷爷、奶奶、姥姥、姥爷也都不放心，总是替他做这做那。他也就没有必要学了。

林叔叔： 所以有人说，独生子女是"小皇帝"。一家人都为一个孩子服务。

三口之家

A family of three

对话二

林东： 对不起，凯丽，你来了很久了吧？我刚起床。

凯丽： 我刚来了半个多小时，在跟你父母聊天呢。你很晚才睡觉吗？

林东： 是的，我在网上跟同学聊天聊到三点。

凯丽： 你们都住校，一个星期回家一次。昨天，你才回家了几个小时，就想他们了？

林东： 我也不知道为什么，跟同学有说不完的话。

凯丽： 那跟你爸爸妈妈呢？

林东： 告诉你一个秘密，要不是爸爸妈妈非要我每个周末回家，我一点都不想回来。在学校里跟同学一起玩，一起聊天，多好啊。

凯丽： 他们一个星期没见你，会很想你的。你难道不想他们吗？

林东：　不是不想，就是跟他们说话很没劲。我爸爸
　　　　见了我就问：考试考到第一名了吗？作业都
　　　　做完了吗？你打算上哪个重点大学？我妈妈
　　　　见了我就说：你在学校要多注意身体，多吃
　　　　蔬菜，多休息，多运动，不要玩电脑玩到太
　　　　晚。

凯丽：　你玩电脑玩到很晚吗？

林东：　怎么可能呢？我们学校管得非常严，每天晚
　　　　上十点关灯，大家都得睡觉。我妈妈就是喜
　　　　欢担心。你父母呢？他们管你吗？

凯丽：　管得不太多。他们有时候也问问我的学习、
　　　　身体、有没有男朋友什么的。

林东：　你有男朋友吗？

凯丽：　这可是我的秘密。

三口之家

🔘 生词

	Simplified	Traditional	Pinyin	Part of Speech	English
1.	做客		zuòkè	v.o.	be a guest, be a visitor
2.	反正		fǎnzhèng	adv.	anyway, in any case, anyhow
3.	懂事		dǒngshì	v.o.	sensible, thoughtful (to describe a child)
4.	独立	獨立	dúlì	adj./n.	independent; independence
5.	怪		guài	v.	blame
6.	放心		fàngxīn	v.o.	feel relieved, rest assured
7.	怕		pà	v.	fear, worry
8.	独生子女	獨生子女	dúshēng zǐnǚ	n.	only child
9.	皇帝		huángdì	n.	emperor
10.	难道	難道	nándào	adv.	can it be that…(used in a question for emphasis)
11.	第一名		dìyīmíng	n.	first, the first place
12.	管		guǎn	v.	manage, control, be in charge of
13.	严	嚴	yán	adj.	strict, rigorous, stern
14.	关灯	關燈	guāndēng	v.o.	turn off light

语言注释

1. 反正 (anyway, in any case)

这个反正不贵，我们再买一个吧。

In any case, it's not expensive. Let's buy another one.

反正他不喜欢放风筝，我们不用请他了。
He doesn't like to fly kites anyway. We don't need to invite him.

2. 要不是 (if not, if it were not for)

要不是你非要我来，今天我就不来了。
I wouldn't have come in today if you hadn't insisted that I do so.

要不是他帮我，我一定不可能把这件事做完。
If it hadn't been for his help, I wouldn't have been able to finish the job.

3. Using 难道···吗？ in a question for emphasis

This structure is used to express a speaker's disbelief and surprise at a situation that is contrary to the speaker's belief or an obvious fact.

难道你不想爸爸妈妈吗？
Can it be that you don't miss your parents?

他难道不知道今天有考试吗？
Is it really possible that he doesn't know about today's test?

学无止境 EXTEND YOUR KNOWLEDGE

We have learned how to say "only child" in Chinese. Here are some words that are associated with the only-child phenomenon in China. Since you know most of the characters already, pinyin is provided only for new characters.

人口	增长 (zēngzhǎng)	出生率 (lǜ)
population	increase	birthrate
晚婚	晚生	少生
later marriage	later childbirth	fewer births
优生	优育	计划生育
healthier childbirth	better childrearing	family planning

YOUR TURN:

Here is what the government encourages the Chinese people to do. Do you understand the meaning?

少生晚生都要优生，生男生女都要优育。

政府办公室

Government offices

中国文化一瞥 A Glimpse into Chinese Culture

Chinese proverbs and idioms

Many proverbs and idioms describe how Chinese parents view their children. Here are a few:

1. wàng zǐ   chéng lóng

望　子　成　龙

hope one's son will turn into a dragon—have a bright future, have great ambitions for one's child, hold high hopes for one's child

2. wàng nǚ   chéng fèng

望 女 成 凤

hope one's daughter will turn into a phoenix—have a bright future, have great ambitions for one's daughter, hold high hopes for one's daughter

IN USE:

A: 这个中学生觉得压力 (yālì, pressure) 很大，因为他父母希望他成为世界上最有名的数学家。

B: 中国不少父母都是望子成龙，望女成凤。

A: The high school student felt a lot of pressure because his parents wanted him to become the most famous mathematician in the world.

B: Many Chinese parents are like this. They hope their children will have a bright future.

3. zhǎng shàng míng zhū

掌 上 明 珠

a bright pearl in the palm—a beloved daughter

IN USE:

小丽是她父母的掌上明珠。

Xiao Li is like a bright pearl in her parents' palm—they treasure her very much.

YOUR TURN:

Use 望子成龙，望女成凤 or 掌上明珠 to describe the following situations.

老王非常喜欢他的小女儿，觉得她又聪明又可爱。	
白老师希望他的儿子将来能成为一个有名的作家。	
他们的女儿是一个律师。他们希望她是世界上最好的律师。	
他们的儿子虽然学习不怎么好，但是很会打篮球。他们都希望他是第二个 Michael Jordan。	
妈妈说小丽唱歌唱得很好，以后一定是一个歌唱家。	

The story of 孟母三迁

在孔子 (Kǒngzi, Confucius) 的弟子 (disciple) 中，孟子 (Mèngzi, Mencius) 是最有名的。孟子小时候，他母亲为了让他有更好的学习环境，搬了三次家。这就是中国历史上一个有名的故事：孟母三迁 (Mèng mǔ sān qiān, Mencius' mother moved houses three times)。

　　孟子小时候，他们家住在一个墓地 (mùdì, graveyard) 旁边。墓地里常常有人来做祭拜 (jìbài, pay tribute)，孟子和他的小朋友觉得很有意思，就常常学着别人做祭拜。孟子的母亲看见了，觉得不能让孩子在这个地方住下去，他们就搬家到城市去。

　　在城市里，每天有人在大街上做买卖 (business)，孟子看到了，觉得做买卖也很有意思，就和小朋友一起学商人 (businessmen) 做买卖。孟子的母亲觉得，这也不是一个好地方，所以她就把家搬到了一个学校附近。

　　搬到学校附近以后，孟子跟以前不一样了。学校的学生每天学习，对人也很客气。孟子就向他们学习，又喜欢读书，对人又客气。孟子的母亲想，这才是我们应该住的地方。

Mencius was one of the most famous Confucian scholars in Chinese history. When he was a little boy, his mother moved three times to create an ideal learning environment for him.

At one time, Mencius' family lived by a graveyard. People frequented the graveyard to pay tribute to the dead. Mencius and his friends thought the ceremony was very interesting and they started to play the game of "paying tribute to the dead." When his mother saw this, she felt the graveyard was not a good place for him to learn, so she moved the family to a city.

In the city, Mencius and the neighboring children mimicked salesmen doing business in the streets. His mother thought the city was not a good place to educate him either, so she moved the family close to a school.

Things were different by a school. Mencius learned etiquette and manners. He also observed the good learning habits of the students. Consequently, Mencius became very interested in learning. His mother was finally relieved because she knew this was the right place for them to live.

YOUR TURN:

　　你觉得你的生活环境怎么影响 (yǐngxiǎng, influence) 了你？

你知道吗？

中国有十三亿 (yì, a hundred million) 人口。有那么多的人要吃饭、穿衣、住房、上学、工作、坐车、看病…，这对中国来说是一个很大的挑战 (tiǎozhàn, challenge)。为了让人口增长得慢一点儿，中国政府在1979年开始了"独生子女"的政策 (zhèngcè, policy)，也就是：一家一个孩子的政策。现在多数的中国家庭都只有一个孩子。

但是，也有一些家庭有两个或者更多的孩子。如果一个家庭生的第一个孩子有健康问题，就可以生第二个孩子。少数民族家庭也可以多生几个孩子。如果男女双方都是独生子女，那么他们结婚以后，也可以生两个孩子。

人山人海

A sea of people in a Beijing street

2.3 大家庭和小家庭
Big Families and Small Families

全家福

🔘 对话一

张奶奶： 你看这张照片，这是我们家的"全家福"。

玛丽娅： 那么多人啊！让我数数，一、二、三、四…，一共有十八个人啊。哪个是您？

张奶奶： 这个是我，那年我八岁，我右边的是我大姐，左边的是三姐。我有四个姐姐，我最小。我们家都是女孩子。

玛丽娅： 那这儿还有几个男孩，他们是谁？

张奶奶： 是我叔叔的孩子。我两个叔叔都没有女儿，只有儿子。你看，这是我大叔叔，这是我小叔叔。坐在中间的这两个人是我爷爷和奶奶。

玛丽娅： 那时候，你们都住在一起吗？

张奶奶：是的，我们一家七口人，大叔叔家五口人，小叔叔家四口人，还有爷爷奶奶，都住在一起。

玛丽娅：你们是不是住在一个很大的房子里？

张奶奶：不太大，所以家里很挤。我住的房间里有两张大床，我们五个姐妹都睡在一个房间里。

玛丽娅：那么多人都在一起吃饭吗？

张奶奶：是的。我们的客厅里放了三个桌子，大人一桌，小孩两桌。客厅里每天有很多人进进出出，说说笑笑，热闹得不得了。有的在那儿做作业，有的做手工，有的玩游戏，有的聊天。有时候客人来了，也去客厅。

玛丽娅：大家庭的生活您喜欢吗？

张奶奶：人多很热闹。要是你想找个人说话，玩游戏，总是可以找到。可是人多事多，这个孩子要上学了，那个要工作了，这个要谈恋爱了，那个要结婚了。想得到一点儿安静是不可能的。人多意见也多，什么事情都是你有你的意见，我有我的意见，要做一个决定不太容易。

玛丽娅：那最后谁做决定呢？

张奶奶：最后总是爷爷为大家做决定。

对话二

明英：立安，你在忙什么？

立安：我在给我弟弟写生日卡。下个星期一是我弟弟的生日。

明英：　你弟弟多大了？

立安：　十四岁了。他在香港上中学。

明英：　你还有别的兄弟姐妹吗？

立安：　我还有两个姐姐。你有兄弟姐妹吗？

明英：　没有。我是独生子女。

立安：　独生子女很好，在家没人跟你竞争。

明英：　你们为哪些事竞争？

立安：　比方说，谁可以跟父母出去，谁可以晚一点
　　　　儿回家，还有玩具、吃的东西、看电视、用
　　　　电脑、零花钱、等等。你一定没有这些问题
　　　　吧？所以我觉得做独生子女挺好的，一定是
　　　　我要什么，父母就给我什么。

明英：　我虽然不需要竞争，可是也有别的问题啊。
　　　　你们家有四个孩子，父母不可能总是管着
　　　　你。我呢，父母二十四小时管着我。他们两
　　　　个人管我一个，还有爷爷奶奶姥姥姥爷也总
　　　　是管我，我被他们管得太多了，一点自由都
　　　　没有。

立安：　那么多人关心你，照顾你也不错啊。

明英：　是啊，我是很幸运。可是有时候没有小朋友
　　　　跟我玩，我只能跟大人玩。爷爷带我去公
　　　　园，我一跑爷爷就说："别跑得太快了，我
　　　　追不上你。"跟大人玩真的很没劲。

立安：　不过有时候，你也不愿意总是跟兄弟姐妹玩
　　　　啊。我弟弟小时候非要跟着我，我走到哪
　　　　儿，他跟到哪儿，每件事都问我"为什
　　　　么"。我不带他出去，他就哭。我父母就

　　　　说："立安，你是哥哥，要好好照顾
　　弟弟。"

明英：　现在他还跟着你吗？

立安：　现在？上次我回家，一跟他说话，他就
　　说："你等一下再跟我说话，好吗？我正在
　　网上跟朋友聊天呢。"

 生词

Simplified	Traditional	Pinyin	Part of Speech	English
1. 全家福		quánjiāfú	n.	photograph of the whole family
2. 数	數	shǔ	v.	count
3. 口		kǒu	m.w.	for number of people in a family
4. 床		chuáng	n.	bed
5. 桌（子）		zhuō(zi)	n.	table
6. 安静	安静	ānjìng	adj./n.	quiet, peaceful; peacefulness
7. 意见	意見	yìjiàn	n.	opinion, view, idea
8. 竞争	競争	jìngzhēng	n./v.	competition; compete
9. 零花钱	零花錢	línghuāqián	n.	pocket money, allowance
10. 等等		děngděng	pron.	etc., and so on
11. 虽然	雖然	suīrán	conj.	although, though
12. 追		zhuī	v.	chase after, catch up with
13. 哭		kū	v.	cry

语言注释

1. Measure word 口

When talking about the number of people in a family, we can use measure word 口. The measure word 个 can also be used, but 口 is more colloquial, especially in northern China.

你家有几口人？　　How many people are in your family?

他家有三口人。　　There are three people in his family.

2. 等等 (etc., and so on, and so forth)

等等 is used at the end of a list.

> 来的人很多，有我姥姥、舅舅、阿姨等等。
>
> Many people came, such as my grandmother, uncle, aunt and so on.

> 为了开晚会，我们准备了汉堡、水果、冰激凌、饮料等等。
>
> For the party, we prepared hamburgers, fruits, ice cream, drinks, etc.

3. 虽然…可是/但是… (although…, though…, even though…)

> 虽然他是独生子女，可是他的同学像他的兄弟姐妹一样。
>
> Although he is an only child, his classmates are like his siblings.

> 虽然天很冷，但是我们还是去公园了。
>
> Even though it was very cold, we went to the park.

学无止境 EXTEND YOUR KNOWLEDGE

We know that Chinese people use many different terms to address family members and relatives. The following two tables show how to address close relatives from the father's and from the mother's families. Pinyin is provided for new characters only.

爸爸家的亲戚

称呼	拼音	和你的关系
爷爷		爸爸的爸爸
奶奶		爸爸的妈妈
伯伯	bóbo	爸爸的哥哥

伯母		伯伯的太太
叔叔		爸爸的弟弟
婶婶	shěnshen	叔叔的太太
姑姑	gūgu	爸爸的姐姐，爸爸的妹妹
姑夫		姑姑的先生 (husband)
堂哥		伯伯、叔叔、姑姑的儿子，年龄比你大。
堂姐		伯伯、叔叔、姑姑的女儿，年龄比你大。
堂弟		伯伯、叔叔、姑姑的儿子，年龄比你小。
堂妹		伯伯、叔叔、姑姑的女儿，年龄比你小。

妈妈家的亲戚

称呼	拼音	和你的关系
姥爷		妈妈的爸爸
姥姥		妈妈的妈妈
舅舅		妈妈的哥哥，妈妈的弟弟
舅妈/舅母		舅舅的太太
阿姨		妈妈的姐姐，妈妈的妹妹
姨夫		阿姨的先生
表哥		舅舅、阿姨的儿子，年龄比你大。
表姐		舅舅、阿姨的女儿，年龄比你大。
表弟		舅舅、阿姨的儿子，年龄比你小。
表妹		舅舅、阿姨的女儿，年龄比你小。

中国文化一瞥 **A Glimpse into Chinese Culture**

Chinese proverbs and idioms

Some proverbs describe many people taking action at the same time.

1. qī   zuǐ   bā   shé
   七   嘴   八   舌

seven mouths and eight tongues—all talking at once, all talking in confusion, lively discussion with everybody trying to get a word in

七嘴八舌
Chatting in a community park

2. qī   shǒu   bā   jiǎo
   七   手   八   脚

seven hands and eight feet—great hurry and bustle, with a lot of people lending a hand

少数民族的妇女在工作
Minority women working together

IN USE:

开班会的时候，同学们七嘴八舌，非常热闹。

During the class meeting, the students were all talking at once and had a lively discussion.

他们家人多。有什么事情，七手八脚一下子就做完了。

There are many people in the family. If something needs to be done, it's done right away with everyone lending a hand.

YOUR TURN:

回答下面的问题：

1. 什么时候同学们会七嘴八舌？
2. 在什么地方你会听到许多人七嘴八舌？
3. 什么时候同学们会七手八脚地做一件事？
4. 在什么地方，你会看到大家七手八脚地帮助别人？

Traditional Chinese sayings about sons

For thousands of years, the Chinese were engaged in agricultural work. Since manpower was valued highly in farming, Chinese people usually valued sons more than daughters. The following sayings reflected this tradition.

多子多福 (fú, good fortune)

the more sons, the more blessings

早生 (give birth to) 儿子早得福

the earlier one has a son, the earlier one is blessed

早得贵子

wishing you will soon have a precious son (often said to newlyweds)

你知道吗？

家庭对中国人来说非常重要。中国现在除了只有两代
(dài, generation) 人的小家庭以外，还有许多家庭是"三代
同堂" (three generations live under one roof)
或者"四代同堂"。

在一般的中国家庭里，父母都出去工作。如果一个家庭是
三代同堂，那么老人（爷爷、奶奶、姥姥、姥爷）就会帮助照
顾孩子。等孩子长大了，也会照顾老人。一个家庭只有两代人
的话，孩子小的时候，父母就常常把他们送到幼儿园去。

中国的传统 (chuántǒng, tradition) 文化是，每个人都应该把家庭
放在第一位。比方说，要是一个家庭有兄弟俩要上学，父母没
有钱，只能送一个孩子去上学，那么他们就会看一看，哪个孩
子的学习比较好。如果哥哥的学习好，弟弟就应该让哥哥去上
学。将来，哥哥从学校毕业了，也不能只关心自己的生活，还
应该关心父母和弟弟的生
活。这种"家庭第一"的
传统让很多中国人在需要
帮助的时候，总是先找自
己的家人和亲戚。比方
说，要是一个人生病了，
需要照顾，他总是先找家
人，再找亲戚。如果找不
到人帮助他，才去找朋
友、邻居和社区。

和姥爷姥姥在一起

2.4 跨国家庭
A Multinational Family

🔘 对话一

玛丽娅： 昨天晚上我看了一个电视节目，说中国的跨国家庭越来越多了。

汤姆： 什么是"跨国家庭"？

玛丽娅： 比方说我们家，我妈妈是法国人，我爸爸是意大利人。他们不是来自一个国家，所以我们家是一个跨国家庭。

凯丽： 哦，是这样。那我家也是。虽然我父母都是在美国出生的，可是我爷爷是德国人，奶奶是法国人，姥姥是加拿大人，姥爷是英国人。我们家是个小联合国。

英国	加拿大
法国	德国

大卫： 我看，跨国家庭不算什么新鲜事。

汤姆： 可能在有些国家不算新鲜事，因为那些国家有许多来自各国的移民。可是在中国，跨国家庭还不太多。你看，我们家的亲戚都是中国人，没有一个外国人。我的邻居也都是中国人。只有一个邻居的女儿，跟一个日本人结婚了。

玛丽娅： 那个电视节目说的跟汤姆差不多。以前中国人都是祖祖辈辈住在一个地方，很少搬家。

现在因为经济发展了，越来越多的人离开家，去别的地方工作，还有人去国外工作。不少外国人也到中国来工作。这样，一些中国人就跟外国人结婚了，中国也有了越来越多的跨国家庭。

一个跨国家庭

大卫：　我觉得跨国家庭很有意思，可能的话，最好我家的每个亲戚都是从不同的国家来的。这样我去看他们的时候，就需要去很多不同的国家。这不是很好玩儿吗？

凯丽：　怎么可能呢？你爸爸和你叔叔，就像你和你哥哥，怎么可能是从两个国家来的呢？

大卫：　我也知道是不可能的，所以我说"可能的话，最好…"。

对话二

汤姆：　凯丽，你说你们家就像是一个小联合国。你的家庭生活是不是很特别？

凯丽：　我觉得我很幸运，因为我们可以吃到许多来自各国的东西。奶奶做的饭和姥姥做的很不

一样。在奶奶家，我们吃德国香肠，还有放
很多奶油的法国菜。到了姥姥家，她常常用
枫糖浆给我们做甜点。

汤姆：　那多有意思啊！我们家不行，到了哪个亲戚
家，吃的都是吃中国饭。

凯丽：　在我们家也庆祝很多节日，除了美国的节
日，我们还庆祝德国的十月节、法国的国庆
日什么的。现在住在中国，所以我们也过中
国的节日。

德国小镇

A small town in Germany

汤姆：　那你们家有没有语言问题？我和杰米刚到中
国的时候，中文不太好。有时候我们听不懂
爷爷奶奶说的话。他们不但说北京话，而且
说得非常快。他们也不懂英文，只要我们说
了一个英文词，他们就听不懂了。

凯丽：　我姥姥姥爷来自加拿大和英国，说英文没有
问题。我爷爷虽然有点儿德国口音，可是英
文还不错。我奶奶说英文就马马虎虎了，她

的英文里有很多法文。而且她一着急就说法
文。我们一点儿也听不懂。除了语言以外，
我们还有别的问题。每个人都觉得自己国家
的东西最好。我要去买衣服，我爷爷一定让
我买德国的，因为他觉得德国做的东西不容
易坏。可是我奶奶一定让我买法国的，她觉
得法国的衣服最漂亮。

汤姆：　虽然我家亲戚都是中国人，可是也一样。我
姥姥姥爷总是觉得上海什么都好，因为他们
是在上海长大的。我爷爷奶奶是北京人，所
以他们说北京是中国最好的城市。

凯丽：　我觉得在跨国家庭里长大挺好的，有机会了
解不同的文化。

汤姆：　我同意。我们的学校也像一个跨国大家庭。
在这儿我们有机会学习各国的文化，非常有
意思。

 生词

	Simplified	Traditional	Pinyin	Part of Speech	English
1.	跨国	跨國	kuàguó	adj.	multinational, transnational
2.	越来越	越來越	yuèláiyuè	adv.	more and more
3.	来自	來自	láizì	v.	come from
4.	算		suàn	v.	be counted as, be considered as
5.	移民		yímín	n./v.	immigrant, immigration; immigrate

6.	外国人	外國人	wàiguórén	n.	foreigner
7.	祖祖辈辈	祖祖輩輩	zǔzǔ bèibèi	n.	for generations, from generation to generation
8.	发展	發展	fāzhǎn	n./v.	development; develop
9.	国外	國外	guówài	n.	abroad, overseas
10.	香肠	香腸	xiāngcháng	n.	sausage
11.	奶油		nǎiyóu	n.	cream
12.	枫糖浆	楓糖漿	fēng tángjiāng	n.	maple syrup
13.	甜点	甜點	tiándiǎn	n.	dessert
14.	口音		kǒuyīn	n.	accent
15.	同意		tóngyì	n./v.	agreement; agree

专名

16.	联合国	聯合國	Liánhéguó	United Nations
17.	十月节	十月節	Shíyuèjié	Oktoberfest
18.	法国国庆日	法國國慶日	Fǎguó Guóqìngrì	Bastille Day

语言注释

越来越 (more and more)

越来越多的人搬到城里来住。
More and more people have moved to the city to live.

他说中文说得越来越好了。
He speaks Chinese better and better.

学无止境 EXTEND YOUR KNOWLEDGE

Many Chinese are fascinated by people who are different from them. They use a variety of words to talk about foreigners. Since it is customary for the Chinese to talk about a person's physical features directly and openly, terms such as "big nose," "round eyes," "fat man" and "potbelly" are not derogatory. One caution: slang should not be used on formal occasions.

外国人 *foreigner*	外国朋友 *foreign friend—* *foreigner*	外国客人 *foreign guest—* *foreigner*	老外 *foreigner (slang)*
西方人 *Westerner*	洋 (yáng) 人 *Westerner* *(old-fashioned)*	大鼻子 *big nose—foreigner* *(slang)*	高鼻子 *high nose—foreigner* *(slang)*

中国文化一瞥 A Glimpse into Chinese Culture

Chinese proverbs and idioms

In ancient China, people usually lived in one place for generations. Leaving one's hometown was rare, and considered a sad event. The following proverbs reflect such sad feelings.

1. lí   xiāng   bèi   jǐng
   离   乡   背   井

leave one's native village, have one's back to the village well— be compelled to leave one's own

village (home), be far away from home

2. piāo   yáng   guò   hǎi
   漂   洋   过   海

travel far away across the sea — go abroad, sail across an ocean

IN USE:

很多年以前，他们一家离乡背井，来到了哈尔滨。

Many years ago, their family left their native village and came to Harbin (Hā'ěrbīn).

经济不好的时候，很多人离乡背井去别的地方找工作。

When the economy is not good, many people leave their homes to look for work elsewhere.

王先生是一九九八年漂洋过海去南非的。

In 1998, Mr. Wang traveled far away across the ocean to South Africa.

两百年以前，就有很多中国人漂洋过海去国外生活。

Two hundred years ago, many Chinese sailed across the ocean to live abroad.

YOUR TURN:

在美国，离乡背井的人多吗？

美国人为什么要离乡背井？

有哪些国家的人漂洋过海到美国来？

如果你可以漂洋过海去国外，你打算去哪个国家？

Lyrics of a folk song

美丽的家乡

我站在高高的山上，
山下是我美丽的家乡。
青山绿水围绕着它，
小鸟在百花中飞翔。

生词

围绕	wéiráo	surround	百花		hundreds of flowers	飞翔	fēixiáng	fly

YOUR TURN:

1. Translate the lyrics into English.

2. Do you know a song that is about someone's hometown? If so, say a few words about that song in Chinese to your class.

3. If you don't know any songs, try to write a short song (4–6 lines) about your hometown in Chinese.

你知道吗？

在过去的几十年中，中国经济发展得很快。许多外国人到中国来工作、学习、生活。2007年，有十八万 (180,000) 左右的外国人在中国工作。[1]

　　除了在中国工作的外国人以外，来中国学习的各国学生也越来越多。2008年，有二十多万外国学生在中国592个大学学习。[2] 这些学生多数来自韩国、美国和日本。

　　如果一个外国人打算在中国长期 (chángqī, long term) 工作和生活，他可以向中国政府申请长期居留证 (jūliú zhèng, residence card)。也有人把"长期居留证"叫作"中国绿卡"。

在中国的外国人

Foreigners in China

---

[1] www.wnpop.gov.cn

[2] "Foreigners studying in China exceeds 200,000 in 2008," www.chinaview.cn, 2009-03-25.

2.5 各种各样的家庭
All Types of Families

🔊 对话一

金顺爱： 下个月五号是我小妹妹的生日，我想给她买一件生日礼物。你说买什么好？

凯丽： 你妹妹多大了？

金顺爱： 两岁。

凯丽： 你妹妹那么小啊？那你给她买个玩具熊猫吧。你有几个兄弟姐妹？

金顺爱： 我有两个弟弟，两个妹妹。只有一个弟弟跟我是同父同母。我八岁的时候，我父母离婚了，后来他们又都再婚了。现在我有一个同母异父的弟弟，还有两个同父异母的妹妹。

凯丽： 那你现在是跟你爸爸还是跟你妈妈一起生活？

金顺爱： 我和我弟弟都跟我妈妈生活。我妈妈是律师，现在在上海工作。我继父是一个中国人，他也是律师。

凯丽： 那你的爸爸在哪儿呢？

金顺爱： 他还住在韩国。他也再婚了，我的继母很年轻，才二十六岁，所以我有两个小妹妹，一个四岁，一个两岁。她们都很可爱。

凯丽： 你常常去韩国看你爸爸吗？

金顺爱： 不常去，只有放暑假和寒假的时候去。不过，我常常给我爸爸打电话，写电邮。对了，我爸爸说，我两个妹妹要养狗，所以上个星期我爸爸送给她们一只小黑狗。

凯丽： 她们一定很高兴吧？

金顺爱：当然了。

 课文

中国的传统是：子女结婚以前，跟父母住在一起。子女结婚以后，有的还跟父母住在一起，有的就离开父母家，建立自己的小家庭。今天，还有不少中国家庭是三代人住在一起的：父母、子女和子女的孩子。也就是说，一个家庭常常有爷爷奶奶、爸爸妈妈和孩子。在这样的家庭里，大家互相照顾。孩子小的时候，爷爷奶奶照顾孩子。爷爷奶奶老了以后，子女和孙子孙女就照顾他们。

　　最近几十年，中国社会变化得很快，家庭也有了很大的变化。许多家庭现在只有两代人：父母和孩子。在中国的城市里，不少子女结婚以后都喜欢过小家庭生活，所以他们就离开了父母家。这样就有了一些只有老人的家庭。还有的年轻人，比较喜欢自由，虽然没有结婚，也离开了父母家，自己搬出去住，结果中国有不少"单身"家庭。另外，有些家庭因为父母离婚，就成了单亲家庭。还有些家庭，因为父母再婚了，原来不是一个家庭的人生活在一起，又建立了一个新家庭。

虽然家庭可能是各种各样的，但是只要家庭里的人互相关心，互相照顾，就能给每个人带来快乐。

一个中国家庭

A Chinese family

🔘 生词

	Simplified	Traditional	Pinyin	Part of Speech	English
1.	同		tóng	*adj.*	same
2.	离婚	離婚	líhūn	*v.o.*	divorce
3.	再婚		zàihūn	*v.o.*	remarry
4.	异	異	yì	*adj.*	different
5.	律师	律師	lǜshī	*n.*	lawyer
6.	继父	繼父	jìfù	*n.*	stepfather
7.	继母	繼母	jìmǔ	*n.*	stepmother
8.	传统	傳統	chuántǒng	*n./adj.*	tradition; traditional
9.	建立		jiànlì	*v.*	establish, set up
10.	代		dài	*n.*	generation

11.	孙子	孫子	sūnzi	*n.*	grandson
12.	孙女	孫女	sūnnǚ	*n.*	granddaughter
13.	最近		zuìjìn	*adj./adv.*	recent; recently
14.	变化	變化	biànhuà	*n./v.*	change; change
15.	年轻	年輕	niánqīng	*adj.*	young
16.	单身	單身	dānshēn	*adj.*	unmarried, single
17.	另外		lìngwài	*adv.*	in addition, moreover, besides
18.	单亲	單親	dānqīn	*n.*	single parent

语言注释

1. Using 对了 to signal that one just remembered something

When a speaker suddenly remembers something, he or she may use the idiomatic expression 对了.

我很喜欢吃意大利饭。对了，离学校不远好像新开了一家饭店，不知道是不是意大利饭店。

I like Italian food. Oh, a new restaurant opened not far from the school, but I am not sure whether it is an Italian restaurant.

好，我们三点在电脑房见。对了，三点我要去见王老师。那我们三点半见吧。

OK, let's meet at 3:00 in the computer lab. Oh, I'm going to see Teacher Wang at 3:00. Let's meet at 3:30 then.

2. 另外 (besides, in addition, moreover)

另外 can be used as an adverb before a verb phrase.

他去超市买了点菜，另外去银行拿出来一点钱。

He went to the supermarket to buy some vegetables. Besides that, he went to the bank to withdraw some money.

我们班有美国学生、中国学生，另外还有一个韩国学生。

Our class has American and Chinese students. In addition, there is a Korean student.

学无止境 EXTEND YOUR KNOWLEDGE

Although the divorce rate is relatively low in China, divorce usually leads to reorganization of the family. Here are some Chinese terms that address members in these reorganized families. Pinyin is provided for new characters only.

称呼	意思	称呼	意思
生父	亲爸爸， birth father	生母	亲妈妈， birth mother
后父	继父	后母	继母
后父/继父的孩子	stepfather's children from previous marriage(s)	后母/继母的孩子	stepmother's children from previous marriage(s)
亲兄弟	同父同母的哥哥或弟弟	亲姐妹	同父同母的姐姐或妹妹
前夫 (fū, husband)	以前的先生	前妻 (qī, wife)	以前的太太

中国文化一瞥 A Glimpse into Chinese Culture

Chinese proverbs and idioms

Some idioms and common phrases reflect the Chinese view of a perfect world. Here are a few. Pinyin is provided only for those phrases with new characters.

1. 天 下 为 公
the whole world as one community

IN USE:

以前中国人把世界叫作"天下"。如果天下是大家的天下，这就是"天下为公"。

In the past the Chinese called the world "under heaven." If everything under heaven belongs to everyone, then "the whole world is one community."

YOUR TURN:

Do you think the following phenomena reflect 天下为公?

	是	不是
有钱的人越来越有钱，没有钱的人越来越没有钱。		
有的国家说应该这样做，因为这样对我们的国家很好。有的国家说不应该这样做，因为这样对我们的国家不好。		
每个孩子到了六七岁，都可以去学校上学。		
这几个国家总是打来打去。		

2. 世 界 大 同
the world is one, the whole world becomes one

IN USE:

现在世界各国的人都可以上网看新闻，我看马上要世界大同了。

Now people from every country can get online to read the news. In my opinion, the whole world will soon become one.

YOUR TURN:

Can you give three examples to show 世界大同？

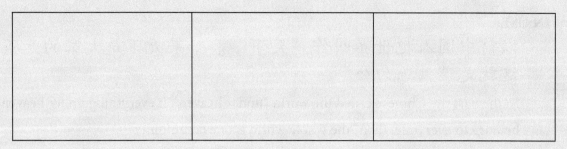

3. 天　下　一　家

the whole world is like one family — the world is one

IN USE:

中国地震 (dìzhèn, earthquake) 以后，许多国家的人都来帮助中国。真是 "天下一家" 啊。

After the earthquake in China, people from many countries came to help China. It was really like "we are one world."

YOUR TURN:

Browse the news and find an example of 天下一家. Tell your class in Chinese what you have found.

4. sì　hǎi　zhī　nèi　jiē　xiōng dì
四　海　之　内　皆　兄　弟

all men are brothers

IN USE:

要是大家都觉得 "四海之内皆兄弟"，就不会有战争 (zhànzhēng, war) 了。

If everyone had believed that "all men are brothers," there wouldn't have been wars.

YOUR TURN:

Browse the news and find an example that shows the opposite of "四海之内皆兄弟". Tell your class in Chinese what you have found.

你知道吗？

中国有一句老话：男大当婚，女大当嫁 (jià, marry a man)。意思是说：男女到了结婚的年龄，应该结婚。中国人觉得结婚是一个人一生 (whole life) 中最重要的大事。为什么呢？因为结婚以后，就要生孩子，就会有一个家庭。有了家庭，在你需要关心、帮助和照顾的时候，家庭都能给你。以前的中国人觉得，不结婚的人是不幸 (bùxìng, unfortunate) 的。

但是，这种关于结婚的想法 (view) 现在有了变化。经济发展以后，社会生活也变化了，社区的服务越来越好，越来越多的人不需要靠 (depend on) 别人生活。结婚不结婚变得不太重要了。不少年轻人喜欢过"单身"的自由生活。还有一些离婚的人也觉得再婚会带来许多麻烦，还是一个人生活比较好。所以现在"单身"的人也比以前多了。

虽然这样，可是多数的中国父母还是希望自己的孩子能结婚。要是孩子大了，还没有男朋友或者女朋友，他们会很着急，一有机会，就会让他们的亲戚朋友帮助孩子找对象 (duìxiàng, potential marriage partner)。

2.6 第二单元复习
Unit 2 Review

对话一

玛丽娅：中秋节你过得好吗？

汤姆：　不错。那天晚上，我的两个舅舅来我们家跟我们一起庆祝中秋节。

玛丽娅：你们除了吃月饼看月亮以外，还做了什么？

汤姆：　没做什么特别的事。他们和我父母聊天，我就坐在旁边听。

玛丽娅：你听到什么有意思的故事了吗？

汤姆：　他们说了很多亲戚家的事。这些亲戚我多半都不认识。他们说到有一个农村的亲戚，现在在北京找到了工作，所以就一个人搬到北京去住，可是他家的人都还在农村。他只有过春节的时候才能回家跟家人见面。

玛丽娅：这多不好啊。他一定很想他的家人吧？

汤姆：　就是啊。他的父母都七十多岁了，两个孩子还在上中学，他的妻子又要工作，又要照顾老人和孩子，忙得不得了。这个亲戚打算要回农村去，开个修车的小公司，这样可以跟家里的人住在一起。可是他的两个孩子不愿意他回去，因为他们都想搬到北京去住。

玛丽娅：他们为什么现在不搬去呢？

汤姆：　好像这个亲戚的工资不太高。没有那么多钱让一家人住在北京。再说，他父母和妻子都喜欢住在农村。

玛丽娅： 这样的家庭在中国一定不少吧?

汤姆： 对。我小舅舅还说，现在不少农村家庭都搬到城里来了。结果，只有老人还住在农村。

玛丽娅： 我想这种情况各个国家都有。为了找到工作，年轻人得搬到有工作的地方去住。我去国外旅行的时候，也常常看到在一些农村地区，多数都是老人，没有太多的年轻人和孩子。

云南农村

A village in Yunnan

对话二

玛丽娅： 张奶奶，您问过黄黄的主人了吗? 它有没有把张爷爷的优盘带回家去?

张奶奶： 楼下的张叔叔和王阿姨说，没见到优盘，不过会帮我们找一找。可是他们那么忙，不知道什么时候才能去帮我找呢。

大卫：　他们的公寓是不是跟您的一样大？

张奶奶：是啊。

大卫：　那找一遍不是很容易吗？不用花很多时间。

张奶奶：要是在我们家可能很快就能找一遍，因为我
　　　　们家比较整齐。在他们家就不那么容易了。

玛丽娅：为什么呢？

张奶奶：他们家的公寓虽然不大，可是哪儿都是东
　　　　西，非常挤。这是因为他们家有五个孩子，
　　　　还养了很多宠物。他们家的宠物除了黄黄以
　　　　外，还有两只小鸟和两只乌龟。

大卫：　现在多数的中国家庭不都只有一个孩子吗？
　　　　他们家怎么有五个呢？

张奶奶：张叔叔和王阿姨有一个女儿，这个女儿已经
　　　　上大学了，住校，不常回家。可是现在还有
　　　　四个小孩子住在他们家。这四个小的都是亲
　　　　戚的孩子。有两个是王阿姨亲戚的孩子。他
　　　　们的父母要去加拿大工作两年，就把他们留
　　　　给王阿姨照顾。另外一个孩子是张叔叔妹妹
　　　　的。因为父母离婚以后都再婚了，这个孩子
　　　　不愿意跟继父住，也不愿意跟继母住，所以
　　　　就被送到张叔叔家来。还有一个是张叔叔弟
　　　　弟的孩子，在上重点中学，张叔叔是这个中
　　　　学的校长，所以这个孩子也住在他们家。

玛丽娅：这么多亲戚的孩子，还有猫、乌龟、小鸟什
　　　　么的，要在他们家找到优盘一定不容易。

生词

Simplified	Traditional	Pinyin	Part of Speech	English
1. 多半		duōbàn	*n.*	majority, most part
2. 农村	農村	nóngcūn	*n.*	countryside, rural area
3. 妻子		qīzi	*n.*	wife

生词扩充 EXPAND YOUR WORD POWER

Many Chinese words are formed by combining two or more characters. If you know the characters in a word, you can often guess the meaning of that word. See if you understand the meaning of the following words.

异同		大同小异		热恋	
大多数		农民		单身宿舍	
独子		酒吧		网吧	
严父		跨国公司		管家	
乡音		零用钱		怕这怕那	
移民家庭		网恋		二婚	
全家照		远亲			

SELF-ASSESSMENT

In Unit 2, you have learned to talk about your family in some detail. You have also learned to describe the "one child" practice in China, the traditional multi-generation family, the modern smaller family, the multinational family, and various types of non-traditional families. Have you achieved the learning goals of Unit 2? After completing the exercises for Unit 2 in your Workbook, fill out the following self-assessment sheet.

Yes/No	*Can you do these things in Chinese?*
	Talk about dating and marriage
	Describe, in some detail, your family members
	Talk in some detail about your personal history
	Use Chinese terms to address your close relatives
	Use Chinese terms to address members of a non-traditional family
	Talk about the "one child" practice in China
	Briefly discuss the advantages and disadvantages of being an only child
	Talk about a typical Chinese family in the past and at present
	Talk about cultural diversity in a family setting
	Describe various types of families

9–10	yes	excellent
6–8	yes	good
1–5	yes	need some work

第三单元：青少年时代

UNIT 3 The Teenage Years

LEARNING GOALS OF UNIT 3

By the end of this unit, you will learn how to:

- Describe and negotiate rules on curfew
- Talk about allowances
- Talk about budgeting and basic money management
- Talk about learning to drive
- Describe rules related to driving
- Describe, in some detail, part-time jobs
- Describe the increasing freedoms and privileges of teenagers
- Talk about responsibilities and obligations in general

3.1 十点以前必须回家
Must Get Home Before Ten O'Clock

🔘 对话一

汤姆： 妈妈，我出去了。

妈妈： 你要去哪儿？

汤姆： 今天是马克十八岁的生日。晚上我们要去
"红房子" 餐厅为他过生日。

上海有名的西餐馆—红房子
Red House—a well-known Western-style restaurant in Shanghai

妈妈：那你吃完饭就早点回来，明天你还有数学考试呢。

汤姆：考试我早就准备好了，今天晚上不用准备了。

妈妈：每次考试前你总是说准备得万无一失了，可是你很少得100分。

汤姆：虽然有时候我得不到100分，但是拿个八九十分是没问题的。反正"八九不离十"就行了。好了，我走了。

妈妈：等一会儿，你几点回来？

汤姆：我也不太清楚。吃完饭后我们可能去看电影，或者去逛商店，也可能去朋友家聊天、玩游戏什么的。

妈妈：这不行。你明天早上还要上学，十点以前一定要回来。

汤姆：现在已经快六点了，十点以前回来时间太紧了，我十一点以前回来吧，行不行？

妈妈：不行，我说十点，就是十点。

汤姆：十点半，怎么样？

妈妈：如果你十点回不来，这两个星期晚上你都不能出去。

汤姆：妈妈，你要讲民主，我的事不能都由你决定。

妈妈：等你过了十八岁，你的事就由你自己决定，可是现在你还没到十八岁，所以就得由我决定。

汤姆：可是我不是小孩子了。晚一点回来没关系啊。

妈妈：等你不是青少年了，随便几点回来都可以。可是今天你十点以前必须回来。

汤姆：好吧，好吧，我十点以前回家。

百乐门—上海有名的夜总会

Paramount—a well-known club in Shanghai, open since the 1930s

对话二

(汤姆和朋友们吃完了晚饭。)

马克： 我们现在去哪儿玩？对了，离这儿不远有个
夜总会，我们要不要去那儿跳舞？

玛丽娅：跳舞挺好玩的。我们去吧。

凯丽： 那个夜总会，去的都是些什么人？

马克： 年轻人挺多的，有大学生，也有一些在公司
工作的白领。

大卫： 高中生能进去吗？

王大明： 好像那个夜总会门口有个牌子，说十八岁以
下的不能进去。

马克： 我已经十八岁了，可以进去了。

凯丽： 可是我们都还没到十八岁，进不去。

马克： 这样的话，我们今天就别去了。那个夜总会
门口总是有不少人，看上去很热门，所以我
老想进去看看。

王大明： 只能等将来了。哎，我们是不是去看电影？

汤姆： 现在已经八点一刻了，我十点以前一定得
回家。

王大明： 啊，已经八点一刻了吗？我妈妈让我八点半
以前就得回家。今天晚上，她请了辅导老师
来帮我准备明天的数学考试。

凯丽： 那你快走吧。

王大明： 没关系，来得及。从这儿坐地铁到我家才五
六分钟。

汤姆： 可是从这儿去地铁站要走五分钟。

大卫： 再说，你家也不住在地铁站里，下了地铁，
还要走几分钟吧。

王大明： 那好吧，我走了。再见！

(王大明走了。)

大卫： 我看我们去逛逛商店吧。这条马路上有一家
不错的电子产品店，我们可以走过去看看。

玛丽娅： 那家商店有什么特别吗？

大卫： 那儿总是有最新最流行的电子产品。

汤姆： 行啊。只要是玩儿，玩什么都行。

凯丽：　那家店远不远？我们也不能玩到太晚，因为
　　　　学校大门十点就关。回去晚了，看门师傅会
　　　　找我们麻烦的。

大卫：　那家店不远，走过去才两三分钟。我们逛完
　　　　了店就回去。

凯丽：　那好吧。

电子产品店

An electronics store in Shanghai

生词

	Simplified	Traditional	Pinyin	Part of Speech	English
1.	青少年		qīngshàonián	*n.*	teenager
2.	时代	時代	shídài	*n.*	time, era
3.	万无一失	萬無一失	wàn wú yī shī	*s.p.*	not a chance of an error, perfectly safe
4.	八九不离十	八九不離十	bā jiǔ bù lí shí	*s.p.*	pretty close, about right
5.	紧	緊	jǐn	*adj.*	tight, close

6.	讲民主	講民主	jiǎng mínzhǔ	v.o.	pay attention to democracy
7.	由		yóu	prep.	by
8.	夜总会	夜總會	yèzǒnghuì	n.	nightclub
9.	白领	白領	báilǐng	n.	white collar (worker)
10.	老		lǎo	adv.	always
11.	来得及	來得及	lái de jí	v.c.	there is still time, in time for
12.	电子	電子	diànzǐ	n.	electronics

语言注释

1. Different meanings of 讲

We have learned the verb 讲, which has the meaning of "tell," "speak," or "explain." For example, 讲故事 (tell a story), 讲课 (give a lesson), 讲演 (give a lecture). 讲 has another meaning of "pay attention to" or "stress." 讲民主 means "pay attention to democracy."

2. 由 (by)

In the passive voice, 由 can be used to introduce the agent of an action. For example:

这件事由你决定。

This will be determined by you.

出国的事由外事 (Foreign Affairs) 办公室办。

Going abroad is handled by the Foreign Affairs office.

We have also learned the preposition 被, which similarly introduces the agent of an action in the passive voice. 被 is generally used for past actions, whereas 由 can be used for past, present and future actions. Another difference is that 被 is often used for a concrete and completed action, and 由 for a process.

菜都被他们吃完了。

They finished all the dishes.   (past, completed)

明天开晚会，吃的东西都由我准备，饮料由你准备。

For tomorrow's party, food will be prepared by me and drinks by you. (future)

3. 老 (always)

老 has the same meaning as 总是. It is more informal and is often used in spoken Chinese.

我跟他出去吃了几次饭，他老说忘了带钱。

He and I went out to eat several times. He always said he forgot to bring any money.

这个学生上课老睡觉，是不是晚上睡得太晚了？

This student always sleeps in class. Isn't it because he goes to bed too late?

4. 来得及 (there is enough time)

来得及 (there is still time, in time, enough time for something)

来不及 (there is no time, not enough time for something)

甲：我的飞机八点半起飞，现在去机场来得及吗？
乙：我看来不及了。

A: My plane takes off at 8:30. Do I still have time to get to the airport?

B: I don't think you have enough time.

我们八点上课，我七点半走应该来得及。

We have classes at 8. I should have plenty of time if I leave at 7:30.

学无止境 EXTEND YOUR KNOWLEDGE

We have learned some words and phrases about "timeliness." Here are a few more related words. Pinyin is provided for new characters only.

准时	及时	提 (tí) 前	提早
on time	in time, timely	ahead of time	ahead of time
早到	早退	迟 (chí) 到	晚到
arrive early	leave early	arrive late	arrive late
推 (tuī) 迟	来不及	耽误 (dānwù)	适时
postpone	not enough time	delay	timely

中国文化一瞥 A Glimpse into Chinese Culture

Chinese proverbs and idioms

Many Chinese proverbs and sayings are about getting prepared. Here are two:

1. yǒu   bèi   wú   huàn

有　备　无　患

be prepared and you won't be sorry; if one is prepared, he will be safe

IN USE:

我把课本上的语法都复习了一遍，有备无患嘛。

I have reviewed all the grammar in the book. It is good to be prepared.

你出去的时候把大门关上，有备无患。

When you leave, close the front gate. It's better to be prepared.

YOUR TURN:

你觉得为了找到合适的工作，怎么做才能有备无患？

2. wáng yáng bǔ   láo

亡　羊　补　牢

mend the fence after the sheep has been stolen—it is never too late to take precautions

IN USE:

虽然你这次考试考得不好，但是可以亡羊补牢。把你做错的
题都再做一遍。

Although you didn't do well on this test, it's not too late to right the wrong. You can re-answer the questions that you got wrong the first time.

YOUR TURN:

Can you use 亡羊补牢 to describe the following actions?

	可以	不可以
1. 他的自行车被小偷偷走了，他要再买一辆新车。		
2. 他的自行车被小偷偷走了，他请警察帮助他找到小偷。		
3. 他的自行车被小偷偷走了，他决定要养一只狗。		
4. 他的自行车被小偷偷走了，他决定以后要把自行车放在他的房子里。		

A Chinese poem from the Southern Song Dynasty (1127–1279)

dōng yè dú shū shì zǐ yù

冬　夜　读　书　示　子　聿

Lù　Yóu　(Nán　Sòng)

陆　游　(南　宋)

Gǔ　　rén　　xué　　wèn　　wú　　yí　　lì,

古　　人　　学　　问　　无　　遗　　力，

shào　zhuàng　gōng　fū　　lǎo　　shǐ　　chéng.

少　　壮　　功　　夫　　老　　始　　成。

Zhǐ　shàng　dé　　lái　　zhōng　jué　　qiǎn,

纸　　上　　得　　来　　终　　觉　　浅，

jué　　zhī　　cǐ　　shì　　yào　　gōng　xíng.

绝　　知　　此　　事　　要　　躬　　行。

这首诗的意思是：

古人为了得到学问，一生都很努力。少年和壮年的努力带来了老年的成功。如果知识是从纸（书）上学到的，总是觉得还不够。要有真的知识，需要去学去用。

People from ancient times spared no effort in acquiring knowledge,

Great effort in younger years leads to success in later life.

Knowledge acquired from paper (books) is always inadequate,

To gain thorough knowledge, one must learn by doing.

YOUR TURN:

Do you have any experiences that show 纸上得来终觉浅，绝知此事要躬行?

你知道吗？

中国人把生日分成特别重要的生日和一般的生日。特别重要的生日是小孩子一岁的生日，还有老人六十岁、七十岁、八十岁、九十岁、一百岁的生日。中国人比较喜欢为小孩和老人庆祝生日。除了庆祝这些重要的生日以外，不少人也过二十岁、三十岁、四十岁和五十岁的生日。

在庆祝这些重要生日的时候，许多中国人会去饭店办生日酒席，请家里人、亲戚、朋友一起来庆祝。在生日酒席上，大家都要吃"寿面"（shòumiàn, longevity noodles）——因为面条是长的，代表了长寿。在老年人的生日酒席上，大家会送给老人"寿桃"（shòutáo, longevity peach）。寿桃不是新鲜的桃子，是做成像桃子一样的点心。这是因为在中国传说中的"老寿星"（Lǎoshòuxīng, the God of Longevity），手里拿着寿桃。

老寿星

A statue of the God of Longevity

3.2 零花钱
Allowances

上海大剧院
Shanghai Grand Theatre

💿 对话一

玛丽娅： 这个周末你想去看芭蕾舞吗？听说俄国芭蕾
舞剧团正在上海大剧院演出《天鹅湖》。

凯丽： 票价一定很贵吧？

玛丽娅： 最便宜的是120元，但是学生票好像只要
80元。

凯丽： 虽然我很想去，但是我这个月的零花钱已经
快用完了。

玛丽娅： 现在离月底还有十天，你已经没有钱了？

凯丽： 是啊，这个月活动特别多，一会儿跟朋友去
吃饭，一会儿去看电影，我又买了几本书，
所以钱就花得差不多了。

玛丽娅： 你父母一个月给你多少零用钱？

凯丽： 一个月三百块。你呢？

玛丽娅： 两百块。

凯丽： 两百块一定不够花吧？现在一张电影票要80元。要是去星巴克喝一杯咖啡，就要30元。两百块一下子就没了。

玛丽娅： 是啊，好在我暑假的时候去打工，挣了一点钱。要不然，200元一定不够。你零用钱不够的时候，怎么办？

凯丽： 我父母给了我一张银行卡，在紧急情况下，我可以去拿钱。但是如果没有紧急情况，我用钱用得多了，他们下个月就不给我那么多钱了。比如，我这个月用了400元，那么下个月，他们只给我200元。如果我用了600元，下个月他们就一分钱都不给我了。

玛丽娅： 要是你非常想去看芭蕾舞，我可以借钱给你。等你有了钱，再还给我好了。

凯丽： 谢谢，我看我还是不去了。如果我这个月就花下个月的钱，那下个月就没钱花了。

对话二

汤姆：你今天看上去挺高兴的，怎么了？

大卫：今天我姥姥给我寄来了50块美元。

汤姆：哇噻，你发财啦。今天是什么特别的日子？

大卫：也不是什么特别的日子，我姥姥一高兴就会给我们寄点小礼物，或者寄点钱什么的。她老说我一个人在上海上学，需要花钱的地方比较多，所以每过一两个月就会给我寄点钱。

汤姆：你父母知道吗？

大卫：这是我跟姥姥之间的秘密。要是我父母知道了，一定就不会给我很多零用钱了。

汤姆：你的零花钱够用吗？

大卫：够用，因为我从来不乱花钱。你呢？

汤姆：我父母正在教我记帐呢。他们说，我每次花钱以后，都应该记下来。这样我就知道我花了多少，还剩多少。要不然，我可能会乱花钱，钱花到哪儿自己都不知道。可是我觉得记帐挺麻烦的。再说，我一个月只有两百块，花到钱没有了，就不花了。

大卫：我觉得你父母说得对。我虽然没有把每次花了多少钱都写下来，但是在月初，我会计划一下，这个月用50元买书，100元出去玩。如果说这个月书买得多了，那我就得少出去玩几次。

汤姆：真有你的。我得好好向你学习学习怎么理财。

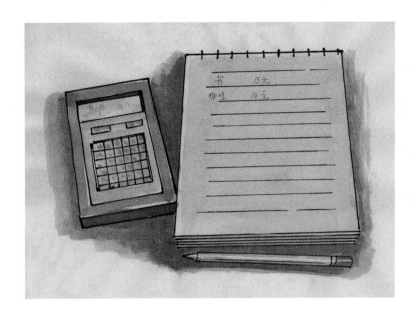

生词

	Simplified	Traditional	Pinyin	Part of Speech	English
1.	芭蕾舞		bāléiwǔ	n.	ballet
2.	剧团	劇團	jùtuán	n.	theatrical company, troupe
3.	剧院	劇院	jùyuàn	n.	theatre, opera house
4.	票价	票價	piàojià	n.	ticket price
5.	月底		yuèdǐ	n.	end of a month
6.	零用钱	零用錢	língyòngqián	n.	pocket money
7.	挣	掙	zhèng	v.	earn (money)
8.	要不然		yàobùrán	conj.	otherwise, or, or else
9.	紧急	緊急	jǐnjí	adj.	urgent, emergent
10.	比如		bǐrú	s.p.	for example, for instance
11.	寄		jì	v.	mail
12.	之间	之間	zhījiān	prep.	between
13.	乱	亂	luàn	adv.	recklessly, randomly
14.	记帐	記帳	jìzhàng	v.o.	keep accounts, keep books
15.	记下来	記下來	jìxiàlai	v.c.	write it down, keep a record

16. 剩		shèng	*v.*	remain, be left over
17. 月初		yuèchū	*n.*	beginning of a month
18. 理财　理财		lǐcái	*v.o.*	manage finance, manage money

专名

| 19. 天鹅湖 天鵝湖 Tiān'é Hú | | | | Swan Lake |

语言注释

1. 要不然 (otherwise)

我应该现在就开始准备高考，要不然就进不了好大学了。

I should start preparing for the college entrance exam now. Otherwise, I won't be able to get into a good university.

我们马上去机场，要不然就来不及了。

Let's go to the airport right way, or else we won't have enough time.

2. 在···情况下 (under the circumstance of)

在一般情况下，机场车每20分钟一班。

Under normal circumstances, the airport shuttle comes every 20 minutes.

在找不到工作的情况下，他决定出国。

Under the circumstance of not being able to find a job, he has decided to go abroad.

3. Using ···好了 at the end of a suggestion

好了 is sometimes added to the end of a suggestion. It softens the tone.

我们明天去好了。

Let's go tomorrow.

你什么时候想去就告诉我好了。

Whenever you'd like to go, please let me know.

4. 乱 (randomly, recklessly)

乱 can be used as an adverb to modify a verb, with the meaning of "recklessly, randomly."

你别把东西乱放。

Don't place things everywhere.

我邻居的狗一天到晚乱叫。

My neighbor's dog barks at random all day long.

5. 真有你的 (you are really something)

The expression 真有你的 is similar to the English expression "You are really something!"

甲：你要的书我都替你带来了。
乙：真有你的。太谢谢了。

A: I have brought all the books you wanted.

B: You are really something! Thank you so much.

甲：你一天就把工作做完了？真有你的。
乙：哪里哪里。

A: Did you finish the job in a day? You are really something!

B: Not really (thank you for saying that).

Sometimes, 真有你的 can be used sarcastically. See the following example:

八点开会，你九点才到，可真有你的。

The meeting started at eight, but you came at nine. You are really something.

学无止境 EXTEND YOUR KNOWLEDGE

Here are some common words that are related to money management. Pinyin is provided for new characters only.

银行卡 *bank card*	信用卡 *credit card*	现金 (jīn) *cash*	现金卡 *debit card*
账户 (zhànghù) *account*	存 (cún) 钱 *deposit money*	取 (qǔ) 钱 *withdraw money*	支 (zhī) 票 *check*
投资 (tóuzī) *investment; invest*	股 (gǔ) 票 *stock*	储蓄 (chǔxù) *saving; save*	大学教育储蓄计划 *college savings plan*

YOUR TURN:

Based on the word list above, can you guess the meaning of the following terms?

退休账户		投资账户	
信用（历）史		银行账户	
投资计划		旅行支票	
存取现金		投资公司	

银行

A Shanghai bank

中国文化一瞥 A Glimpse into Chinese Culture

Chinese proverbs and idioms

Here are some proverbs and idioms about how people spend money.

1. huī   jīn   rú   tǔ

挥   金   如   土

scatter one's gold around as though it were dust—spend money like water,

spend one's money lavishly

IN USE:

他挥金如土，不到一年就把家里的钱花完了，还问银行借了很多钱。

He spent money like water. In less than a year, he spent all of his family's money and also borrowed a lot from banks.

为了得到最好的足球队员，这个足球队挥金如土。

To get the best soccer player, the soccer team spent money lavishly.

YOUR TURN:

你知道谁挥金如土？这个人挥金如土以后，有什么结果？

2. dà   shǒu   dà   jiǎo

大   手   大   脚

spend extravagantly, wasteful

IN USE:

他花钱大手大脚。结果没到月底就没钱了。

He was wasteful when spending money. As a result, he ran out of money before the end of the month.

YOUR TURN:

Can you use 大手大脚 to describe the following situations?

	可以	不可以
1. 虽然他的工资不高，但是为了让女朋友高兴，他为她买了1000元的外套，800元的裙子，还送给她一台新电脑。		
2. 她父母刚给她300元零花钱，她就去买手机。因为300元不够，她还向朋友借了200元。		
3. 王明每个月的工资是3000元，每个月她的钱都花不完。		
4. 白老师非常喜欢买衣服。虽然她还有很多新衣服没有穿过，但是她看到了喜欢的衣服就要买。		

3. ài   cái   rú   mìng

爱   财   如   命

love one's wealth as if it were one's life—regard money as the most important thing

(this proverb is used to describe a miser)

IN USE:

他爱财如命，结婚三十年了，一件礼物都没有送给过他太太。

He is a miser. He has been married for thirty years and has not given his wife even one gift.

YOUR TURN:

1. 你觉得跟谁交朋友比较快乐？爱财如命的人还是大手大脚的人？为什么？

2. 如果一个家庭有两个孩子，一个爱财如命，一个大手大脚，你觉得哪个孩子会给父母带来比较多的问题？

The story of 一毛不拔 (bá)

墨子(Mòzǐ, 公元前470-391)和杨朱(Yáng Zhū)是战国时期(公元前476-221)的哲学家(zhéxuéjiā, philosopher)。那时候，因为有许多战争(zhànzhēng, war)，人民的生活很痛苦(tòngkǔ, miserable)。许多哲学家都希望再也不要有战争。墨子要大家"兼爱"(jiān'ài, love without differentiation)，杨朱要大家好好保护(bǎohù, protect)自己。

有一天，墨子的一个学生问杨朱："如果从你身上拔(bá, pull)一根毛，可以保护天下的人，你愿意这么做吗？"

杨朱回答："一根毛不可能解决(jiějué, solve)大家的问题。"

墨子的学生又问："如果可能，你愿意从身上拔一根毛吗？"

杨朱没有回答，因为他不愿意。

"一毛不拔"的成语就是这么来的。这个成语开始的时候用来说那些非常自私(zìsī, selfish)的人，后来用来说那些对钱非常小气(stingy)的人。

Mozi (470–391 BC) and Yang Zhu (c. 400 BC) were philosophers in the Warring States period (476–221 BC). At that time, frequent wars were destroying the lives of many Chinese. Philosophers devoted their energies to stopping further wars. Whereas Mozi advocated loving one's fellow countrymen without differentiation, Yang Zhu felt the most important thing in life was to protect oneself.

One day, a student of Mozi asked Master Yang, "If one strand of your hair would benefit everyone on earth, would you pull it out?"

Master Yang replied, "A single hair definitely will not solve everyone's problems."

Mozi's student asked again, "If it would, are you willing to pull out one strand of your hair?"

Master Yang didn't answer, as he didn't want to pull out a hair for anyone.

This is the origin of the proverb 一毛不拔 (too stingy to pull out a hair, extremely stingy). The proverb at first described extremely selfish people. Later it was used to describe people who are extremely stingy.

你知道吗？

大 多数的中国父母都给孩子零花钱。许多家长一高兴就会给孩子一点零花钱。到了过节、过生日，孩子也会得到一些零花钱。

在国外，许多高中生都是通过(tōngguò, through)做家务(domestic chores)得到父母给的零花钱。在中国不一样，孩子一般不用帮助做家务事就能得到零花钱。很多中国高中生觉得，他们的学习已经很忙了，不应该再做家务事了。他们的父母好像也是这么想的。可是，中国父母喜欢用钱来奖励(jiǎnglì, reward)孩子的学习。如果考试考得好了，父母常常会奖励给孩子一点钱。

零花钱不够用的时候，多数的学生会问父母要钱。虽然中国父母的工资不高，但是因为现在很多孩子都是独生子女，所以父母一般都会给他们钱，有的还会给孩子不少钱，让孩子觉得"想要就有"。

多数的中国父母都教育孩子不要乱花钱，但是有些高中生常常互相攀比(pānbǐ, compare oneself with others)，看谁穿最酷的运动鞋，谁用最贵的手机，谁有最新的游戏机。结果有的学生只想买名牌(brand name)，花钱大手大脚。不少中国家长觉得，教育孩子怎么理财是非常重要的。

3.3 学开车
Learning to Drive

对话一

凯丽： 周末你们想去哪儿玩儿？

玛丽娅： 除了购物中心和几个公园以外，上海没有什么特别好玩的地方。

凯丽： 听说浙江有一些地方挺好玩的。比如安吉。

安吉风景

A scene from Anji in Zhejiang Province

大卫： 要是你们想去，我们可以坐旅游车去。

凯丽： 坐旅游车比较贵。有没有直接去那儿的公共汽车？

大卫： 好像没有。去安吉，我们先要坐火车，再换几次公共汽车，我看一天都到不了那儿。

汤姆： 去安吉最好自己开车。这样，只要三小时左右就到了。

凯丽： 开车？我们一不会开车，二没有车。

大卫： 就是，我们都没学过开车。听说美国的高中
教学生怎么开车，可是我们学校没有这样
的课。

汤姆： 我觉得每个高中都应该有驾驶课。会开车多
方便啊！想去哪儿，就去哪儿。想什么时候
去，就什么时候去。

玛丽娅： 可是我觉得在大城市里，会不会开车都没有
关系，公共交通很方便。开车也有开车的问
题。比如，交通很堵，停车也不容易。

汤姆： 在上海，我们可以用公共交通，可是如果打
算去郊游，自己开车还是挺不错的。再说，
开车给你带来的那种自由的感觉，多好啊！

大卫： 最好再开一辆很快的跑车，那感觉就更
好了。

玛丽娅： 好了，别做梦了。这个周末去不去安吉？

凯丽： 算了，还是以后再说吧。

北京街景

A street scene in Beijing

对话二

玛丽娅： 美国的高中生什么时候可以开始学开车？

汤姆： 十六岁左右。一般的高中都可以让学生修驾驶者教育课和驾驶者培训课。

玛丽娅： 是不是上完了课就可以开车了？

汤姆： 不是的。他们还要参加路考。通过了路考，才可以开车。

玛丽娅： 也就是说，在美国十六岁就可以拿到驾照了，是吗？

汤姆： 对，如果你上完了课，路考也通过了，而且你父母同意你拿驾照的话，那么你可以拿到一个临时驾照。

玛丽娅： 什么时候才可以拿到正式驾照呢？

汤姆： 十八岁。

玛丽娅： 世界上不少国家都是要到了十八岁才可以开始开车。美国多不错啊！十六岁就可以开车了。

汤姆： 你知道在中国，要到什么年龄才能拿到驾照吗？

玛丽娅： 也是十八岁。我哥哥快十八岁了，很想学开车，因为中国的学校没有驾驶课，所以他正在找驾驶学校呢。

汤姆： 中国的驾驶学校收十八岁以下的学生吗？我也很想学开车。

玛丽娅： 好像不收。安东尼已经问过三四个驾驶学校了，他们都只培训成年人。

汤姆：　如果你知道哪个学校收十八岁以下的学生，
　　　　别忘了告诉我。我一定去报名。
玛丽娅：好的。

中国驾照

Image of a Chinese driver's license

中国的驾驶学校

A driving school in China

 生词

	Simplified	Traditional	Pinyin	Part of Speech	English
1.	旅游车	旅遊車	lǚyóuchē	*n.*	tour bus
2.	驾驶	駕駛	jiàshǐ	*v.*	drive
3.	停车	停車	tíngchē	*v.o.*	park (a car)
4.	郊游	郊遊	jiāoyóu	*v.*	go on an excursion
5.	感觉	感覺	gǎnjué	*n.*	feeling
6.	跑车	跑車	pǎochē	*n.*	sports car
7.	做梦	作夢	zuòmèng	*v.o.*	dream
8.	算了		suàn le	*s.p.*	forget it, leave it at that
9.	驾驶者	駕駛者	jiàshǐzhě	*n.*	driver
10.	培训	培訓	péixùn	*n./v.*	training; train
11.	路考		lùkǎo	*n./v.*	road test, driving test; take a road test
12.	通过	通過	tōngguò	*v./prep.*	pass; through, by means of
13.	驾照	駕照	jiàzhào	*abbr.*	driver's license
14.	临时	臨時	línshí	*adj.*	temporary
15.	正式		zhèngshì	*adj.*	official, formal
16.	收		shōu	*v.*	accept, admit, receive
17.	成年人		chéngniánrén	*n.*	adult

专名

18.	浙江		Zhèjiāng		a province in China
19.	安吉		Ānjí		a place in Zhejiang province

语言注释

1. 比如 (for example)

We learned 比方说 in Lesson 1.4. 比如 has the same meaning as 比方说. 比方说 is often used in spoken Chinese.

人民广场附近可去的地方不少，比如上海博物馆、上海大剧院、人民公园什么的。

There are some places worth going near the People's Square, such as the Shanghai Museum, the Shanghai Grand Theatre, the People's Park, etc.

外文书店有许多不同语言的书，比如英语、法语、日语、汉语、意大利语等等。

The Foreign Language Bookstore has books in many languages, such as English, French, Japanese, Chinese, Italian, etc.

2. …没有关系 (it doesn't matter if…, it doesn't make any difference if…)

To express the meaning "it doesn't matter/it doesn't make any difference if one does this or that," we need to put an adjective or a verb in its affirmative and negative form before 没有关系.

明天你去不去都没有关系。

It doesn't matter if you go (or not) tomorrow.

我有没有告诉你都没有关系，因为你从来都不听我说的。

It doesn't make any difference whether I have told you or not, because you never listen to what I say.

贵不贵没有关系，你替我买到就好。

Whether it is expensive doesn't matter. It's great you've bought it for me.

房间大不大没有关系，但是要干净。

It doesn't matter if the room is big or not, but it has to be clean.

3. 算了 (forget it, leave it at that)

算了，外面下这么大的雨，我们怎么打网球？
Oh, forget it. It's raining so heavily. How can we play tennis?

你不想去就算了。
If you don't want to go, let's forget it.

学无止境 EXTEND YOUR KNOWLEDGE

Here are some words related to driving. Pinyin is provided for new characters only.

起动 start the car	倒 (dào) 车 back up the car	转弯/拐弯 make a turn
掉 (diào) 头 make a U-turn	超 (chāo) 车 pass a car	路口 crossroads, exit
路边 road side	车道 car lane	换车道 change lanes
直线 (xiàn) straight line	红绿灯 (dēng) traffic lights	公路 highway

中国文化一瞥 A Glimpse into Chinese Culture

Chinese proverbs and idioms

Since the Chinese value real actions, here are some proverbs that are related to unrealistic wishes and illusions.

1. huà　bǐng　chōng jī
画　饼　充　饥
draw cakes to satisfy hunger—feed on illusions

IN USE:

广告 (guǎnggào, commercial, advertisement) 说，这种药能帮助学生学习。吃了药以后，考试就能考得很好。这个广告不是画饼充饥吗？

The commercial said this drug can help students learn. After taking the drug, students can do well in a test. Isn't the commercial like drawing a cake to satisfy hunger?

小王虽然现在没有工作，但是他常常对别人说，如果他现在有一个大公司，他一定会很有钱。我看小王是在画饼充饥。

Although Xiao Wang doesn't have a job at present, he often tells people that if he owned a big company, he would be very rich. In my opinion, Xiao Wang is living on illusions.

YOUR TURN:

Can you tell one story of 画饼充饥? (Someone who lives on illusions, not on reality.)

2. yī   zhěn   huáng liáng
一   枕   黄   粱

head on the pillow while millet is cooked—a short and sweet dream

IN USE:

我成了非常有名的作家，写了许多书。可是那只是一枕黄粱。

I became a well-known author and wrote many books. But it was only a sweet dream.

好了，好了，你成为电视台经理不是真的，是一枕黄粱。

That's enough. Your becoming a manager of the TV station is not real, but a dream.

YOUR TURN:

Describe a great dream you had that has little to do with reality. You may end your description with the following sentence: 可是那是一枕黄粱。

3. mèng huàn   pào   yǐng
梦   幻   泡   影

a dreamy illusion and a shadow in a bubble—hallucinations, illusion

IN USE:

你的发财计划是梦幻泡影。

Your plan to get rich is just an illusion.

他老想演电影，当名人。他父母说这都是梦幻泡影。

He always thinks about acting in a movie and becoming a celebrity. His parents say all this is an illusion.

YOUR TURN:

Name onc or two things you have heard of that are examples of 梦幻泡影. Explain why you believe so.

The story of 一枕黄粱

卢生 (Lú Shēng) 是唐朝 (Táng Cháo, Tang Dynasty, 公元618–907年) 的一个学者 (xuézhě, scholar)。他老觉得自己又聪明又能干，可是没有机会用他的才能 (talent)。有一次，他在外边旅行。天快要黑了，他决定去一个小旅馆 (hotel) 住一个晚上。他进了旅馆，看到旅馆的主人正在用黄粱 (millet) 做晚饭。卢生等着吃晚饭，慢慢地睡着了。他梦见自己跟一个非常漂亮的女人结婚了，有了五个儿子。他成了高官 (gāoguān, high-ranking official)，他的儿子也成了高官。他又梦见自己已经八十多岁了，病得很重，快要死 (sǐ, die) 了……这时候，卢生醒 (xǐng, wake up) 了。晚饭黄粱还没有做好，他这才知道自己做了一个梦。

Mr. Lu Sheng was a scholar in the Tang Dynasty. He had always felt that he had great talents but didn't have the opportunity to use them. One day when he was traveling, he checked into a hotel. The hotel owner was cooking some millet for dinner. While waiting for the dinner to be cooked, Mr. Lu felt asleep. He dreamed he married a beautiful woman and had five sons. He became a high-ranking official, and so did his five sons. Then he was in his eighties and became seriously ill. He was on his deathbed… Then, Mr. Lu woke up. He found the millet was still cooking and all was but a dream.

你知道吗？

中国的教育可以被分成初等 (chūděng, elementary level)、中等 (secondary)、和高等 (higher) 教育。

初等教育包括 (bāokuò, include) 幼儿园和小学。中国的幼儿园有三四个年级：大班（6-7岁）、中班（5-6岁）、小班（4-5岁）、小小班（3-4岁）。中国的小学一般有六个年级。中国孩子12岁或13岁从小学毕业。

中等教育包括初中、高中、中专 (zhuān, vocational) 和技术 (jìshù, technical) 学校。中国的初中有三个年级：初一、初二、初三。高中也有三个年级：高一、高二、高三。中专和技术学校一般要上三四年才能毕业。中专和技校(abbreviation of 技术学校)学生毕业以后，一般不上大学，直接去工作。

高等教育包括大学和大专。大学和大专的不同是：大专只要上两年，大学要上四年。大学有四个年级：大一、大二、大三、大四。

中国有"九年义务 (yìwù, compulsory) 教育"。每个孩子都应该在学校学习九年，念到初中毕业，才能去工作。

小学生

大学校园
At a university campus

3.4   兼职
A Part-time Job

对话一

玛丽娅：大卫，昨天下课以后，你急急忙忙地离开了
学校，去哪儿了？

大卫：哦，我找到了一个兼职的工作，当法语
家教。昨天去跟学生见面了。

玛丽娅：是吗？你的学生上几年级？

大卫：她叫红红，今年六岁，在上幼儿园。不过她
父母说，学外文越早越好。

玛丽娅：你每个星期要去几次？

大卫：两次，每次一两个小时。

玛丽娅：你要给她上课吗？用什么课本？

大卫：她父母说，我不用给红红上课，就是陪她
玩，给她讲讲故事。这个工作很轻松。再
说，从学校去她家也很方便。她家就住在学
校对面的那个小区里。我骑自行车过去，才
三四分钟。

玛丽娅：你怎么想起来要当家教了？

大卫：我本来也没想到要去兼职。有一天，我在学
校门口等公共汽车，红红和她妈妈也在等
车，我们说了一会儿话。红红的妈妈一听我
是法国人，就问我愿意不愿意给红红当家
教。我觉得当家教，一个星期也花不了多少
时间，还可以挣一点儿零花钱，就同意了。

玛丽娅： 我觉得兼职挺不错的。虽然中国的高中生一般都不打工，可是在国外，高中生兼职是很平常的事。

大卫： 那你打算兼职吗？

玛丽娅： 如果有合适的工作，我也想去兼职。

最好的汉语老师

想在这个暑假继续学习汉语吗?想轻松快乐地说好汉语吗?就请跟着我一起学习汉语吧。请给我打电话吧：

Fanny ，1177076。

Fanny 有汉语教学经验，对外汉语专业辅导老师，可辅导汉语初级（口语、正音、听说），初中等 HSK（听力、语法、综合），中高级汉语视听说，高级 HSK（听力、口试、作文），汉语流行语等。

家教广告

An advertisement for providing Chinese tutoring

对话二

(玛丽娅给张经理打电话。)

玛丽娅： 喂，请问张经理在吗？

张经理： 我就是，请问您是哪位？

玛丽娅： 我叫玛丽娅。我的邻居马京生先生让我打电话给您，请问你们公司是不是正在招一名英文翻译？我对这个工作很有兴趣。

张经理： 哦，马京生告诉你了吧？这是一个临时的工作。

玛丽娅： 他告诉我了。他还说，你们需要把公司的网页翻译成英文。

张经理： 是的，除了翻译网页以外，我有时候还需要一个翻译帮我看看英文电子邮件。你的英文怎么样？

玛丽娅： 虽然我是在意大利出生的，可是我跟父母在美国和英国住了几年，我从小就说英文，英文还不错。

张经理： 你不是中国人啊？你说中文说得那么好，没有一点外国口音，我还以为你是中国人呢。我可不行，学了八九年英文了，英文还是马马虎虎的，听说读写都不好。我当然很欢迎你来当翻译，可是你知道，我的公司非常小，只有三个人，我不可能给你全天的工作。

玛丽娅： 没关系。我现在是高中生，不能全天工作。我只想下课以后，兼兼职。

张经理： 那太好了。你一个星期来工作四五个小时就行了。工作时间很灵活，什么时候有空，就什么时候过来。不过，你在上高中，出来打工会不会影响学习？

玛丽娅： 一个星期工作四五个小时不会影响学习的。

张经理： 那好。工资是一个小时二十元，月底发工资。

玛丽娅： 好，没问题。这个星期五下午三点以后我有空，可以去工作吗？

张经理： 当然可以。你知道我们公司的地址吗？

玛丽娅： 知道，马京生都已经告诉我了，你们公司就
在他公司的旁边，是吧?

张经理： 对，没错。那我们星期五下午见。

玛丽娅： 好的，再见。

中国公司

A Chinese company

生词

	Simplified	Traditional	Pinyin	Part of Speech	English
1.	急忙		jímáng	*adv.*	in a hurry, hastily
2.	兼职	兼職	jiānzhí	*v.o.*	get a part-time job
3.	家教		jiājiào	*n.*	tutor
4.	年级	年級	niánjí	*n.*	grade, year (in school)
5.	小区	小區	xiǎoqū	*n.*	complex, residential area
6.	想起来	想起來	xiǎngqǐlai	*v.c.*	think of, remember, recall
7.	本来	本來	běnlái	*adv.*	originally, at first
8.	愿意	願意	yuànyì	*o.v.*	be willing to
9.	先生		xiānsheng	*n.*	Mr. (title), teacher, husband
10.	招		zhāo	*v.*	recruit, enroll
11.	网页	網頁	wǎngyè	*n.*	web page
12.	以为	以為	yǐwéi	*v.*	assume, think, believe

13. 全天		quántiān	*n.*	all day, full time
14. 灵活	靈活	línghuó	*adj.*	flexible, agile
15. 影响	影響	yǐngxiǎng	*n./v.*	influence; affect
16. 发	發	fā	*v.*	distribute, issue, give out

语言注释

1. Duplication of a word

Sometimes, to make the language more vivid, we may duplicate an adjective or an adverb, such as 大大的，白白的，慢慢地，好好地⋯ If the adjective or the adverb has two characters (A+B), the duplication pattern is AABB, such as 急急忙忙，高高兴兴，快快乐乐⋯

We can also duplicate two-character verbs. The pattern is ABAB: 休息休息，检查检查，运动运动⋯ If the two-character verb is a combination of a verb and an object, then the pattern becomes AAB: 睡睡觉，打打球，兼兼职⋯

你急急忙忙地要去哪儿？
Where are you going in such a hurry?

我的小狗安安全全地回来了。
My puppy came back safely.

你身体不好，可以在家好好地休息休息，
多睡睡觉。
You are not feeling well. You can take a good rest and have more sleep at home.

2. 本来 (originally, at first)

他本来要去海南岛，后来决定去云南了。
At first, he was going to Hainan Island. Later he decided to go to Yunnan.

你本来就应该把书带来。不带书，我们怎么准备
考试啊？
You should have brought your book. Otherwise, how can we prepare for the test?

学无止境 **EXTEND YOUR KNOWLEDGE**

The following words refer to different kinds of employment. Pinyin is provided for new characters only.

全职 *full-time job*	半职 *part-time job*	临时工 *temporary worker*
合 (hé) 同工 *contract worker*	零工 *odd jobs*	钟点工 *hourly worker*
个体户 (hù) *self-employed*	蓝领 *blue collar (manual work)*	粉领 *pink collar (service job)*
白领 *while collar (office job)*	金 (jīn) 领 *gold collar (corporate executive)*	自由职业 (zhíyè) *freelance*

中国文化一瞥 **A Glimpse into Chinese Culture**

Chinese proverbs and idioms

Some proverbs describe people's attitudes towards work. Here are a few.

1. jiǎo tà shí dì
脚 踏 实 地
stand on solid ground—be down to earth, do solid work

IN USE:

他总是脚踏实地地工作，所以同事都很喜欢他。
He always does solid work. That's why his colleagues all like him.

在工作中要脚踏实地，把应该做的工作都做好。
One should be down to earth at a job, and fulfill all of the job's responsibilities.

YOUR TURN:

Can you use 脚踏实地 to describe the following employees?

张明、王红、高小丽、金中元在一个公司工作。张明不是很喜欢他的工作，所以他有些事做得又好又快，有些事做得马马虎虎。经理批评他，他说，"天下没有十全十美的事，八九不离十就可以了。"

王红觉得她的工作有点儿太容易了，她正在找别的工作。但是她把应该做的事都做完了，而且做得很好。做完了自己的工作以后，她有时候还帮助别人工作。

高小丽觉得她的工作非常有意思，她工作得很努力。她的工作也做得很好。不过有时候在上班的时候她喜欢上网看看新闻，写写电邮，不过她上网的时间不太长，每次十分钟左右。

金中元觉得自己非常聪明，他总是花很多时间去跟别人谈公司应该有什么样的计划。结果，他常常没有时间做完自己的工作。

	张明	王红	高小丽	金中元
脚踏实地吗？				

2. sān tiān dǎ yú, liǎng tiān shài wǎng
　 三　 天　 打　 鱼，　两　 天　 晒　 网

fish for three days and dry the fish net for two days—inconsistent in work or study

IN USE:

玛丽今天要学钢琴，明天要学小提琴，后天又要学画画。真是三天打鱼，两天晒网，什么都学不好。

Mary at one time wanted to learn piano, then changed to violin, and later switched to painting. It's like going fishing for three days and drying out the fish net for two days. She can't learn anything well.

YOUR TURN:

你认识三天打鱼，两天晒网的人吗？为什么你说这个人是三天打鱼，两天晒网？

3. hǔ tóu shé wěi
虎 头 蛇 尾

a tiger's head and a snake's tail—a fine start but a poor finish, start out well but not continue well

IN USE:

甲：我弟弟做事总是虎头蛇尾。

乙：那你弟弟比我弟弟好。你弟弟还有头有尾。我弟弟做事是没头没尾。我不知道他是不是开始了，也不知道是不是做完了。

A: When my brother does something, it always has a grand start but a poor finish.

B: Your brother is better than my brother. At least he has a start and an end. When my brother does something, there is no start or end to it. I don't know if he has started or if he has finished.

YOUR TURN:

Complete the following sentences, making them examples of 虎头蛇尾：

1. 大卫决定这个月要看完三本书，但是＿＿＿＿＿＿＿＿＿＿＿
＿＿＿＿＿＿＿＿＿。

2. 汤姆说他要把数学书从头到尾复习一遍，可是＿＿＿＿＿＿＿
＿＿＿＿＿＿＿。

3. 月初，凯丽计划这个月要开始记账，可是＿＿＿＿＿＿＿＿
＿＿＿＿＿＿＿。

4. 玛丽娅想她应该去上海博物馆参观一天，把那儿的东西都好好地看一看。但是＿＿＿＿＿＿＿＿＿＿＿＿＿＿＿＿。

你知道吗?

中国的学校一年有两个学期。秋季(jì,秋天的学期)从9月1日开始,一直到第二年的1月底。这时候,中国人都在准备过春节,学校也开始放寒假。寒假有三四个星期。春季(春天的学期)总是在过了春节以后开始,一般从2月底到7月初。暑假比较长,有六七个星期。

中国的中学生要学许多课程,比如:汉语、数学、物理、化学、地理、外语、历史、音乐、体育等等。他们一个星期上30-35节课,每天还有一两个小时的自学(self study)时间。除了学习以外,中学生也参加课外活动,比如运动队、兴趣小组、学生社团等等。

在长城的高中生
High school students at the Great Wall

3.5 自由和责任
Freedom and Responsibility

🔘 对话一

汤姆： 最近我父母常常对我说，现在你长大了，可以做一些以前不能做的事。但是你应该知道，做每件事都需要负责任。比方说，如果我们给你零花钱，你应该计划花在哪儿，花多少，不能乱花。如果我们晚上让你出去玩，你应该知道什么时候必须回家…

凯丽： 哦，我懂了。他们的意思是，"世界上没有免费的午餐。"有时候我们好像得到了更多的自由，其实自由不是免费的午餐，为了自由，我们要负更多的责任。比如，如果我们可以开车了，就必须注意安全，别出事故。

汤姆： 你怎么那么理解我父母的意思？你说的跟他们说的一样。

凯丽： 其实，我父母也常常跟我说这些。他们还特别关心我是不是在谈恋爱。他们说，谈恋爱可以给一个人带来很多快乐，也可以带来很多麻烦。他们让我做每件事情，都要想想后果。如果做一件事情，会带来不好的后果，那就不应该去做。

汤姆： 你父母很开通，还跟你说谈恋爱的事。我妈妈可保守了，总是跟我说，她和我爸爸是大学毕业以后才开始谈恋爱的。上高中不应该谈恋

爱，应该好好学习。还叫我学习中国的高中
生，说他们在高中的时候只关心高考，只注意
学习。要是我在高中就开始谈恋爱，一定会影
响我的学习的。

凯丽：我觉得不一定。两个人也可以在学习上互相帮
助啊。

汤姆：我也是这么跟我妈妈说的。可是我妈妈说，要
是我非要谈恋爱，就必须找一个学习好的女
生，这样我的学习就不会受到坏影响。

凯丽：你妈妈真有意思。

高中生

💿 对话二

大卫：　玛丽娅，你找到兼职的工作了吗？

玛丽娅：找到了，现在我在帮一个小公司翻译网页，
　　　　还帮公司的经理看看英文电子邮件。

大卫：　你喜欢那个工作吗？

玛丽娅：很喜欢。可是有时候觉得责任挺大的。这个公司的张经理是我邻居的朋友。他一看我是外国人就说，太好了，我们请了个外国人来当翻译，这样我们公司的英文网页一定是十全十美。他这么一说，让我觉得压力很大。要是我没做到十全十美，就都是我的责任了。

大卫：你是说，翻译完了以后，没有人帮你看一看吗？

玛丽娅：是的。开始我把翻译完了的东西带回家，让我爸爸帮我检查一下。可是我爸爸为了让我学会负责任，从来不替我看，老让我自己检查，自己改错。我请安东尼帮我检查，他就学我爸爸："玛丽娅，你应该为自己做的事负责。"我真没想到，兼职会有那么多的责任。早知道这样，我应该去找一个责任轻一点儿的工作。

大卫：什么工作都要负责任。就拿我的工作来说吧，虽然听上去只是陪红红玩玩，可是也有很多责任。要是她说中文，我就得提醒她说法文。跟她在一起，我要注意她的安全。那天她跟我出去玩儿，在路上乱跑，差一点被自行车撞到。吓了我一跳。

玛丽娅：看小孩的责任很重。

大卫：不过，我们要看到好的一面。发了工资以后，我们花钱比以前自由多了吧？

玛丽娅：你说得对。昨天我拿到了工资，我请你去喝一杯咖啡吧。

 生词

	Simplified	Traditional	Pinyin	Part of Speech	English
1.	长大	長大	zhǎngdà	v.c.	grow up
2.	责任	責任	zérèn	n.	responsibility
3.	免费	免費	miǎnfèi	adj.	free, free of charge
4.	午餐		wǔcān	n.	lunch
5.	其实	其實	qíshí	adv.	actually, in reality, in fact
6.	后果	後果	hòuguǒ	n.	result, consequence
7.	开通	開通	kāitōng	adj.	open-minded, liberal
8.	保守		bǎoshǒu	adj.	conservative
9.	受到		shòudào	v.	be subject to
10.	改		gǎi	v.	correct, change, revise
11.	提醒		tíxǐng	v.	remind
12.	吓一跳	嚇一跳	xiàyītiào	v.o.	be startled, be frightened
13.	一面		yīmiàn	n.	one side

语言注释

1. 其实 (in fact, as a matter of fact)

他说他懂了，其实不一定都懂了。

He said he understood, but actually he may not have understood everything.

写汉字其实不难，就是要多练习练习。

Writing Chinese characters is actually not difficult, but it needs some practice.

2. 拿···来说 (speaking of, with regard to, as far as... is concerned)

The set phrase 拿···来说 is used to introduce a topic. It is usually placed at the beginning of a sentence.

拿中国的高中生来说，他们要通过高考才能进大学。

Speaking of high school students in China, they need to pass the college entrance exam before going to college.

拿运动来说，我最喜欢的是打篮球。

With regard to sports, my favorite is basketball.

学无止境 EXTEND YOUR KNOWLEDGE

Here are some additional words for describing a person's worldview. Pinyin is provided for new characters only.

传统	过时	守 (shǒu) 旧
traditional	*outdated*	*sticks to the old ways*
开明	前卫	现代
open-minded, liberal	*forward-thinking*	*modern*
激 (jī) 进	左	右
radical	*left*	*right*
极端 (duān)	温和	中庸 (yōng)
extreme	*moderate*	*middle of the road, moderate*

中国文化一瞥 A Glimpse into Chinese Culture

Chinese proverbs and idioms

Many Chinese proverbs express meanings by way of analogy. Here are a few.

1. huǒ   shāo   méi   máo

火   烧   眉   毛

eyebrows catch on fire—extremely urgent

IN USE:

飞机马上就要起飞了，可是我们还在等票，真是火烧眉毛。

The plane is to take off soon but we are still waiting for tickets. It really feels like our eyebrows are on fire.

你为什么总是到了考试这天才开始准备呢？有必要每次都这样火烧眉毛吗？

Why do you always start preparing on the day of the test? Is it necessary to create such extreme urgency every time?

YOUR TURN:

1. 你觉得什么情况对你来说是火烧眉毛？
2. 在火烧眉毛的时候，你会做什么？

2. jī   fēi   dàn   dǎ

鸡   飞   蛋   打

the hen has flown away and the eggs in the coop are broken—all is lost,

come out empty-handed

IN USE:

他花了很多钱为女朋友买礼物。结果，他的钱都花完了。但是女朋友又找到了别的男朋友，不和他谈恋爱了。他是鸡飞蛋打，什么都没了。

He spent a lot of money buying his girlfriend a gift. As a result, he spent all his money, but his girlfriend found another boyfriend and stopped dating him. It's like the hen has flown away and the eggs in the coop are broken—he came out empty-handed.

YOUR TURN:

Can you use 鸡飞蛋打 to describe the following situations?

	可以	不可以
1. 他的钱都用来买车了。可是他的车一买来就坏了，而且修车师傅说，这辆车修不好了。		
2. 小明想让妹妹替他做作业，就把他最喜欢的音乐CD送给他妹妹。可是他妹妹把作业都做错了，小明得了零分。		
3. 我的自行车被小偷偷走以后，我马上报告了警察。		
4. 汤姆的电脑有了病毒，电脑上的文件都打不开了。他只能用学校的电脑，可是学校的电脑也有了病毒，现在他优盘上的文件也都打不开了。		

3. gǒu jí tiào qiáng

狗　急　跳　墙

a dog will leap over a wall in desperation—one will take desperate measures if pushed to the wall (this proverb usually has a negative connotation)

IN USE:

这个坏人看到警察来了，狗急跳墙，从二楼跳下去，结果摔坏了腿。

When the bad guy saw the police were coming, in desperation he jumped down from the second floor. As a result he broke his leg.

YOUR TURN:

Complete the following two scenarios so that they can be used as examples of 狗急跳墙.

1. 小偷在偷自行车的时候，被人看到了，他狗急跳墙，＿＿＿
＿＿＿＿＿＿＿＿＿＿＿＿＿＿＿＿＿。

2. 许多人在追两个坏人，坏人上山以后，就迷路了，找不到下山的路，他们狗急跳墙＿＿＿＿＿＿＿＿＿＿
＿＿＿＿＿＿＿＿＿＿＿＿＿＿＿。

你知道吗?

跟　　许多别的国家一样，在中国一个人到了18岁，就是成年人了。许多青少年时代不能做的事，到了18岁就能做了，比如选举、就业 (jiùyè, employment)、驾车、参军 (cānjūn, join the military) 等等。但是中国也有跟别的国家不一样的地方。虽然18岁是成年人了，可是不能结婚。中国法定(legal)的结婚年龄是：女的20岁，男的22岁。这是因为中国的人口比较多，所以政府希望大家晚一点儿结婚，晚一点儿生孩子。

因为中国非常大，每个地方的情况都不同。有时候，有些不到法定年龄的青少年也找得到工作，特别是在农村。农村的孩子常常很小就帮助父母工作。有些家庭自己开了商店、公司，也会让孩子很早就参加工作。

3.6 第三单元复习
Unit 3 Review

课文

一些中国的报纸报道说，因为中国的中学作业太多，所以有一半左右的中学生每天睡觉的时间不到七个小时。这不但影响了学生的健康，也影响了他们的学习。

广东有一名中学生说："我现在每天晚上最早12点睡觉，早上6点30分起床。"他每天最多睡六七个小时，可是还是他们班睡觉睡得多的。他有一个同学，因为成绩不太好，晚上常常睡不好觉，每晚只能睡三个小时，所以白天学习没有精神。

另外一个中学生说，这学期他上五门课。只要每门课的老师一天给一个小时的作业，五门课就有五个小时的作业。写得再快也要写到晚上十一点。因为每天睡得很晚，等到下午上课的时候，他老想睡觉。

有一位学生家长说，虽然他的孩子在上小学六年级，但是每天晚上要六点半才到家。吃完晚饭七点开始做作业，一直做到十二点才能做完。第二天早上六点就必须起床了。这位家长很担心孩子的身体健康。

还有一位学生家长说，他的孩子现在上高中一年级，但是已经每天做作业做到晚上十一点。前几天，为了准备英文考试，每天要学习到十二点。因为睡觉睡得不够，结果孩子病了。

中国的报纸说，为了学生的健康，学校应该少给学生一些作业。

对话

张奶奶：玛丽娅，告诉你一个好消息，张爷爷的优盘找到了。

玛丽娅：是吗？是在哪儿找到的？是不是在黄黄的家？

张奶奶： 不是的。那天我看到黄黄到三楼的白叔叔家去了，我就想，除了黄黄家以外，我还应该问问别的邻居，黄黄有没有把东西带到他们家去。所以我就一家一家地去问。问到了六楼的王奶奶家，王奶奶说她一点儿都不懂电脑，不知道什么是优盘，但是她把黄黄带到她家去的东西都放在一个盒子里。她把盒子拿出来，让我看看有没有我要找的东西。结果我就在她那儿找到了优盘。

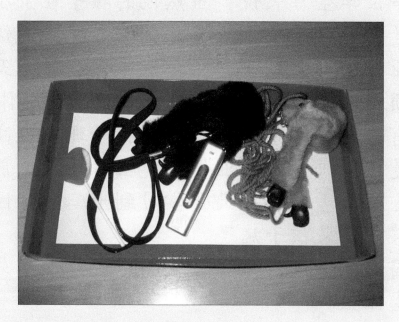

王奶奶的盒子

玛丽娅： 太好了。那黄黄是怎么把优盘拿走的？

张奶奶： 张爷爷的优盘上有一根绳子。猫常常很喜欢玩绳子，可能黄黄在玩绳子的时候，就把优盘带走了。

玛丽娅： 谢天谢地，它把优盘带到王奶奶家去了。要是带到一个没有人去的地方，我们怎么找得到呢？

张奶奶： 你说得对。

玛丽娅： 那个优盘没坏吧？

张奶奶： 没有。张爷爷拿到优盘以后，马上放到电脑上去看，一点都没坏，张爷爷写的小说都在那儿。他非常高兴，现在每天从早到晚都在写，我想很快就能写完了。

玛丽娅： 太好了！

张奶奶： 所以我们要谢谢你和大卫。要不是你们想到可能是黄黄，我们可能还找不到那个优盘呢。

玛丽娅： 要谢的话，应该谢谢大卫。他这个侦探当得挺不错的。

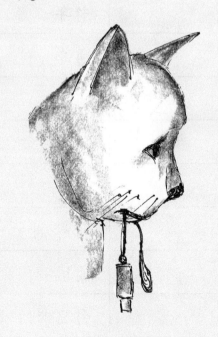

生词

	Simplified	Traditional	Pinyin	Part of Speech	English
1.	报道	報道	bàodào	*n./v.*	(news) report; report
2.	精神		jīngshén	*n.*	spirit, mind, energy
3.	家长	家長	jiāzhǎng	*n.*	parent
4.	消息		xiāoxí	*n.*	news
5.	根		gēn	*m.w.*	*for long and thin objects*
6.	绳子	繩子	shéngzi	*n.*	rope, string

生词扩充 EXPAND YOUR WORD POWER

Many Chinese words are formed by combining two or more characters. If you know the characters in a word, you can often guess the meaning of that word. See if you understand the meaning of the following words.

少年		青年	
中年		老年	
家长会		通车	
通话		通信	
年初		年底	
老是		兼课	
免票		歌舞剧	
长大成人		校区	
梦想		白日梦	

SELF-ASSESSMENT

In Unit 3, you have learned to talk about the increasing freedoms and opportunities, as well as the increasing responsibilities and obligations that teenagers have. You have also learned how to describe monthly allowances, curfew rules, part-time jobs, and driving rules. Have you achieved the learning goals of Unit 3? After completing the exercises for Unit 3 in your Workbook, fill out the following self-assessment sheet.

Yes/No	*Can you say and write these things in Chinese?*
	Describe and negotiate rules on curfew
	Talk about allowances
	Talk about budgeting and basic money management
	Talk about learning to drive
	Describe rules related to driving
	Describe, in some detail, part-time jobs
	Describe the increasing freedoms and privileges of teenagers
	Talk about responsibilities and obligations in general

7–8 yes excellent
4–6 yes good
1–3 yes need some work

第四单元： 学校生活

UNIT 4 School Life

LEARNING GOALS OF UNIT 4

By the end of this unit, you will learn how to:

- Read and understand general public announcements
- Talk about sports events
- Name some basic sports equipment
- Name basic cooking utensils and kitchen equipment
- Name some basic toiletries
- Describe how to organize an activity
- Describe, in some detail, a place's history
- Describe, in some detail, an itinerary
- Describe, in some detail, a day's program or activities

4.1 运动会
A Sports Meet

对话

大卫： 下个星期五学校要开运动会，体育老师让我们班负责准备运动器材。

凯丽： 开运动会需要很多运动器材吧。难道那么多器材都由我们班准备吗？

大卫： 是的。别的班有别的班的工作，有的要准备比赛场地，有的要负责运动员休息室。

凯丽： 今年的运动会是不是只有田径和体操比赛？

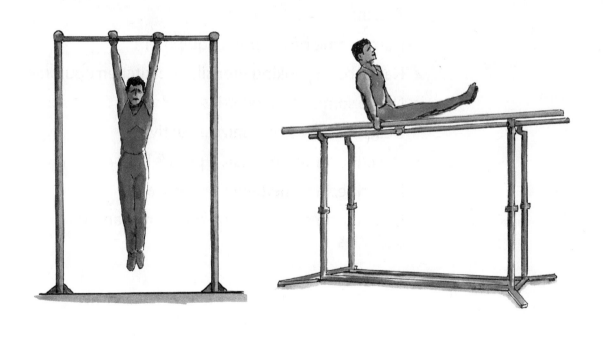

大卫： 不，还有球类比赛。我听玛丽娅说，要把班上的同学分成三个小组，每个小组准备一种比赛器材。

凯丽： 玛丽娅的主意不错，这样每个小组都有工作重点，不容易丢三落四。

大卫： 我比较有力气，应该去体操组，因为体操器材都比较重。

凯丽： 你知道这次一共有多少个球类比赛项目吗？

大卫： 有篮球、排球、羽毛球、乒乓球和网球。

凯丽： 哦，那我们除了准备球和球拍以外，别的就不用准备了吧？

大卫： 我们还要在教室楼的前边放四张乒乓桌。

凯丽： 四张乒乓桌？放得下吗？

大卫： 开运动会那天，教室楼前不能停自行车，应该放得下。你看，这是运动会的介绍。星期五要同时举行各种球类比赛，乒乓球比赛在教室楼前边举行，羽毛球在体育馆，篮球在篮球场，排球在图书馆后边。

凯丽： 这么多比赛同时举行，到时候一定会很热闹。

 课文

上海国际学校春季运动会

各位家长、各位老师、各位同学：大家好！

　　欢迎您来参加上海国际学校春季运动会。今年的运动会有40多个比赛项目，有200多名师生要参加比赛。下面是今天比赛的场地和时间：

田径比赛（男女团体和个人）
时间：　　上午8点半到下午3点
地点：　　学校操场

体操比赛（男女团体和个人）
时间：　　上午8点半到11点半
地点：　　学校体育馆

球类比赛（男女团体和个人）
时间：　　下午1点到4点
地点：　　乒乓球（教室楼前边）
　　　　　篮球（篮球场）
　　　　　羽毛球（体育馆）
　　　　　排球（图书馆后边）

　　为了方便大家，学生餐厅全天供应茶水和点心，11:45到1:15供应午饭。另外，教室楼的一楼有运动员休息室，二楼有家长和师生休息室。如果您需要其他服务，请跟服务人员联系——他们都戴着蓝色的棒球帽。

　　祝运动员得到好成绩！祝运动会举办成功！

春季运动会组织小组
3月30日

 生词

	Simplified	Traditional	Pinyin	Part of Speech	English
1.	运动会	運動會	yùndònghuì	n.	sports meet
2.	器材		qìcái	n.	equipment
3.	场地	場地	chǎngdì	n.	area, space, place
4.	休息室		xiūxīshì	n.	lounge, break room
5.	田径	田徑	tiánjìng	n.	track and field
6.	体操	體操	tǐcāo	n.	gymnastics
7.	球类	球類	qiúlèi	n.	category of ball games
8.	分		fēn	v.	divide, separate
9.	主意		zhǔyì	n.	idea
10.	重点	重點	zhòngdiǎn	n.	emphasis, focal point
11.	丢三落四		diū sān là sì	s.p.	forgetful, miss this or that
12.	力气	力氣	lìqi	n.	strength
13.	项目	項目	xiàngmù	n.	item, (sports) event
14.	排球		páiqiú	n.	volleyball
15.	羽毛球		yǔmáoqiú	n.	badminton
16.	乒乓球		pīngpāngqiú	n.	table tennis, ping-pong
17.	球拍		qiúpāi	n.	racket, bat
18.	同时	同時	tóngshí	adv.	simultaneously, at the same time
19.	团体	團體	tuántǐ	n.	group, team

| 20. | 个人 | 個人 | gèrén | *n.* | individual |
| 21. | 供应 | 供應 | gōngyìng | *n./v.* | supply |

语言注释

1. 成 in a complement of result

In Lesson 5.5 of *Huanying*, Volume 2, we learned that certain prepositions can serve as complements of result. One of these prepositions is 成, which has the meaning of transforming something "into" something different. See the following examples:

我们可以分成四个小组。
We (our group) can be divided into four groups.

他把小说改成了电影。
He adapted the novel into a movie.

请你把这些句子翻译成汉语。
Please translate these sentences into Chinese.

这个小问题变成了一个大问题。
This has changed from a minor issue into a major one.

2. 下 in a potential complement

We learned the basic structure of a potential complement in Lesson 1.3. The word 下 is used in a potential complement with the meaning of "having the capacity/room/space" for something. For example:

这里放得下四张桌子吗?
Is there enough room to put four tables here?

我吃得太多了，吃不下了。
I've eaten too much and can't eat any more (there isn't any more room for food).

这张纸写不下那么多句子。
There is not enough space on the paper to write that many sentences.

我家门口只停得下两辆车。
There is only room for parking two cars in front of my house.

学无止境 EXTEND YOUR KNOWLEDGE

The following words are about sports events. Pinyin is provided for new words only.

初赛 *preliminary*	半决赛 *semifinals*	决赛 *finals*	排名 *ranking*
男子团体赛 *men's team competition*	女子团体赛 *women's team competition*	男子个人赛 *men's individual competition*	女子个人赛 *women's individual competition*
冠军 (guànjūn) *champion, first place*	亚军 (yàjūn) *second place*	季军 (jìjūn) *third place*	得分 *score, to score*
金牌 *gold medal*	银牌 *silver medal*	铜 (tóng) 牌 *bronze medal*	前六名 *the top six*

Based on the words you have just learned, can you guess the meaning of the following phrases?

乒乓球决赛		男子排球冠军	
游泳亚军		女子体操团体赛	
跳远第一名		进入前八名	
女子跳水金牌		男子滑冰银牌	
棒球初赛		排名第五	

中国文化一瞥 A Glimpse into Chinese Culture

Chinese proverbs and idioms

The following are some proverbs that can be used when talking about sports and other types of situations:

1.zhēng xiān kǒng hòu
争　先　恐　后
strive to be the first and fear to lag behind—rush to the front

IN USE:

1. 短跑比赛的时候，运动员们争先恐后地跑向终点(zhōngdiǎn, the finish line)。

   In the short-distance race, the athletes rushed to be the first to reach the finish line.

2. 每年过春节以前，火车站总是有许多人争先恐后地买火车票。

   Every year before the Spring Festival, the train station is filled with people in a rush to be the first to buy train tickets.

YOUR TURN:

1. 你看到过有人争先恐后地买东西吗？他们在买什么？
2. 你觉得什么时候你会争先恐后地去做一件事？

2. jiàn bù rú fēi
健　步　如　飞
walk fast as if on wings—walk fast and vigorously

IN USE:

王爷爷虽然八十岁了，可是还是健步如飞。

Even though Grandpa Wang is 80 years old, he still walks fast and vigorously.

YOUR TURN:

在你的家人和朋友中，谁常常健步如飞？你呢？

The next two proverbs both have something to do with shooting skills:

3. bǎi   bù   chuān yáng

百 步 穿 杨

shoot an arrow through a willow leaf a hundred paces away—
shoot with great precision; superior marksmanship

4. bǎi   fā   bǎi   zhòng

百 发 百 中

fire at the target a hundred times without a single miss—
hit the target at every shot; never miss one's target

IN USE:

这些射击 (shèjī, shooting) 运动员一个个都是百步穿杨，
百发百中。

None of these shooting athletes ever misses a shot.

我觉得林东真是个数学天才。每次数学考试他都是
百发百中，得到满分。

I think Lin Dong is a math genius. He never misses anything on a math test and always
gets perfect scores.

YOUR TURN:

如果一个人能做到百步穿杨，百发百中，请你选择他最需要
的是什么，为什么？

Please select the factor that someone needs most to achieve "never missing a target," and
explain why in Chinese.

朋友	老师	天才	健康	爱情
钱	家庭	时间	兴趣	学校

The origin of 百步穿杨

传说在春秋时期 (公元前770–476年)，有一个非常出色 (chūsè, superior) 的射手 (shèshǒu, archer)，叫养由基 (Yǎng Yóu Jī)。他可以在一百步 (bù, step) 以外射中杨树叶 (yángshùyè, willow leaf)，而且他是百发百中。如果一个人做什么事都有成功的把握 (bǎwò, assurance)，我们就可以用"百步穿杨"或者"百发百中"来形容 (xíngróng, describe) 他。

It was said that during the Spring and Autumn Period (770–476 BC), there was a superior archer, Yang You Ji. He could shoot an arrow through a willow leaf at a distance of one hundred paces and he never missed a target. Nowadays, the two proverbs are used to describe someone who is sure of success at everything he or she does.

你知道吗？

在 中国的城市里，从小学生到大学生，每个星期都要上一次体育课。虽然许多学校没有健身房，但是差不多每个学校都有操场。在上体育课的时候，体育老师会教大家打球，比如篮球、排球、羽毛球、乒乓球、足球。网球和棒球在中国还不太流行，而且很多学校没有网球场。除了打球以外，学生也会学习体操、游泳和田径。常见的田径活动有跳高、跳远、长跑和短跑。因为这些活动都在室外 (outdoors)，如果下雨，大家就可以打乒乓球或者下棋 (xiàqí, play chess)。

不少学校每年要举行一次运动会。到了开运动会的那一天，各个年级的学生可以参加年级组的比赛。多数的比赛项目是田径比赛，也有一些球类和体操比赛。

高中生在操场上

4.2 国际文化日
International Culture Day

🔘 对话一

明英：　学校马上要举办国际文化日了，我们汉语班要介绍中国文化。中国文化有许多方面，我们应该介绍哪一方面呢？

汤姆：　这个问题提得好。我参加过不少国际文化活动，可是有些活动太一般了，总是听听报告，看看外国电影，或者大家唱唱歌，跳跳舞。我们班的活动应该有点儿新意。

凯丽：　比方说…

汤姆：　比方说我们可以用不同的活动来介绍文化的一个方面。中国人不是特别喜欢"食文化"吗？我们为什么不介绍一下"食文化"呢？

大卫：　什么是"十"文化，十种文化吗？

汤姆：　不，"食"是"食品"的食，就是关于吃的东西。

明英：　中国人是特别重视吃什么，怎么吃。也重视食品和健康的关系。你打算怎么介绍？

汤姆：　我们可以组织一个烹调表演。

大卫：　烹调表演算不上有什么新意。

汤姆：　　烹调表演只是活动之一。我们可以好好计划计划，再加上一些别的活动。比方说，我们可以介绍中国各地的环境，说一说那个地方的食品有哪些特点。

明英：　　好主意。我们需要先研究一下中国各地的菜有什么不同，然后我们可以分成几个小组，让每个小组做一个地方的菜，比如广东菜、四川菜、上海菜等等。

玛丽娅：　对，每个小组还可以介绍那个地区的地理环境和气候，因为地理环境和气候都会影响农业出产，也决定了那个地区的饮食。

汤姆：　　介绍完了以后，就举行烹调比赛。每个小组不但要表演怎么做菜，而且还要把做好的菜让观众尝一尝。最后我们请观众投票选举哪个小组的菜做得最好吃。

大卫：　　行，我们就这么做。

对话二

玛丽娅：丁老师说，国际文化日那天只有我们班要举
　　　　行烹调表演，所以我们可以用学生餐厅的厨
　　　　房。我们可以先去厨房看一下，那里有没有
　　　　我们需要的东西。

（在厨房里。）

明英：你们看，这儿有盘子、杯子和刀叉，那儿还
　　　有很多筷子。不过，好像没有餐巾纸，我们
　　　应该准备一些餐巾纸。

大卫：我看做饭的锅子够了，
　　　可是这儿只有一个大
　　　炒菜锅，我们有四个
　　　烹调小组，还需要
　　　三个。

凯丽：厨房的炒菜锅又大又重，做菜不方便，我们
　　　还是去借四个小一点儿的炒菜锅吧。

明英：好，我正在写我们需要的东西："餐巾纸、
　　　四个炒菜锅"，还需要什么别的吗？

大卫：我们组还需要一个蒸笼。

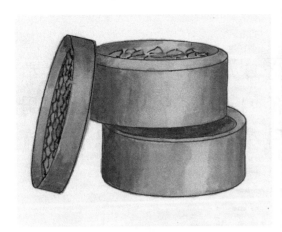

广东点心

汤姆：   你是不是在广东组？广东人做点心常常需要
         蒸笼。我们组要做烤肉，所以最好有一个烤
         箱。

玛丽娅： 那儿有两个大烤箱。

汤姆：   哪儿？

玛丽娅： 就在微波炉的旁边。

明英：   汤姆，你们小组要做哪个地区的菜？怎么要
         做烤肉？我在中国饭店很少吃到烤肉。

汤姆：   我们组决定要做中国新疆少数民族的饭菜。
         那里的少数民族做的烤肉好吃极了。哎，你
         们上海组要做什么菜？

明英：   因为上海好吃的菜很多，每次讨论，大家都
         七嘴八舌，我们到现在还没做出决定。

 生词

	Simplified	Traditional	Pinyin	Part of Speech	English
1.	新意		xīnyì	n.	novel ideas, fresh ideas
2.	食		shí	n./v.	food; eat

3.	食品		shípǐn	*n.*	food, food item
4.	重视	重視	zhòngshì	*v.*	take something seriously, value
5.	之一		zhī yī	*s.p.*	one of...
6.	加上		jiāshàng	*v.*	add
7.	特点	特點	tèdiǎn	*n.*	special feature
8.	气候	氣候	qìhòu	*n.*	climate
9.	农业	農業	nóngyè	*n.*	agriculture
10.	出产	出產	chūchǎn	*n./v.*	product; produce
11.	举行	舉行	jǔxíng	*n.*	hold, stage
12.	选举	選舉	xuǎnjǔ	*n./v.*	election; elect
13.	餐巾纸	餐巾紙	cānjīnzhǐ	*n.*	paper napkin
14.	锅子	鍋子	guōzi	*n.*	pan, pot
15.	炒菜锅	炒菜鍋	chǎocàiguō	*n.*	wok, frying pan
16.	蒸笼	蒸籠	zhēnglóng	*n.*	steamer
17.	烤肉		kǎoròu	*n./v.*	barbecue(d) meat, roast(ed) meat
18.	烤箱		kǎoxiāng	*n.*	oven (for baking, roasting)
19.	微波炉	微波爐	wēibōlú	*n.*	microwave oven
20.	七嘴八舌		qīzuǐ bāshé	*s.p.*	all talking at once [see Unit 2.3, EYK]

专名

21.	新疆		Xīnjiāng		an autonomous region in China

语言注释

1. …之一 (one of...)

When describing something (a noun) as being "one of" a group, we add 之一 after the noun describing the larger group. See the following examples:

南京是中国的大城市之一。

Nanjing is one of China's large cities.

历史课是我最喜欢的课之一。

History is one of the courses that I like most.

那个饭店最有名的菜之一是西湖醋鱼。

One of the best-known dishes in that restaurant is West Lake fish in vinegar sauce.

文化日的活动之一是看电影。

One of the activities on Culture Day is watching a movie.

2. 算不上 (can't be considered)

虽然今天的考试算不上难，但是我考得还是不太好。

Although today's test couldn't be considered difficult, I didn't do very well.

我们学校的球队算不上是上海最好的。

Our school's team can't be considered the best in Shanghai.

学无止境 EXTEND YOUR KNOWLEDGE

We have learned how to say the names of some commonly used kitchen utensils. Here are a few more words for things that you see in a kitchen. Pinyin is provided for new characters only.

水壶 (hú)	咖啡壶 (hú)	茶壶 (hú)	菜刀
water kettle	coffeepot	teapot	cutting/chopping knife
砧板 (zhēnbǎn)	刨(bào)子	开罐 (guàn) 刀	剪 (jiǎn) 刀
cutting board	peeler	can opener	scissors
篮子	炉 (lú) 子	洗碗 (wǎn) 机	冰箱
basket	oven (stovetop)	dishwasher	refrigerator

中国文化一瞥 A Glimpse into Chinese Culture

Chinese proverbs and idioms

The following proverbs are about diversity.

1. bǎi huā qí fàng, bǎi jiā zhēng míng
百 花 齐 放，百 家 争 鸣

(let) a hundred flowers bloom and a hundred schools of thoughts

contend — encourage artistic and/or intellectual diversity

IN USE:

1. 为了让社会进步，就应该百花齐放，百家争鸣。
   For society to develop, artistic and/or intellectual diversity should be allowed to flourish.

2. 我们公司在发展新产品的时候，总是让工程师们
   百花齐放，百家争鸣。
   When our company develops new products, engineers are always allowed to express different opinions (diverse views are encouraged).

YOUR TURN:

Can you use 百花齐放，百家争鸣 to describe the following situations?

	可以	不可以
1. 开中秋晚会的时候，同学们七嘴八舌，都说今年的月饼非常好吃。		
2. 为了决定文化日的活动，我们开了一个班会，同学们提了很多不同的建议。		
3. 我妈妈一会儿说要去饭店办酒席，一会儿说要在家里请客。随便妈妈说什么，爸爸都同意。		
4. 同学们可以决定要表演什么节目：唱歌，跳舞，演话剧，拉小提琴，弹钢琴等等，都可以。		

2. duō zī   duō cǎi

多　姿　多　彩

varied and colorful

IN USE:

1. 云南的少数民族有多姿多彩的文化历史。
   The minority groups in Yunnan have varied and colorful cultural histories.

2. 社区服务日的活动多姿多彩。
   There are various activities on Community Service Day.

YOUR TURN:

美国是一个多民族的国家，你参加过哪些多姿多彩的文化活动？

中国的八大菜系 The eight major cuisines of China

因为中国地方很大，各地做的菜都各有特点。一般来说，中国菜被分为八大菜系 (càixì, cuisine)。它们是：四川菜系、广东菜系、山东菜系、福建 (Fújiàn) 菜系、浙江菜系、江苏菜系、湖南菜系和安徽 (Ānhuī) 菜系。

China is a huge country and has many regional cuisines. Generally speaking, there are eight major cuisines in China. They are: Sichuan cuisine, Guandong cuisine, Shandong cuisine, Fujian cuisine, Zhejiang cuisine, Jiangsu cuisine, Hunan cuisine and Anhui cuisine.

YOUR TURN:

在地图上找一找，这八个地方在中国的什么地方（中部，南部，东南，西北…）

	在中国的…		在中国的…
四川		广东	
山东		福建	
浙江		江苏	
湖南		安徽	

你知道吗？

多数的中国人说到开晚会，就想到吃饭。为了庆祝生日、节日、结婚纪念日、毕业，许多中国人都去饭店办酒席。

去参加酒席，需要注意一些礼节 (etiquette)，比如谁第一个坐下来，坐在什么地方合适。一般来说，要让最重要 (important) 的客人先坐下来，还要让这位客人坐在面对房门的座位上。不太重要的人可以坐在背 (bèi, back) 对房门的座位上。为了表示 (biǎoshì, express) 客气，许多人都要坐在背对房门的座位上。所以在酒席开始以前，不少中国人会为了谁先坐，坐在哪儿花一些时间。

大家都坐下来以后，服务员就开始上菜 (serve the dishes)。先上冷菜。冷菜常常有四个到八个。然后是四个、六个或八个热炒 (hot stir-fried dishes)。热炒应该跟冷菜一样多，或者更多。比方说，如果有四个冷菜，那么最少也要有四个热炒。当然，你决定上八个热炒也可以。等大家差不多吃完了冷菜和热炒以后，服务员就会上米饭和汤，这表示酒席快要结束了。最后上的是甜食：一点儿水果或者甜汤。

在离开酒席以前，客人一定会告诉主人 (host)，这个酒席好极了。主人一定会客气地说："哪里哪里。"

北京有名的饭店

4.3　校外考察
A Field Trip

対话一

凯丽：　　昨天下午我没找到你，你去哪儿了？

玛丽娅：　我们历史课的学生去校外考察了。这几天我们正在学习上海历史，所以白老师带我们去外滩了。

外滩

凯丽：　　外滩有什么特别的历史吗？

玛丽娅：　白老师说，1844年英国人开始用外滩作为码头，还开了不少公司，外滩就开始发展了。到了1848年，在黄浦江边造了一条大马路，这条马路的名字叫 The Bund。

凯丽：　　原来是这样，怪不得外国人常常把外滩叫作 The Bund。

玛丽娅：从十九世纪中开始，上海的外国公司和外国银行越来越多，外滩地区成了上海的金融和商业中心，在那里造了很多商业大楼。

凯丽：你是说外滩那些大楼都是十九世纪造的吗？

玛丽娅：不，外滩是从十九世纪开始发展的，可是多数的大楼都是在二十年代或者三十年代造的。

凯丽：你知道外滩一共有多少大楼吗？

玛丽娅：白老师说，在外滩和外滩附近的马路上，一共有五六十座大楼，有英国式、法国式、西班牙式、希腊式等等。现在这些大楼都是上海政府要保护的历史建筑。

外滩的大楼

凯丽：现在谁在用这些大楼？

玛丽娅：有些大楼是政府的办公楼。还有一些大楼里有公司、银行、饭店、商店。

凯丽：对了，外滩还有黄浦公园。黄浦公园是什么时候建立的？

玛丽娅：黄浦公园是上海最老的一个公园，是1868年建立的。

凯丽：历史课的社会考察听上去很有意思，让你学到了那么多外滩的历史。

玛丽娅：要是你想了解外滩的历史，黄浦公园里有一个外滩历史纪念馆，里边有很多历史照片，介绍了外滩和上海的发展历史。

凯丽：是吗？下次去外滩，我一定要去那个纪念馆看一看。

 对话二

张先生：欢迎上海国际学校的师生来东海国际社区参观。我是东海国际社区的负责人，姓张。

同学们：张先生好！

张先生：大家好。我先给你们介绍一下社区的情况。东海国际社区是1995年建立的。在这以前，这里都是菜地。

上海的一个社区

汤姆： 菜地？这里以前没有建筑吗？

张先生： 对，这些大楼和马路都是1995年以后造的。大家知道，从九十年代开始，上海经济发展得很快，建立了许多新公司和新工厂。

上海的一个工厂

我们这个地区现在有100多个公司和工厂。为了方便，在这儿工作的人都希望能住得离公司和工厂近一些，所以就建立了东海国际社区。

大卫： 为什么叫国际社区呢？是不是有很多外国人住在这儿？

张先生： 对，现在有二十多个国家六百多家居民住在东海国际社区。我们社区的生活环境非常好，绿化多，空气好，购物交通服务都很方便。

玛丽娅： 刚才我们在社区门口看到很多白色的面包车，上面写着东海国际社区。为什么你们有那么多车子？

张先生： 那是我们社区的班车。每十分钟有一班车去地铁站。居民只要坐上了地铁，二十分钟就能到人民广场。另外每二十分钟有一班车去附近的超市，方便居民买东西。

凯丽： 除了这些高楼以外，那儿的那些小房子也是你们社区的吗？

张先生：是的。我们不但有公寓楼，还有别墅。我们可以过去看一下，这些别墅有的是西班牙式的，有的是法国式的。

汤姆： 住在这儿的居民买东西方便吗？

张先生：超市离这儿坐车要十分钟。但是如果居民只需要一般的服务，我们有一个东海社区服务中心，那儿有商店、银行、邮局、饭店等等。我们看完了别墅，可以去服务中心参观一下。好，请大家跟我来。

生词

	Simplified	Traditional	Pinyin	Part of Speech	English
1.	校外		xiàowài	*n.*	out of school, off campus
2.	考察		kǎochá	*n./v.*	investigation; investigate
3.	码头	碼頭	mǎtóu	*n.*	dock
4.	造		zào	*v.*	build
5.	世纪	世紀	shìjì	*n.*	century
6.	金融		jīnróng	n.	finance
7.	商业	商業	shāngyè	n.	commerce, business
8.	年代		niándài	*n.*	decade of a century, years, time
9.	座		zuò	*m.w.*	for mountains, large buildings
10.	式		shì	*n.*	style, type

11.	保护	保護	bǎohù	n./v.	protection; protect
12.	建筑	建築	jiànzhù	n./v.	architecture; build
13.	纪念馆	紀念館	jìniànguǎn	n.	memorial museum, memorial hall
14.	菜地		càidì	n.	vegetable plot
15.	工厂	工廠	gōngchǎng	n.	factory
16.	绿化	綠化	lǜhuà	n./v.	greenbelt; make area green with plants
17.	空气	空氣	kōngqì	n.	air
18.	面包车	麵包車	miànbāochē	n.	van
19.	公寓		gōngyù	n.	apartment
20.	别墅		biéshù	n.	villa, single family house

专名

21.	外滩		Wàitān	The Bund
22.	黄浦江		Huángpǔjiāng	Huangpu River
23.	希腊		Xīlà	Greece
24.	黄浦公园	黃浦公園	Huángpǔ Gōngyuán	Huangpu Park

语言注释

1. Time expressions for centuries and decades (世纪、年代)

We use 世纪 to talk about centuries:

二十世纪　　　　the 20th century

二十一世纪　　　the 21st century

年代 is used to talk about decades:

九十年代 the 90's

五十年代 the 50's

To be more specific, we can say:

十九世纪八十年代 the 1880's

二十世纪七十年代 the 1970's

2. 跟 (following)

We have learned that 跟 has the meaning of "with." It also has the meaning of "following, after." For example:

跟我来。 Come after me (follow me).

跟我念拼音。 Read the pinyin after me.

学无止境 EXTEND YOUR KNOWLEDGE

We have now learned some words describing different industries. Here are a few more. Pinyin is provided for new characters only.

工业	轻工业	重工业
industry	light industry	heavy industry
手工业	服务业	高科技 (jì) 产业
handicraft industry	service industry	high-tech industry
娱乐业	建筑业	餐饮业
entertainment industry	construction industry	restaurant industry
房地产业	医药业	旅游业
real estate industry	pharmaceutical industry	tourism industry

YOUR TURN:

你住的地方有哪些产业 (industry)？请把主要的五个产业写下来：

中国文化一瞥 A Glimpse into Chinese Culture

Chinese proverbs and idioms

The following sayings are about neighbors.

1. lín   lǐ   xiāng zhù
邻 里 相 助

neighbors help neighbors; people in the same neighborhood help each other

IN USE:

在我们社区，邻里相助是常见的事。

In our community, it is common for people in the same neighborhood to help each other.

YOUR TURN:

1. Please give an example of 邻里相助。
2. 你做过"邻里相助"的事吗？请把你做的事告诉大家。

2. zuǒ lín yòu shè
左 邻 右 舍

next-door neighbors; neighboring families

IN USE:

1. 我需要帮助的时候，左邻右舍都来帮忙。
   When I needed help, my next-door neighbors came to help.
2. 她家的左邻右舍都养宠物。
   Her next-door neighbors all have pets.

YOUR TURN:

请向大家介绍一下你家的左邻右舍。

3. yuǎn qīn bù rú jìn lín
远 亲 不 如 近 邻
a distant relative is not as good as a close neighbor

IN USE:

远亲不如近邻。邻居互相帮助是应该的。

A distant relative is not as good as a close neighbor. Neighbors should help each other.

YOUR TURN:

你同意"远亲不如近邻"的说法吗？为什么？

Some common sayings about helping each other:

人人为我，我为人人。　　Everyone helps me and I help everyone.

人人爱我，我爱人人。　　Everyone loves me and I love everyone.

为人民服务。　　　　　　Serve the people.

你知道吗？

黄浦江把上海分成浦东和浦西。上海的市中心—南京路和外滩都在浦西。在上海的外滩，有一个有名的公园，叫黄浦公园。黄浦公园是1868年8月建立的，它的东边是黄浦江，北边是苏州河，这是上海最早建造的公园。黄浦公园的原名 (original name) 是 Public Park (公共花园)，后来又改 (gǎi, change) 成"外滩公园"。1946年改成"黄浦公园"以后，这个名字就一直用到现在。

黄浦江

　　在黄浦公园的中间，有一个"外滩广场"。各类文化活动和庆祝活动常常在外滩广场举行。每年在这儿有几十场的广场音乐会，吸引 (xīyǐn, attract) 了很多国内外的游客。在黄浦公园里，还有一个"外滩历史纪念馆"。纪念馆里有许多照片，介绍了外滩和上海发展的历史。纪念馆的开放时间是每天上午10点到下午2点。去那儿参观的人很多，因为一个小小的纪念馆介绍了一个大城市100多年的历史。

黄浦江边的码头

4.4 去南京
Going to Nanjing

 课文

通知

同学们：

　　这个周末，汉语班的老师和同学要去南京参加华东地区的"中学生汉语演讲大赛"。演讲大赛将在南京大学举行，有三千多名学生要参加今年的比赛。

　　为了方便大家，学校已经为我们订好了一辆大客车，送我们直接去南京大学。大客车定于星期五下午三点出发，七点左右到达南京。到南京以后，我们将住在"南京明日大酒店"。以下是我们在南京的行程安排：

星期六	7点	在明日大酒店吃早饭
	8点	出发去南京大学
	9点-17点	参加中学生汉语演讲大赛
	18点	参观南京夫子庙，吃晚饭，逛夜市
	21点	回饭店
星期日	7点	在明日大酒店吃早饭
	8点	出发去钟山风景区
	9点-15点	参观钟山风景区
	19点	回到上海国际学校

这个周末南京的天气是晴天，最高气温15-17度，最低气温7-10度。请大家根据天气情况，准备合适的衣服。

班长：玛丽娅
三月二十日

石象路

The Sacred Way at the Ming Tombs in Nanjing

南京的夫子庙

🔘 对话

玛丽娅：这个周末我们要去南京，你的行李都准备好了吗？

凯丽：准备好了。你看，我就只带这个背包。

玛丽娅：这个背包那么小，放得下很多东西吗？

凯丽：我们一共才去两天，不用带很多东西。

玛丽娅：我看我得带一个拉杆箱，不然我的东西放不下。

凯丽：拉杆箱？你要带很多东西吗？

玛丽娅：也不太多，两套衣服、两双鞋子、帽子、太阳眼镜、几本书、笔记本、汉语词典、一些吃的东西。我还打算把笔记本电脑、MP3播放机、手机和游戏机都带去。对了，我还要带一些洗漱用品。

凯丽：这个机那个机的，你带这些去干什么？

玛丽娅：有了电脑，晚上可以上网；有了手机，可以打电话发短信；有了MP3和游戏机，在去南京的路上可以玩儿。我觉得这些东西都会用到。

凯丽：那你为什么要带两双鞋子呢？

玛丽娅：我穿一双球鞋，可是还要带一双皮鞋，因为去参加演讲比赛的时候需要穿得漂亮一点儿。另外我还要带一双拖鞋，在房间里可以穿。

凯丽：我看你没必要带拖鞋，中国的饭店不但有洗漱用品，而且还有拖鞋。

玛丽娅：　我知道，可是饭店的牙刷、牙膏、梳子、拖
鞋都是一次性的。我自己带这些东西，不是
比较环保吗？

凯丽：　　好吧，那你就带一个大箱子吧。

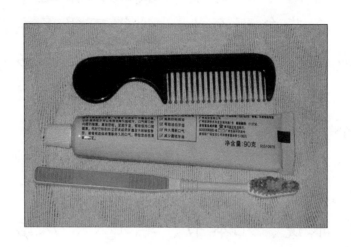

🔘 生词

	Simplified	Traditional	Pinyin	Part of Speech	English
1.	客车	客車	kèchē	n.	bus (charter)
2.	于	於	yú	prep.	in, at (a time, place)
3.	以下		yǐxià	prep.	below, under
4.	行程		xíngchéng	n.	itinerary
5.	夜市		yèshì	n.	night market
6.	根据	根據	gēnjù	prep.	according to, on the basis of
7.	背包		bèibāo	n.	backpack
8.	拉杆箱	拉桿箱	lāgānxiāng	n.	wheeled luggage
9.	笔记本	筆記本	bǐjìběn	n.	notebook
10.	洗漱		xǐshù	v.	wash one's face and rinse one's mouth
11.	球鞋		qiúxié	n.	sports shoes

12. 皮鞋		píxié	*n.*	leather shoes
13. 拖鞋		tuōxié	*n.*	slippers
14. 牙刷		yáshuā	*n.*	toothbrush
15. 牙膏		yágāo	*n.*	toothpaste
16. 梳子		shūzi	*n.*	comb
17. 一次性		yīcìxìng	*adj./n.*	disposable; one time
18. 环保	環保	huánbǎo	*n.*	environmental protection

专名

19. 华东	華東	Huádōng	East China
20. 夫子庙	夫子廟	Fūzimiào	Confucius Temple
21. 钟山 风景区	鍾山 風景區	Zhōngshān fēngjǐngqū	Zhongshan Scenic Area

语言注释

1. 于 (at, in, from...)

于 is similar to 在. It is used in formal written Chinese.

毕业典礼定于星期六上午十点举行。

The graduation ceremony is to be held at 10 a.m. on Saturday.

这位老作家1933年生于北京。

This old author was born in Beijing in 1933.

2. 以下 (below, under)

以下是文化日活动的计划。

Below is the plan for the Culture Day activities.

请大家看以下的图片。

Please take a look at the picture below.

3. 根据 (according to, based on)

你可以根据工作情况，决定哪天去休假。

Based on your situation at work, you can decide which day to take off.

根据地图，我们应该往左拐。

According to the map, we should turn left.

学无止境 EXTEND YOUR KNOWLEDGE

The following words are for toiletries. Pinyin is provided for new characters only.

肥皂 (féizào) *soap*	洗发 (fà) 液 (yè) *shampoo*	护发素 (sù) *conditioner*
电吹 (chuī) 风 *hair dryer*	洗手液 (yè) *hand soap*	卫生纸 *toilet paper*
面纸 *facial tissue*	镜 (jìng) 子 *mirror*	剃 (tì) 须 (xū) 刀 *razor*
剃 (tì) 须 (xū) 膏 *shaving cream*	香水 *perfume*	棉 (mián) 签 (qiān) *cotton swab*
棉 (mián) 球 *cotton ball*	牙线 (xiàn) *dental floss*	牙签 (qiān) *toothpick*
面霜 (shuāng) *facial cream*	防晒霜 (fángshàishuāng) *sunscreen*	漱口液 (yè) *mouthwash*

YOUR TURN:

Think of three additional toiletries that are not listed above. Find out how to say them in Chinese from Chinese speakers or dictionaries, and share them with your class.

中国文化一瞥 A Glimpse into Chinese Culture

Chinese proverbs and idioms

The following proverbs are about feeling happy.

1. huān shēng xiào yǔ
欢 声 笑 语
cheering and laughing

IN USE:

在晚会上，哪儿都是欢声笑语。
Everywhere at the party there is cheering and laughing.

YOUR TURN:

请说出三个你能听到欢声笑语的地方。

2. 欢 天 喜 地
full of joy; overjoyed; be elated and happy

IN USE:

1. 过春节的时候，小孩子们欢天喜地。
   Children are full of joy during the Spring Festival.

2. 他父母欢天喜地地告诉每个人，"我们的孩子考上北京大学了。"
   His parents were overjoyed and told everyone: "Our son has been admitted to Beijing University."

YOUR TURN:

什么事情会让你欢天喜地？

3. xǐ   qì   yáng   yáng

喜   气   洋   洋

look cheerful; look delighted; full of joy

IN USE:

这几天他喜气洋洋的，因为他的好朋友要从法国来看他。

He looks cheerful these days because his best friend is coming to visit him from France.

YOUR TURN:

请你注意一下，在你的同学和朋友里，谁看上去喜气洋洋？
问一下他/她为什么那么高兴？

4. xǐ   xiào   yán   kāi

喜   笑   颜   开

beaming with happy smiles; one's face lit up with happiness

IN USE:

1. 张爷爷喜笑颜开，因为他的优盘找到了。

   Grandpa Zhang is beaming with happy smiles, because he has found his USB drive.

2. 我们学校的足球队得了冠军，运动员们喜笑颜开。

   Our school's soccer team won the championship and the athletes were all full of

   smiles.

YOUR TURN:

请你说一件你经历过的事。在这件事里，必须有一个人或者
几个人"喜笑颜开"。

The secret to happiness

Some Chinese people say the secret to happiness is to remember these three sayings:

助人为乐	zhù rén wéi lè	find pleasure in helping others
知足常乐	zhī zú cháng lè	to be content is to be happy
自得其乐	zì dé qí lè	enjoy yourself, find joy in your own way

YOUR TURN:

1. 你觉得这三个秘密一样重要还是其中一个更重要？为什么？

2. 你知道在别的语言中，有没有关于一个人得到快乐的说法？

你知道吗？

南京是中国有名的古都 (ancient capital city)。2400多年以前，在公元前472年，越王就把首都建立在南京，那时候南京叫"越城"。后来又有十个朝代 (cháodài, dynasty) 和中华民国 (Republic of China) 先后把南京作为首都。"南京"这个名字是从明代 (Ming Dynasty) 开始的。因为南京有两千多年的历史，又是许多朝代的首都，所以经济、文化发展得很快，成为全国的经济中心和文化中心之一。如果你去南京参观，可以看到许多历史文化的景点。钟山风景区的景点记录了南京两千年左右的历史。

南京最有名的大学是南京大学。南京大学成立于1902年，已经有100多年的历史了。今天的南京大学有两个校区，有四万名左右学生。其中两千多名是外国学生。他们在南京大学学习汉语和其他的学科 (major)。

夫子庙夜景

中山陵

Sun Yat-sen Mausoleum

4.5 家长开放日
Open House Day for Parents

 课文

家长开放日活动介绍

各位家长：

　　欢迎您前来参加上海国际学校的家长开放日。为了让您更好地了解学校的教学情况，我校今天五月六日（星期五）上午8:30到下午3:30举办家长开放日。以下是开放日的活动安排：

1. 全校教师的课程都对家长开放，家长可以去各个班级听课。

2. 家长可以在8:30，10:30，或12:30去学校大礼堂听校长介绍我校的教学情况。

3. 初三家长可以在9:30–10:30去教学楼三楼的大教室。初三的教师要报告我校初中毕业考试和高中招生的情况，并听取家长对学校工作的意见和建议。

4. 高三家长可以在9:30–10:30去学校礼堂。高三的教师要报告高考信息，回答家长关于高考的问题，并听取家长对学校工作的意见和建议。

5. 学校体育馆全天有学生书画、作文、科学实验展览。

6. 下午2:00在学校大礼堂有学生表演。

7. 学校图书馆全天有教师教案、论文的展览。

8. 学生食堂、宿舍、体育馆、图书馆、电子阅览室、电脑房、活动中心全天对家长开放。

非常感谢您参加家长开放日的各种活动，请多提意见和建议。

上海国际学校
五月六日

 对话

玛丽娅：这个星期五是我们学校的家长开放日。那天，有不少学生家长要来我们学校听课，听报告，参观，看展览。

汤姆：　我们那天还上课吗？

玛丽娅： 上午要上课。那天所有的课都对家长开放，家长可以随便到哪个教室去听课。

大卫： 除了听课以外，家长还可以参加别的活动吗？

玛丽娅： 星期五学校有报告、展览、参观、表演什么的。我们上完课以后，还需要跟家长座谈。家长们不但想从老师那儿了解学校的教学情况，也想听听我们学生的看法。

凯丽： 我们乐队跟戏剧社和合唱团的同学还要表演节目。我要去弹钢琴。

玛丽娅： 那天下午我们会很忙，有些同学要去表演，有些要去开座谈会，还有一些要在学校的各个地方接待家长。同时，我们班还参加了在体育馆举办的书画、作文、和科学实验展览，需要一些同学去做讲解员。

大卫： 大家是不是可以自愿报名参加各种活动？

玛丽娅： 自愿报名最好，这样每个人都可以做自己感兴趣的事。大卫，你想做什么？

大卫： 我去参加座谈会吧。

玛丽娅： 太好了，我们班的座谈会就由你负责吧，想参加座谈会的同学可以去你那里报名。谁负责展览的讲解工作呢？汤姆，你能负责吗？

汤姆： 对不起，我已经有安排了，要去电脑房帮助老师接待家长。

凯丽： 明英这几天一直在准备书画展览，我看就由她负责吧。

玛丽娅： 好，那就这样吧。

生词

	Simplified	Traditional	Pinyin	Part of Speech	English
1.	开放	開放	kāifàng	*adj./v.*	open, open-minded; to open
2.	全		quán	*adj./adv.*	entire; all, completely
3.	班级	班級	bānjí	*n.*	class
4.	招生		zhāoshēng	*v.o.*	admit students
5.	听取	聽取	tīngqǔ	*v.*	listen to
6.	书画	書畫	shūhuà	*n.*	calligraphy and painting
7.	作文		zuòwén	*n.*	composition
8.	实验	實驗	shíyàn	*n./v.*	experiment
9.	展览	展覽	zhǎnlǎn	*n./v.*	exhibition; exhibit
10.	教案		jiào'àn	*n.*	lesson plan
11.	论文	論文	lùnwén	*n.*	research paper, thesis
12.	阅览室	閱覽室	yuèlǎnshì	*n.*	reading room
13.	所有		suǒyǒu	*adj.*	(including) all
14.	座谈	座談	zuòtán	*v.*	discuss freely
15.	看法		kànfǎ	*n.*	opinion, idea
16.	座谈会	座談會	zuòtánhuì	*n.*	open discussion
17.	接待		jiēdài	*n./v.*	reception; receive
18.	讲解员	講解員	jiǎngjiěyuán	*n.*	guide (for exhibit)
19.	自愿	自願	zìyuàn	*v.*	volunteer
20.	讲解	講解	jiǎngjiě	*v.*	explain, interpret

语言注释

1. 全 (entire, all)

全 can be used either as an adjective or an adverb. As an adjective, it has the meaning of "entire." Usually, 全 should only apply to singular nouns. For example:

全国　　the entire country

全班　　the entire class

全校　　the entire school

When it is used as an adverb, 全 has the meaning of "completely, all." It can be used with or without 都. For example:

他们全来了。
They all came.

这些字我全都不认识。
I don't know any of these words.

2. 所有 (all, including all)

When referring to an entire group of items/people, 所有 is used before the noun, with the meaning of "including all."

所有的课都满了。
All of the classes are full.

所有来参观的人都说这儿的风景美极了。
All those who come to visit say the scenery is extremely beautiful here.

学无止境 EXTEND YOUR KNOWLEDGE

The following words are about different forms of Chinese folk art (民间艺术). Pinyin is provided for new characters only.

书法 *Chinese calligraphy*	剪 (jiǎn) 纸 *paper cutout*	水墨 (mò) 画 *ink painting*
篆刻 (zhuànkè) *seal cutting*	泥 (ní) 人 *clay figurine*	景泰 (tài) 蓝 *cloisonné enamel*
刺绣 (cìxiù) *embroidery*	木 (mù) 雕 *wood carving*	石 (shí) 雕 *stone carving*
玉 (yù) 雕 *jade carving*	蜡染 (làrǎn) *wax printing*	布 (bù) 艺 *arts and crafts made of fabrics*

 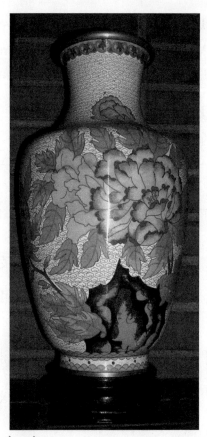

刺绣，景泰蓝

中国文化一瞥 A Glimpse into Chinese Culture

Chinese proverbs and idioms

The following two proverbs both have something to do with painting, and each has a story behind it. People now use both proverbs to describe many situations that are not necessarily about painting.

1. huà lóng diǎn jīng
画   龙   点   睛

bring a painted dragon to life by putting in the pupils of its eyes — add the finishing touch;
add the critical touch that brings a work of art or writing to life

IN USE:

张老师：　　这篇文章写得好极了，特别是最后两个句子。

玛丽娅：　　最后两个句子是大卫写的。他为这篇文章
　　　　　　画龙点睛。

Teacher Zhang: This article is very well written, particularly the last two sentences.

Maria: The last two sentences were written by David, who added in the critical touch and brought the article to life.

YOUR TURN:

Can you use 画龙点睛 to describe the following situations?

	可以	不可以
1. 文化日的时候，我们大家一起做了一个长城的录像。张老师看了以后说我们做得非常好。		
2. 文化日的时候，我们大家一起做中国饮食的录像。汤姆为录像加了一些音乐。我们的录像现在看上去好极了。		

3. 我给小弟拍的照片看上去有点乱，因为旁边有许多树啊、车啊、人啊什么的。大卫帮我用电脑软件把这些都去掉了，现在照片上只有小弟一个人，看上去非常好。		
4. 张老师说我写的文章不太好，他让我把几个句子再写一遍。我写了以后，他说比以前好一点儿了。		

The story of 画龙点睛

传说公元500年左右，有一位有名的画家，叫张僧繇(Zhāng Sēngyóu)。他画的东西都跟真的一样。有一天，他去参观一个庙 (miào, temple)，在墙上画了四条龙 (lóng, dragon)，可是他没有给这四条龙画眼睛。有人问他："这几条龙为什么没有眼睛呢？"张先生回答说："只要我画上眼睛，这些龙就都会飞走。"听张先生这么说，旁边的人都大笑起来，他们觉得张僧繇疯 (fēng, crazy) 了。张先生什么也没有说，拿起笔来，为两条龙点上了眼睛。他刚画完，乌云 (wūyún, dark cloud) 就来了，雷电 (léidiàn, thunder and lightning) 也来了，这两条龙飞到天上去了。大家都目瞪口呆 (mù dèng kǒu dāi, stunned speechless)。"画龙点睛"的意思是：为一件作品 (work of art) 加上最关键 (guānjiàn, critical) 的最后一笔，让这件作品变得更好。

According to the legend, Zhang Sengyou was a famous artist who lived around 500 AD. He was able to draw things that looked exactly like their real counterparts. One day while touring a temple, he painted four dragons on the wall, but he didn't paint eyes on the dragons. Someone asked him why the dragons didn't have eyes. Master Zhang replied, "If I add eyes to the dragons, they will fly away." On hearing this, everyone laughed and thought he was crazy. Master Zhang didn't say a thing but instead used his brush to add eyes to two dragons.

As soon as he finished, clouds came, then thunder and lightning came, and the two dragons flew into the sky. Everyone was speechless. Since then, the expression "bring a painted dragon to life by putting in the pupils of its eyes" is used to describe adding the final or critical touch that brings a work of art or writing to life.

2. huà shé tiān zú

画　蛇　添　足

paint a snake with feet—unnecessary; an unnecessary and redundant act

IN USE:

孩子做完学校的作业以后，有些家长还给孩子更多的作业。我觉得这是画蛇添足。

After their children finish their homework from school, some parents give them more homework. I think it is unnecessary.

YOUR TURN:

你做过画蛇添足的事情吗？

The story of 画蛇添足

两千多年以前，在战国时期，有一个楚国人在办祭祀 (jìsì, offering sacrifice to the dead)。祭祀完了以后，他给下人 (servants) 一壶 (hú, jar) 酒。这些下人看到这壶酒只够一个人喝，不够那么多人喝，就决定要举行一个画蛇 (shé, snake) 的比赛。谁第一把蛇画完，谁就可以喝那壶酒。一个人很快就画完了。他看到别人还在画，就决定为蛇加上几只脚。这时候，第二个人也画完了，就把那壶酒拿去喝了。第二个人对第一个人说："蛇没有脚。你为什么要为蛇画脚呢？"

"画蛇添足"这个成语告诉我们，不应该做不用做的事。做那些不用做的事不但浪费 (làngfèi, waste) 时间，而且还影响你达到原来的目的 (mùdì, goal)。

Over two thousand years ago, in the Warring States Period, a man in the State of Chu was offering a sacrifice to his ancestors. After the ceremony, the man gave a jar of wine to his servants. The servants thought the wine was only enough for one person, and not enough for all of them. They decided to hold a competition to draw pictures of snakes and the one who finished the picture first would drink the wine. One of them finished the snake quickly. Seeing that the others were still busy drawing, he added feet to the snake. At this moment another man finished drawing, snatched the jar, and drank the wine, saying, "A snake doesn't have feet. How can you add feet to a snake?"

This story was later used to tell people not to do unnecessary things. Unnecessary acts are not only wasteful, but also may hinder you from reaching your original goal.

你知道吗?

中国的中小学有一个半小时的午休 (lunch break) 时间。以前不少中小学生都回家去吃午饭，因为他们家都住得不远。可是现在情况有点儿不一样了。多数的学生都在学生餐厅吃午饭。他们吃的是"盒饭"。盒饭里有米饭、一点儿汤，还有两个菜。菜是蔬菜，再加上一点儿鱼肉。

学生不回家吃午饭的原因 (reasons) 很多。原因之一是因为城市发展得很快。许多家庭觉得市中心的老房子太小，就搬家到离市中心比较远的新公寓里去住，因为新公寓比较大。不少在市中心的学校还在原来的地方，所以有些学生需要坐公共交通来学校上学。有的学生需要坐一两个小时的公共汽车或地铁才能到学校。原因之二是差不多所有学生的妈妈现在都在外边工作，她们没有时间为孩子做午饭。原因之三是，有些学生家长想，如果孩子不回家吃饭，他们就会有更多的时间可以做作业。

现在许多学生都是"独生子女"，没有机会跟同龄人 (peers) 玩。午休时间让大家可以自由地跟朋友说话，玩游戏。这时候，他们不用担心学校的作业，也不用担心家长来管他们。所以午休时间可以说是学生的"自由活动时间"。

4.6 第四单元复习
Unit 4 Review

课文

这是大卫写的博客：

今天我们学校举行了国际文化日活动。全校的老师和同学都参加了。我们国际学校有来自三十多个国家和地区的学生和老师，国际文化日是我们了解各国文化的大好机会。

每个外语班的同学都准备了一些活动来介绍他们正在学习的语言和文化。有些外语是几个国家的语言，这个班的同学就选其中一个国家的情况来介绍。比如，美国、英国、新西兰、澳大利亚都说英文，去年英语班介绍了美国，今年就主要介绍澳大利亚。我们汉语班的同学介绍了中国文化，还有日语班、德语班、法语班、西班牙语班、阿拉伯语班都介绍了不同国家的情况。

我觉得我们汉语班的活动很有意思，也特别受大家的欢迎。今天我们重点介绍的是中国的"食文化"。以前我只知道中国菜的味道不太一样。有的中国菜有点儿辣，有的有点儿甜。这次我们班的同学先介绍了各地的农业出产、地理环境和气候对饮食的影响，然后我们分成四个小组做了四个地方的菜。我们做了广东菜、新疆菜、上海菜、和山东菜。我在山东组，我们做了包子和饺子。广东组做了很多点心，上海组做了上海有名的"小笼包子"，新疆组做了烤肉。我们把做好的菜让观众尝一尝，然后请他们投票选举出最好吃的菜。结果新疆组得了38票，山东组得了36票，上海组和广东组都得了33票。新疆组赢了。虽然我们组没有赢，但是我还是觉得我们组做的饺子是最好吃的，比饺子店做的要好吃多了。

虾饺

对话

大卫： 今天我上网的时候看到，网上有一个国际数学竞赛。全世界有几十万的中小学生都打算参加这个竞赛。

凯丽： 是吗？这是一个什么样的数学竞赛？为什么有那么多人要参加？

大卫： 这个竞赛叫"国际网上数学竞赛"，是2007年由澳大利亚一家教育网站开始举办的。来自一百个左右国家的中小学生已经参加过这个竞赛，做了几千万个数学题。这个数学竞赛主要是比赛口算的能力。

汤姆： 你是说，学生不能用纸和笔来做数学题吗？

大卫： 对。

凯丽： 这听上去有点儿难。

大卫： 不一定，因为这个教育网站会根据学生的年龄把他们分到不同的比赛组。要是你是小学生，就做小学的数学题。是中学生，就做中学的数学题。

凯丽： 哦，是这样。

明英： 要是我想参加，怎么报名？要交报名费吗？

大卫： 不需要。这个网上数学竞赛是免费的。想参加竞赛的中小学生，可以直接上网报名。

凯丽： 那竞赛的时候，是许多人一起比赛吗？

大卫： 我也不太清楚，网上说，这个网站会让两个或者更多的学生一起在网上比赛口算的能力，看谁算得又快又准确。这个数学竞赛常常有几千个学生同时在网上参加。如果一个学生算得又快又好，就可以多得分。

明英： 这个竞赛是用英文讲解的吗？如果用英文，许多中国的中小学生可能不会去参加吧？

大卫： 竞赛是用英文的。但是我觉得，现在中国中小学生的英文越来越好，可能参加的人也会越来越多。对了，我看到说，这两年，北京、上海、天津一些国际学校的学生已经开始参加竞赛了。

凯丽： 是吗？那我们也上网去看看。

生词

Simplified	Traditional	Pinyin	Part of Speech	English
1. 博客		bókè	*n.*	web log, blog
2. 得		dé	*v.*	get, obtain
3. 赢		yíng	*v.*	win
4. 竞赛	競賽	jìngsài	*n.*	competition, contest
5. 口算		kǒusuàn	*v.*	say the result aloud after solving a math problem in one's head
6. 不一定		bùyīdìng	*adv.*	not necessarily
7. 准确	準確	zhǔnquè	*adj./n.*	accurate; accuracy

专名

8. 新西兰	新西蘭	Xīnxīlán		New Zealand
9. 澳大利亚	澳大利亞	Àodàlìyà		Australia
10. 阿拉伯		Ālābó		Arabic; Arab

生词扩充 EXPAND YOUR WORD POWER

Many Chinese words are formed by combining two or more characters. If you know the characters in a word, you can often guess the meaning of that word. See if you understand the meaning of the following words.

羽毛球拍		网球拍	
赛场		运动鞋	
雨鞋		跳高	
跳远		长跑	
短跑		全校	
全厂		展览会	
意见箱		市中心	
新式		建造	
服务日		绿化日	
考察团		校外活动	
得分		得票	
难题		重点项目	

SELF-ASSESSMENT

In Unit 4, you have learned to read general public announcements, name some commonly used daily necessities, talk briefly about a place's history, and describe events with some detail. Have you achieved the learning goals of Unit 4? After completing the exercises for Unit 4 in your Workbook, fill out the following self-assessment sheet.

Yes/No	*Can you say and write these things in Chinese?*
	Read and understand general public announcements
	Talk about sports events
	Name some basic sports equipment
	Name basic cooking utensils and kitchen equipment
	Name some basic toiletries
	Describe how to organize an activity
	Describe, in some detail, a place's history
	Describe, in some detail, an itinerary
	Describe, in some detail, a day's program or activities

7–9	yes	excellent
4–6	yes	good
1–3	yes	need some work

附錄
APPENDIX

對話、課文（繁體字版）
Dialogues and Texts in Traditional Characters

Unit 1.1 對話一

湯姆： 你好，我叫湯姆。你是新來的吧？我好像沒見過你。

明英： 你好！我叫明英。很高興認識你。我是這個學期轉學來上海國際學校的。

湯姆： 你以前在哪個學校？

明英： 北京第四中學。

湯姆： 哇噻，那麼厲害啊？北京第四中學是有名的好學校，能進北京四中可不容易。能認識你這麼聰明的人，非常幸運，也非常高興。

明英： 別開玩笑了。

湯姆： 你是怎麼考進北京四中的？

明英： 是這樣的，我父母都是美國大學的教授，去年在北京做研究，所以我就在北京四中借讀了一年。

湯姆： 那你怎麼又到上海來了呢？

明英： 今年我父母來上海歷史博物館做研究，我們就把家搬到上海來了。你呢？你一直在這個國際學校上學嗎？

湯姆： 對。我是在美國舊金山出生的。四年前，我爸爸到上海來工作，我就跟父母來中國了。來上海以後，我一直在這兒上學，因為我父母覺得上國際學校可以讓我一邊學英語一邊學漢語，不會影響我將來回美國上大學。你也是美國人吧？

明英： 對。可是我是在中國出生的，兩歲的時候跟父母去了美國。我是在美國上的小學和初中，所以現在我的中文沒有英文好。去年我父母帶我來中國，就是希望我能好好地學習中文。你的中文好還是英文好？

湯姆： 我的英文比較好。可是這兩年，我的中文也進步很快。對了，將來你打算回美國上大學嗎？

明英： 這個我還沒決定。我很喜歡北京。要是有機會，我可能會報名上北京大學。你呢？

湯姆： 我也挺喜歡中國的，我的朋友又都在中國。和你一樣，我也可能會在中國上大學。

Unit 1.1 對話二

湯姆： 凱麗，來，我給你介紹一下，這是新來的同學，明英。

凱麗： 你好，我叫凱麗。歡迎你來我們學校。

明英： 你好，認識你很高興。

湯姆： 凱麗是我的好朋友，特別理解我。她可聰明了，今年暑假，她上了一個準備高考的暑期學校，現在是我們班的數學天才。

凱麗： 好了，湯姆，別甜言蜜語了。有甚麼事，你就說吧。

湯姆： 你看，我說你最理解我了嘛。你能把《數學高考題分析》借給我看看嗎？

凱麗： 當然可以。明英，你看，我知道湯姆說我好是為了借書。

明英： 也不完全是吧。可能湯姆真的覺得你非常聰明。

湯姆： 謝謝你，明英，我又找到了一個特別理解我的人。

凱麗： 我明天可以把書帶來給你。

明英： 那本書很不錯，我把裡邊的題都做了一遍。

凱麗： 是嗎？你用多長時間做完的？

明英： 兩三個星期吧。因為我喜歡數學，一有空兒就做。

湯姆： 真的？我多麼幸運啊！兩個數學天才都是我朋友。

明英： 又開玩笑了。我們互相學習吧。

Unit 1.2 對話

凱麗： 要選新班長了，我覺得你當班長挺合適的。你想參加競選嗎？

瑪麗婭： 我得好好想想。當班長需要跟同學老師打交道，需要為大家服務，是一個學習為人處事的好机會。

凱麗： 我覺得你又聰明又能幹，學習好，喜歡運動，還常常幫助別人。你應該參加競選。

瑪麗婭： 我有的優點你都有，你怎麼不參加競選呢？

凱麗： 當班長第一得願意聽大家說話，不能著急。第二要能領導大家一起工作。第三做事要做得又快又好。可是我有時候一聽別人說的跟我想的不一樣，我就會著急。再說，有時候我做事做得挺慢的。所以我當班長不合適。你比我能幹多了。

瑪麗婭： 哪裡哪裡。我沒有你說的那麼能幹。

凱麗： 你就別客氣了，你一定能好好領導我們班的。

瑪麗婭： 好吧，我回家以後，先準備一下，寫一個競選演講。等我把演講寫好了，你能幫我看一看嗎？

凱麗： 當然可以。大衛和湯姆也能幫你。我們還會發電郵給大家，讓大家選你。對了，我們還應該做幾個"瑪麗婭，加油！"的牌子，把這些牌子挂在教室和學生餐廳裡。有我們當你的競選助手，你一定能競選成功。

瑪麗婭： 真的嗎？太謝謝你了。

Unit 1.2 課文

同學們、老師們：

你們好！我叫瑪麗婭羅西尼。我在競選當班長。班長是很重要的工作。如果有了一個好班長，一個班就能進步得比較快。大家常常說，我努力、聰明、能幹、愛幫助別人。這些優點能讓我好好地為大家服務。

我們上海國際學校是一個特別的學校，因為大家是從許多不同國家來的，有不同的文化。我是在義大利出生的，因為父母的工作，我在很多國家住過：美國、英國、法國、韓國、巴西、南非。五年以前，我們又搬家來到上海這個國際大城市。因為我去過很多國家，跟不同國家的人打過交道，看到過許多不同的文化，我特別能理解國際學生的需要。我覺得一個班長只有理解了班裡的同學才能領導一個班。

　　大家都知道，我不但自己的學習成績很好，而且還常常幫助別的同學。我當了班長以後，會把大家的學習需要告訴老師，讓我們的學習進步得更快。

　　除了學習以外，我還參加許多體育和娛樂活動。我當了班長以後，會組織更多的體育和文化活動，讓大家來參加。只有身體健康，我們才能更努力地學習。

　　在過去的兩年中，我做過義工，也打過工。我當了班長以後，會領導大家更好地為社區服務，把我們的世界變得更美好。

　　當然，大家一定知道我還有一個優點 -- 我組織的晚會是學校裡最受歡迎的。你們都還記得高三同學的畢業招待會，和在我家開過的晚會吧？要是我當了班長，那麼下一次我們班的晚會一定會是你參加過的最難忘的晚會。

　　同學們，請投我一票，謝謝大家！

Unit 1.3 對話一

凱麗：　明英，這學期的課你都選好了吧？

明英：　是的，我選了英語、數學、化學、物理、歷史和體育。可是我不是很喜歡歷史課，想換一門。你知道怎麼換課嗎？

凱麗：　你需要填寫一張退課加課表。你先寫上要退甚麼課，然後再寫上你要加的課、上課的時間和老師的姓名就可以了。今天好像是可以退課加課的最後一天，你知道去哪兒拿表嗎？

明英：　在教務處嗎？

凱麗：　對，圖書館和電腦房也有退課加課表。

明英：　謝謝。我們是不是一個學期要上四門必修課和兩門選修課？

凱麗：　是的。

明英：　在我們學校，除了外語課以外，還有哪些是選修課？

凱麗：　還有美術、音樂、健康教育、地理甚麼的。

明英：　地理課聽上去很有意思。

凱麗：　是啊。教地理課的張老師上課上得非常好。每個學期都有很多學生要上他的課，常常是學期還沒有開始，他的課已經滿了。

明英：　是嗎？如果我上不了張老師的地理課，那我就選經濟
　　　　學。教經濟學的老師怎麼樣？

凱麗：　不太清楚，因為我沒有上過經濟學。你可以問問大衛，
　　　　他上過。

Unit 1.3 對話二

瑪麗婭：這個學期你上幾門課？

大衛：　七門。

瑪麗婭：那麼多啊？除了必修課以外，你上哪些選修課？

大衛：　我上地理和電腦。

瑪麗婭：這麼多課裡，你最喜歡哪門課？

大衛：　我的課都不錯，可是我最喜歡地理課。教地理課的是張
　　　　老師。他教地理教了二十多年了。上課的時候，他常常
　　　　講故事。他不但告訴我們一個地方的地理環境，還告訴
　　　　我們那兒的歷史。那門課的作業挺多的，我們每個星期
　　　　都需要上網做研究，了解地理環境怎麼影響了一個地區
　　　　的經濟和文化。你呢？你最喜歡甚麼課？

瑪麗婭：除了歷史課以外，別的課我都喜歡。

大衛：　這個學期誰教歷史？

瑪麗婭：是那個新來的白老師。她講課的時候，從來不看著學
　　　　生，也不注意我們聽得懂聽不懂，就看著書說啊說啊。
　　　　同學們就自己做自己的事，有人用手機發短信，有人畫
　　　　畫兒，有人做作業，還有人睡覺。

大衛：　是嗎？上這門課聽上去跟玩兒一樣，是不是很容易？

瑪麗婭：不容易。每天白老師給我們很多作業，讓我們看書背
　　　　書。每次考試都很長，有五十個問題。要是你不背書，
　　　　就回答不了。這門課開學的時候有二十五個學生，現在
　　　　不少人已經退課了，只有十四個人了。

大衛：　那你怎麼不退課呢？

瑪麗婭：我也想過要退課，可是有一天白老師對我們說，她大學
　　　　剛畢業，還在學習怎麼教書，希望我們能幫助她，給她
　　　　一個學習的機會。你想，老師都這麼說了，我還好意思
　　　　退課嗎？

大衛：　是啊。那你跟她說過她上課的問題了嗎？

瑪麗婭：說過了，可是白老師好像理解不了我們的學習需要。她常說，在大學的時候，她老師也是每天讓她背書。要是她背得了，我們也一定背得了。

大衛：　我看，你現在可真是進退兩難啊。

Unit 1.4 對話一

大衛：　今天下午，各個學生社團要向大家介紹情況。你去嗎？

凱麗：　當然去。這個學期你參加了幾個社團？

大衛：　我還沒決定參加哪一個。你有甚麼好建議嗎？

凱麗：　你那麼喜歡運動，為甚麼不參加一個運動隊呢？

大衛：　參加了運動隊，就得每個星期去訓練。我喜歡的運動太多了，又比較喜歡自由，所以還是不參加運動隊的好。這樣我有空的時候，可以喜歡玩甚麼就玩甚麼。

凱麗：　那參加戲劇社吧。你比較外向，又對戲劇有興趣。

大衛：　不行，不行。我唱歌唱不好，跳舞跳不好，哪能當演員呢？

凱麗：　不會唱歌跳舞沒關系，你可以演話劇。比方說，你可以在話劇裡演一個偵探。你又高又瘦，穿上一件長大衣，再戴上一頂帽子，一定很像那個有名的英國偵探。

大衛：　好了好了，別開玩笑了。

凱麗：　對了,你不是也很喜歡電腦嗎？怎麼不參加電腦興趣小組呢？聽說電腦小組正在計劃做一個機器人。

大衛：　是嗎？今天下午我一定要去聽一聽電腦小組的介紹。

Unit 1.4 對話二

凱麗：　湯姆，這個學期你還參加數學興趣小組嗎？

湯姆：　對。數學小組對我的學習挺有幫助的。我們每次活動，都會有一位數學老師來參加。這位老師會給我們分析一些比較難的數學題，然後讓我們做。做完了以後，老師會檢查我們做得對不對。每次活動，我都能學到一些新知識。

凱麗：　聽上去很有意思。

湯姆： 你不是也很喜歡數學嗎？為甚麼不來參加數學興趣小組？

凱麗： 這學期不行，我已經參加了學校的樂隊。

湯姆： 樂隊不是一個星期活動一次嗎？這不會影響你參加數學興趣小組的。

凱麗： 可是我還參加了棒球隊。棒球隊一個星期要訓練兩個下午。你呢？這個學期還在學校的網球隊打網球嗎？

湯姆： 我已經退出網球隊了。網球隊來了一位新教練，以前是國家隊的網球運動員。他覺得我們的訓練時間太少，要我們每天訓練兩個小時。你想，我們又不是運動員，哪有那麼多時間訓練？特別是現在，每天有許多作業，還常常要考試，所以我退出了。

凱麗： 那你除了數學興趣小組以外，不參加別的社團了嗎？

湯姆： 我還參加了美國學生俱樂部。俱樂部裡都是美國來的學生，我們每個月活動兩次，都是很輕松的活動，比方說，看電影、聽音樂、去美國餐廳吃飯、開晚會甚麼的。又輕松又好玩。

Unit 1.5 對話一

瑪麗婭： 謝謝大家選我當班長。今天開班會我們要討論兩件事：第一件是關於作業的問題，有些同學覺得現在的作業太多了，也有同學覺得不多不少。第二件是關於中國文化講座活動。好，請大家說吧。

同學一： 現在學習壓力挺大的，每門課的老師都給我們很多作業。有時候，我從下課以後就開始做作業，一直要做到晚上十二點鐘。除了上課以外，我每天做作業就要做六七個小時。能不能請老師少給我們一些作業？

湯姆： 你說得對。作業越少越好。

瑪麗婭： 你也要花六七個小時做作業嗎？

湯姆： 不，我每天兩三個小時就能把作業做完。不過，要是沒有作業，我不就可以多參加一些別的活動了嗎？

凱麗： 你兩三個小時就能做完作業，還抱怨甚麼呀。

瑪麗婭： 請問大家一般每天要花多少時間做作業？

同學一： 六七個小時。

凱麗： 我一般要花三四個小時。

大衛： 我也只要三四個小時。

同學一： 為甚麼我花的時間比你們多呢？

湯姆： 是不是因為你做作業的時候特別認真，做好了還要檢查三四遍？

同學一： 不檢查怎麼行呢？我得不到100分，就會玩不好，睡不好。

瑪麗婭： 好吧，聽上去大家的學習方法不太一樣，不一定是作業太多的問題。

湯姆： 瑪麗婭，你可真是一言中的。

Unit 1.5 對話二

瑪麗婭： 現在我們請大衛給我們介紹這個學期中國文化講座的情況。

大衛： 大家好。這個學期我們班打算組織四次講座。講座的時間是每個月第一個星期一的下午四點半。

湯姆： 這些講座是關於甚麼的？

大衛： 這個學期的四個話題是：一、中國的電影歷史；二、飲食文化；三、現代畫；四、太极拳和健康。大家覺得這幾個話題怎麼樣？

湯姆： 第四個話題好像是給老年人準備的。打太极拳是老年人的運動。不信，你早上到公園去看看，在那兒打太极拳的都是老人。

凱麗： 我覺得湯姆說得對。能不能換個話題？

大衛： 當然可以，大家有甚麼建議嗎？

明英： 能不能請人來給我們談談在中國上大學的情況？

瑪麗婭： 我的鄰居是個大學生，我可以把他請來。

大衛： 你的鄰居是法國人吧？他的漢語說得怎麼樣？

瑪麗婭： 他是在法國出生的，可是三歲就離開了法國，跟父母到中國來了。他是在北京上的小學和中學，漢語講得非常好，聽上去跟中國人一樣。

湯姆：　我也可以請我的鄰居，她是中國人，現在是音樂學院的
　　　　學生。她好像在學習鋼琴，我常常聽到她在家一邊彈鋼
　　　　琴一邊唱歌。下課以後，她在一個俱樂部打工，可能是
　　　　在那兒彈鋼琴，也可能是在那兒唱歌。我不太清楚。
大衛：　沒關系，如果你鄰居來了，她可以告訴我們她在做
　　　　甚麼。

Unit 1.6 課文

（這是湯姆給爺爺奶奶寫的電子郵件。）

New	Reply	Reply All	Forward	Delete	Print

爺爺奶奶：你們好！

　　奶奶的電子郵件收到了。奶奶說爺爺正在學習電腦打字，學會了就給我們寫電郵。爺爺學得怎麼樣了？

　　學校九月一日開學了。這個學期，我比以前更忙了。因為再過兩年我們就要參加高考，所以老師們非常注意我們的學習，每天給我們很多作業。我們班有的同學每天要花六七個小時做作業。我做作業做得很快，但是每天還要花三四個小時。

　　這個學期我上了六門課，四門是必修課，兩門是選修課。我最喜歡的是數學課。教我們數學的王老師以前在兩個重點中學教過書，聽說他的不少學生現在成了大學的數學教授。王老師的教學方法非常好。他能把一個很難的問題一下子就講清楚。講完了以後，他就讓我們馬上練習做題。跟有些老師不一樣，他給的作業不太多。可是數學作業不容易，需要我花時間去想，去做。

　　除了上課以外，我還參加了學校的數學興趣小組和美國學生俱樂部。每個月有一個周末，我去"老人愛,愛老人"組織做半天義工。暑假的時候，我在那個組織做過義工，認識了幾位老人，跟他們成了好朋友，他們希望我能常常去看看他們，所以現在我每個月去看他們一次。

　　杰米說，他要給你們寫電子郵件，把他的秘密告訴你們。我不知道他的秘密是甚麼，因為他還沒有告訴我。

　　爸爸媽媽都很好，也很忙。他們讓我問你們好！

　　　　　　　　　　　　　　　　　　　　　　　　湯姆

Unit 1.6 對話

大衛： 張爺爺，請您看一下這張圖片，你認識這個人嗎？

張爺爺： 這個人是誰啊？我看不太清楚，我的眼鏡呢？

瑪麗婭： 您的眼鏡在這兒呢。

張爺爺： 人老了，看近的東西，沒有眼鏡就看不清楚了。哦，這個人有點兒像小高，可是小高比這張圖片上的人好看多了。

瑪麗婭： 張爺爺，這是我一邊聽看門師傅說一邊畫的，我畫得不太好。這個小高是誰？

張奶奶： 小高啊，他是我們老鄰居的孩子。他出生以後，身體不太好，常常因為生病不能去幼兒園，他父母工作又非常忙，所以我常常照顧他。他就跟我自己的孩子一樣。

大衛： 他常常來看你們嗎？

張奶奶： 對，以前他每個星期都要來一兩次。怎麼了？你們認識小高嗎？

瑪麗婭： 哦，是這樣的，我們很想知道張爺爺丟了優盤的那一天，有沒有人來過你們家。看門師傅說，小高來過，可是因為你們在睡覺，他就走了。

張爺爺： 對，對。那天小高是要來跟我們說再見的。他那天下午就要坐飛機去加拿大，因為我們在睡覺，就沒見到他。他現在正在加拿大學習呢。上個星期，他還給我來了電郵，說他馬上要高中畢業了，想到美國去上大學。

張奶奶： 瑪麗婭，等小高回來，你可以見見小高。小高畫畫兒畫得可好了。你看，這張畫兒是他畫的。

瑪麗婭： 這只貓很可愛。

張奶奶： 這是我們樓下鄰居養的貓，叫"黃黃"。黃黃很友好。從一樓到九樓，它哪兒都去過。只要你家的門開著，它就會進去。夏天的時候，我常常把大門開著，所以它常常來我們家。

張爺爺： 黃黃還喜歡把這家的東西帶到那家去，把那家的東西帶到這家來。要是我們家多了甚麼東西，我們就知道是黃黃帶來的。它帶來的東西可多了，有襪子啊、糖啊、餅乾啊、小玩具啊甚麼的，有一次它還帶來了半條魚。

大衛：　　哎，張爺爺，你的優盤會不會是黃黃拿走的呢？

張奶奶：　對啊，我們怎麼沒想到呢？我們應該一家一家地去問問。

Unit 2.1 對話一

（星期一瑪麗婭在學校見到了湯姆。）

瑪麗婭：　星期天我給你發短信，請你去看電影，你怎麼沒回？

湯姆：　　哦，我把手機忘在家裡了。昨天為了慶祝我姥姥和姥爺結婚四十周年，我們一家都去美心酒家參加酒席了。

瑪麗婭：　你姥姥姥爺不是住在北京嗎？

湯姆：　　是的。不過他們上個星期來上海看親戚朋友了。我姥姥姥爺都是上海人，後來因為工作，才把家搬到北京去的。所以他們的很多親戚朋友還住在上海。

瑪麗婭：　有多少人去參加酒席？

湯姆：　　一百多人。多數是親戚，還有一些是姥姥姥爺在上海的朋友。

瑪麗婭：　那麼多人一定很熱鬧吧？

湯姆：　　當然熱鬧了。我姥姥有四個兄弟姐妹，我姥爺有六個兄弟姐妹，住在上海的都來了。他們的子女，只要是在上海的，也都來參加了。

瑪麗婭：　你媽媽有兄弟姐妹嗎？

湯姆：　　她有一個妹妹，兩個弟弟。星期日的酒席就是他們四個人組織的。

瑪麗婭：　他們都住在上海嗎？

湯姆：　　不，我媽媽的兩個弟弟住在上海，妹妹住在北京。

瑪麗婭：　聽上去，以前的中國家庭，孩子都不少。

湯姆：　　是啊，可是現在不一樣了。一般的中國家庭只有一個孩子。星期六的時候，來的老人比孩子多。

瑪麗婭：　這麼多親戚，你都認識嗎？

湯姆：　　有一半以上我都不認識。

瑪麗婭：　那麼多親戚朋友來參加酒席，你姥姥姥爺一定很高興吧？

湯姆： 對。我姥爺特別喜歡唱歌。昨天他高興得不得了，一下子唱了五首歌。我把他的表演都錄了像。下次你來我家，我給你看錄像。

瑪麗婭： 好。

Unit 2.1 對話二

湯姆： 媽媽，星期天我聽姥姥說，她跟姥爺是中學同學。

媽媽： 對，那時候，他們不在一個班，可是都參加了學校的合唱團，後來就成了好朋友。

湯姆： 他們在中學就結婚了嗎？

媽媽： 在中國不能那麼早就結婚。中國的結婚年齡是：男的二十二歲以上，女的二十歲以上。

湯姆： 你和爸爸不是常常說，我們在中學最好不要談戀愛，要一心一意學習嗎？怎麼姥姥姥爺在中學就談戀愛了呢？

媽媽： 他們是中學畢業以後開始談的。那時候，姥姥在上海的一個幼兒園當老師，姥爺去北京上大學了，他們倆就互相寫信。越寫越有話說，慢慢地就談戀愛了。

湯姆： 他們不打電話嗎？

媽媽： 四十多年以前，一般的中國家庭都沒有電話。

湯姆： 那他們是甚麼時候結婚的呢？

媽媽： 姥爺大學畢業以後又過了兩年，他們才結婚。因為姥爺的工作在北京，所以姥姥就搬到北京去了。

湯姆： 那你是在北京出生的嗎？

媽媽： 是的，我和你舅舅阿姨都是在北京出生的，我們的小學、中學也都是在北京上的。

湯姆： 那兩個舅舅怎麼都搬到上海來了呢？

媽媽： 大舅舅是在上海上的大學，畢業以後就在上海工作。小舅舅前幾年在上海找到了他喜歡的工作，就把家搬過來了。

湯姆： 哦，是這樣。

Unit 2.2 對話一

（星期六，凱麗去林叔叔家做客。）

凱麗： 林叔叔林阿姨好！

林叔叔：凱麗，快進來，請坐。我給你去拿飲料。

凱麗： 謝謝林叔叔。林東呢？他出去了嗎？

林阿姨：他還在睡覺呢。

林叔叔：甚麼？都十點了，他還沒起床？

林阿姨：他啊，昨天晚上做作業做到半夜。我讓他做完作業就睡覺，可是他不聽，一直在網上跟朋友聊天，到兩三點鐘才睡覺。反正今天他不用去上學，晚一點起床也沒有關系。

林叔叔：林東這個孩子啊，就是不懂事。我常說，要是林東能像凱麗那樣獨立，能把自己照顧好就好了。林東到現在還像個小孩，吃飯要我們幫他做，房間要我們幫他打掃，衣服要我們幫他洗，買東西要我們幫他買，出門要我們告訴他坐甚麼車。

凱麗： 你們可以教林東怎麼做。我父母總是讓我自己先試著做，要是我做不好，他們才幫我。這樣練習了幾次，我就會做了。

林叔叔：凱麗說得對。我們不能怪林東不獨立，是我們自己不放心，做甚麼事都怕他做不了，做不好。

林阿姨：對啊，還有爺爺、奶奶、姥姥、姥爺也都不放心，總是替他做這做那。他也就沒有必要學了。

林叔叔：所以有人說，獨生子女是"小皇帝"。一家人都為一個孩子服務。

Unit 2.2 對話二

林東： 對不起，凱麗，你來了很久了吧？我剛起床。

凱麗： 我剛來了半個多小時，在跟你父母聊天呢。你很晚才睡覺嗎？

林東： 是的，我在網上跟同學聊天聊到三點。

凱麗： 你們都住校，一個星期回家一次。昨天，你才回家了幾個小時，就想他們了？

林東： 我也不知道為甚麼，跟同學有說不完的話。

凱麗： 那跟你爸爸媽媽呢？

林東： 告訴你一個秘密，要不是爸爸媽媽非要我每個周末回家，我一點都不想回來。在學校裡跟同學一起玩，一起聊天，多好啊。

凱麗： 他們一個星期沒見你，會很想你的。你難道不想他們嗎？

林東： 不是不想，就是跟他們說話很沒勁。我爸爸見了我就問：考試考到第一名了嗎？作業都做完了嗎？你打算上哪個重點大學？我媽媽見了我就說：你在學校要多注意身體，多吃蔬菜，多休息，多運動，不要玩電腦玩到太晚。

凱麗： 你玩電腦玩到很晚嗎？

林東： 怎麼可能呢？我們學校管得非常嚴，每天晚上十點關燈，大家都得睡覺。我媽媽就是喜歡擔心。你父母呢？他們管你嗎？

凱麗： 管得不太多。他們有時候也問問我的學習、身體、有沒有男朋友甚麼的。

林東： 你有男朋友嗎？

凱麗： 這可是我的秘密。

Unit 2.3 對話一

張奶奶： 你看這張照片，這是我們家的"全家福"。

瑪麗婭： 那麼多人啊！讓我數數，一、二、三、四…，一共有十八個人啊。哪個是您？

張奶奶： 這個是我，那年我八歲，我右邊的是我大姐，左邊的是三姐。我有四個姐姐，我最小。我們家都是女孩子。

瑪麗婭： 那這兒還有幾個男孩，他們是誰？

張奶奶： 是我叔叔的孩子。我兩個叔叔都沒有女兒，只有兒子。你看，這是我大叔叔，這是我小叔叔。坐在中間的這兩個人是我爺爺和奶奶。

瑪麗婭： 那時候，你們都住在一起嗎？

張奶奶： 是的，我們一家七口人，大叔叔家五口人，小叔叔家四口人，還有爺爺奶奶，都住在一起。

瑪麗婭： 你們是不是住在一個很大的房子裡？

張奶奶： 不太大，所以家裡很擠。我住的房間裡有兩張大床，我們五個姐妹都睡在一個房間裡。

瑪麗婭： 那麼多人都在一起吃飯嗎？

張奶奶： 是的。我們的客廳裡放了三個桌子，大人一桌，小孩兩桌。客廳裡每天有很多人進進出出，說說笑笑，熱鬧得不得了。有的在那兒做作業，有的做手工，有的玩游戲，有的聊天。有時候客人來了，也去客廳。

瑪麗婭： 大家庭的生活您喜歡嗎？

張奶奶： 人多很熱鬧。要是你想找個人說話，玩游戲，總是可以找到。可是人多事多，這個孩子要上學了，那個要工作了，這個要談戀愛了，那個要結婚了。想得到一點兒安靜是不可能的。人多意見也多，甚麼事情都是你有你的意見，我有我的意見，要做一個決定不太容易。

瑪麗婭： 那最後誰做決定呢？

張奶奶： 最後總是爺爺為大家做決定。

Unit 2.3 對話二

明英： 立安，你在忙甚麼？

立安： 我在給我弟弟寫生日卡。下個星期一是我弟弟的生日。

明英： 你弟弟多大了？

立安： 十四歲了。他在香港上中學。

明英： 你還有別的兄弟姐妹嗎？

立安： 我還有兩個姐姐。你有兄弟姐妹嗎？

明英： 沒有。我是獨生子女。

立安： 獨生子女很好，在家沒人跟你競爭。

明英： 你們為哪些事競爭？

立安： 比方說，誰可以跟父母出去，誰可以晚一點兒回家，還有玩具、吃的東西、看電視、用電腦、零花錢、等等。你一定沒有這些問題吧？所以我覺得做獨生子女挺好的，一定是我要甚麼，父母就給我甚麼。

明英：我雖然不需要競爭，可是也有別的問題啊。你們家有四個孩子，父母不可能總是管著你。我呢，父母二十四小時管著我。他們兩個人管我一個，還有爺爺奶奶姥姥姥爺也總是管我，我被他們管得太多了，一點自由都沒有。

立安：那麼多人關心你，照顧你也不錯啊。

明英：是啊，我是很幸運。可是有時候沒有小朋友跟我玩，我只能跟大人玩。爺爺帶我去公園，我一跑爺爺就說："別跑得太快了，我追不上你。"跟大人玩真的很沒勁。

立安：不過有時候，你也不願意總是跟兄弟姐妹玩啊。我弟弟小時候非要跟著我，我走到哪兒，他跟到哪兒，每件事都問我"為甚麼"。我不帶他出去，他就哭。我父母就說："立安，你是哥哥，要好好照顧弟弟。"

明英：現在他還跟著你嗎？

立安：現在？上次我回家，一跟他說話，他就說："你等一下再跟我說話，好嗎？我正在網上跟朋友聊天呢。"

Unit 2.4 對話一

瑪麗婭：昨天晚上我看了一個電視節目，說中國的跨國家庭越來越多了。

湯姆：甚麼是"跨國家庭"？

瑪麗婭：比方說我們家，我媽媽是法國人，我爸爸是意大利人。他們不是來自一個國家，所以我們家是一個跨國家庭。

凱麗：哦，是這樣。那我家也是。雖然我父母都是在美國出生的，可是我爺爺是德國人，奶奶是法國人，姥姥是加拿大人，姥爺是英國人。我們家是個小聯合國。

大衛：我看，跨國家庭不算甚麼新鮮事。

湯姆：可能在有些國家不算新鮮事，因為那些國家有許多來自各國的移民。可是在中國，跨國家庭還不太多。你看，我們家的親戚都是中國人，沒有一個外國人。我的鄰居也都是中國人。只有一個鄰居的女兒，跟一個日本人結婚了。

瑪麗婭：　那個電視節目說的跟湯姆差不多。以前中國人都是祖祖輩輩住在一個地方，很少搬家。現在因為經濟發展了，越來越多的人離開家，去別的地方工作，還有人去國外工作。不少外國人也到中國來工作。這樣，一些中國人就跟外國人結婚了，中國也有了越來越多的跨國家庭。

大衛：　我覺得跨國家庭很有意思，可能的話，最好我家的每個親戚都是從不同的國家來的。這樣我去看他們的時候，就需要去很多不同的國家。這不是很好玩兒嗎？

凱麗：　怎麼可能呢？你爸爸和你叔叔，就像你和你哥哥，怎麼可能是從兩個國家來的呢？

大衛：　我也知道是不可能的，所以我說"可能的話，最好…"。

Unit 2.4 對話二

湯姆：　凱麗，你說你們家就像是一個小聯合國。你的家庭生活是不是很特別？

凱麗：　我覺得我很幸運，因為我們可以吃到許多來自各國的東西。奶奶做的飯和姥姥做的很不一樣。在奶奶家，我們吃德國香腸，還有放很多奶油的法國菜。到了姥姥家，她常常用楓糖漿給我們做甜點。

湯姆：　那多有意思啊！我們家不行，到了哪個親戚家，吃的都是吃中國飯。

凱麗：　在我們家也慶祝很多節日，除了美國的節日，我們還慶祝德國的十月節、法國的國慶日甚麼的。現在住在中國，所以我們也過中國的節日。

湯姆：　那你們家有沒有語言問題？我和杰米剛到中國的時候，中文不太好。有時候我們聽不懂爺爺奶奶說的話。他們不但說北京話，而且說得非常快。他們也不懂英文，只要我們說了一個英文詞，他們就聽不懂了。

凱麗：　我姥姥姥爺來自加拿大和英國，說英文沒有問題。我爺爺雖然有點兒德國口音，可是英文還不錯。我奶奶說英文就馬馬虎虎了，她的英文裡有很多法文。而且她一著急就說法文。我們一點兒也聽不懂。除了語言以外，我們還有別的問題。每個人都覺得自己國家的東西最好。我要去買衣服，我爺爺一定讓我買德國的，因為他覺得德國做的東西不容易坏。可是我奶奶一定讓我買法國的，她覺得法國的衣服最漂亮。

湯姆：　雖然我家親戚都是中國人，可是也一樣。我姥姥姥爺總是覺得上海甚麼都好，因為他們是在上海長大的。我爺爺奶奶是北京人，所以他們說北京是中國最好的城市。

凱麗：　我覺得在跨國家庭裡長大挺好的，有機會了解不同的文化。

湯姆：　我同意。我們的學校也像一個跨國大家庭。在這兒我們有機會學習各國的文化，非常有意思。

Unit 2.5 對話

金順愛：　下個月五號是我小妹妹的生日，我想給她買一件生日禮物。你說買甚麼好？

凱麗：　你妹妹多大了？

金順愛：　兩歲。

凱麗：　你妹妹那麼小啊？那你給她買個玩具熊貓吧。你有幾個兄弟姐妹？

金順愛：　我有兩個弟弟，兩個妹妹。只有一個弟弟跟我是同父同母。我八歲的時候，我父母離婚了，後來他們又都再婚了。現在我有一個同母异父的弟弟，還有兩個同父异母的妹妹。

凱麗：　那你現在是跟你爸爸還是跟你媽媽一起生活？

金順愛：　我和我弟弟都跟我媽媽生活。我媽媽是律師，現在在上海工作。我繼父是一個中國人，他也是律師。

凱麗：　那你的爸爸在哪兒呢？

金順愛：　他還住在韓國。他也再婚了，我的繼母很年輕，才二十六歲，所以我有兩個小妹妹，一個四歲，一個兩歲。她們都很可愛。

凱麗：　你常常去韓國看你爸爸嗎？

金順愛：　不常去，只有放暑假和寒假的時候去。不過，我常常給我爸爸打電話，寫電郵。對了，我爸爸說，我兩個妹妹要養狗，所以上個星期我爸爸送給她們一只小黑狗。

凱麗： 她們一定很高興吧？

金順愛：當然了。

Unit 2.5 課文

中國的傳統是：子女結婚以前，跟父母住在一起。子女結婚以後，有的還跟父母住在一起，有的就離開父母家，建立自己的小家庭。今天，還有不少中國家庭是三代人住在一起的：父母、子女和子女的孩子。也就是說，一個家庭常常有爺爺奶奶、爸爸媽媽和孩子。在這樣的家庭裡，大家互相照顧。孩子小的時候，爺爺奶奶照顧孩子。爺爺奶奶老了以後，子女和孫子孫女就照顧他們。

最近幾十年，中國社會變化得很快，家庭也有了很大的變化。許多家庭現在只有兩代人：父母和孩子。在中國的城市裡，不少子女結婚以後都喜歡過小家庭生活，所以他們就離開了父母家。這樣就有了一些只有老人的家庭。還有的年輕人，比較喜歡自由，雖然沒有結婚，也離開了父母家，自己搬出去住，結果中國有不少“單身”家庭。另外，有些家庭因為父母離婚，就成了單親家庭。還有些家庭，因為父母再婚了，原來不是一個家庭的人生活在一起，又建立了一個新家庭。

雖然家庭可能是各種各樣的，但是只要家庭裡的人互相關心、互相照顧，就能給每個人帶來快樂。

Unit 2.6 對話一

瑪麗婭：中秋節你過得好嗎？

湯姆： 不錯。那天晚上，我的兩個舅舅來我們家跟我們一起慶祝中秋節。

瑪麗婭：你們除了吃月餅看月亮以外，還做了甚麼？

湯姆： 沒做甚麼特別的事。他們和我父母聊天，我就坐在旁邊聽。

瑪麗婭：你聽到甚麼有意思的故事了嗎？

湯姆： 他們說了很多親戚家的事。這些親戚我多半都不認識。他們說到有一個農村的親戚，現在在北京找到了工作，所以就一個人搬到北京去住，可是他家的人都還在農村。他只有過春節的時候才能回家跟家人見面。

瑪麗婭： 這多不好啊。他一定很想他的家人吧？

湯姆： 就是啊。他的父母都七十多歲了，兩個孩子還在上中學，他的妻子又要工作，又要照顧老人和孩子，忙得不得了。這個親戚打算要回農村去，開個修車的小公司，這樣可以跟家裡的人住在一起。可是他的兩個孩子不願意他回去，因為他們都想搬到北京去住。

瑪麗婭： 他們為甚麼現在不搬去呢？

湯姆： 好像這個親戚的工資不太高。沒有那麼多錢讓一家人住在北京。再說，他父母和妻子都喜歡住在農村。

瑪麗婭： 這樣的家庭在中國一定不少吧？

湯姆： 對。我小舅舅還說，現在不少農村家庭都搬到城裡來了。結果，只有老人還住在農村。

瑪麗婭： 我想這種情況各個國家都有。為了找到工作，年輕人得搬到有工作的地方去住。我去國外旅行的時候，也常常看到在一些農村地區，多數都是老人，沒有太多的年輕人和孩子。

Unit 2.6 對話二

瑪麗婭： 張奶奶，您問過黃黃的主人了嗎？它有沒有把張爺爺的優盤帶回家去？

張奶奶： 樓下的張叔叔和王阿姨說，沒見到優盤，不過會幫我們找一找。可是他們那麼忙，不知道甚麼時候才能去幫我找呢。

大衛： 他們的公寓是不是跟您的一樣大？

張奶奶： 是啊。

大衛： 那找一遍不是很容易嗎？不用花很多時間。

張奶奶： 要是在我們家可能很快就能找一遍，因為我們家比較整齊。在他們家就不那麼容易了。

瑪麗婭： 為甚麼呢？

張奶奶： 他們家的公寓雖然不大，可是哪兒都是東西，非常擠。這是因為他們家有五個孩子，還養了很多寵物。他們家的寵物除了黃黃以外，還有兩隻小鳥和兩隻烏龜。

大衛： 現在多數的中國家庭不都只有一個孩子嗎？他們家怎麼有五個呢？

張奶奶：　張叔叔和王阿姨有一個女兒，這個女兒已經上大學了，住校，不常回家。可是現在還有四個小孩子住在他們家。這四個小的都是親戚的孩子。有兩個是王阿姨親戚的孩子。他們的父母要去加拿大工作兩年，就把他們留給王阿姨照顧。另外一個孩子是張叔叔妹妹的。因為父母離婚以後都再婚了，這個孩子不願意跟繼父住，也不願意跟繼母住，所以就被送到張叔叔家來。還有一個是張叔叔弟弟的孩子，在上重點中學，張叔叔是這個中學的校長，所以這個孩子也住在他們家。

瑪麗婭：　這麼多親戚的孩子，還有貓、烏龜、小鳥甚麼的，要在他們家找到優盤一定不容易。

Unit 3.1 對話一

湯姆：　媽媽，我出去了。

媽媽：　你要去哪兒？

湯姆：　今天是馬克十八歲的生日。晚上我們要去"紅房子"餐廳為他過生日。

媽媽：　那你吃完飯就早點回來，明天你還有數學考試呢。

湯姆：　考試我早就準備好了，今天晚上不用準備了。

媽媽：　每次考試前你總是說準備得萬無一失了，可是你很少得100分。

湯姆：　雖然有時候我得不到100分，但是拿個八九十分是沒問題的。反正"八九不離十"就行了。好了，我走了。

媽媽：　等一會兒，你幾點回來？

湯姆：　我也不太清楚。吃完飯後我們可能去看電影，或者去逛商店，也可能去朋友家聊天，玩游戲甚麼的。

媽媽：　這不行。你明天早上還要上學，十點以前一定要回來。

湯姆：　現在已經快六點了，十點以前回來時間太緊了，我十一點以前回來吧，行不行？

媽媽：　不行，我說十點，就是十點。

湯姆：　十點半，怎麼樣？

媽媽：　如果你十點回不來，這兩個星期晚上你都不能出去。

湯姆：　媽媽，你要講民主，我的事不能都由你決定。

媽媽： 等你過了十八歲，你的事就由你自己決定，可是現在你
還沒到十八歲，所以就得由我決定。

湯姆： 可是我不是小孩子了。晚一點回來沒關系啊。

媽媽： 等你不是青少年了，隨便幾點回來都可以。可是今天你
十點以前必須回來。

湯姆： 好吧，好吧，我十點以前回家。

Unit 3.1 對話二

(湯姆和朋友們吃完了晚飯。)

馬克： 我們現在去哪兒玩？對了，離這兒不遠有個夜總會，我
們要不要去那兒跳舞？

瑪麗婭： 跳舞挺好玩的。我們去吧。

凱麗： 那個夜總會，去的都是些甚麼人？

馬克： 年輕人挺多的，有大學生、也有一些在公司工作的白
領。

大衛： 高中生能進去嗎？

王大明： 好像那個夜總會門口有個牌子，說十八歲以下的不能進
去。

馬克： 我已經十八歲了，可以進去了。

凱麗： 可是我們都還沒到十八歲，進不去。

馬克： 這樣的話，我們今天就別去了。那個夜總會門口總是有
不少人，看上去很熱門，所以我老想進去看看。

王大明： 只能等將來了。哎，我們是不是去看電影？

湯姆： 現在已經八點一刻了，我十點以前一定得回家。

王大明： 啊，已經八點一刻了嗎？我媽媽讓我八點半以前就得回
家。今天晚上，她請了輔導老師來幫我準備明天的數學
考試。

凱麗： 那你快走吧。

王大明： 沒關系，來得及。從這兒坐地鐵到我家才五六分鐘。

湯姆： 可是從這兒去地鐵站要走五分鐘。

大衛： 再說，你家也不住在地鐵站裡，下了地鐵，還要走幾分
鐘吧。

王大明： 那好吧，我走了。再見！

（王大明走了。）

大衛：　我看我們去逛逛店吧。這條馬路上有一家不錯的電子產品店，我們可以走過去看看。

瑪麗婭：那家商店有甚麼特別嗎？

大衛：　那兒總是有最新最流行的電子產品。

湯姆：　行啊。只要是玩兒，玩甚麼都行。

凱麗：　那家店遠不遠？我們也不能玩到太晚，因為學校大門十點就關。回去晚了，看門師傅會找我們麻煩的。

大衛：　那家店不遠，走過去才兩三分鐘。我們逛完了店就回去。

凱麗：　那好吧。

Unit 3.2 對話一

瑪麗婭：這個周末你想去看芭蕾舞嗎？聽說俄國芭蕾舞劇團正在上海大劇院演出《天鵝湖》。

凱麗：　票价一定很貴吧？

瑪麗婭：最便宜的是120元，但是學生票好像只要80元。

凱麗：　雖然我很想去，但是我這個月的零花錢已經快用完了。

瑪麗婭：現在離月底還有十天，你已經沒有錢了？

凱麗：　是啊，這個月活動特別多，一會兒跟朋友去吃飯，一會兒去看電影，我又買了幾本書，所以錢就花得差不多了。

瑪麗婭：你父母一個月給你多少零用錢？

凱麗：　一個月三百塊。你呢？

瑪麗婭：兩百塊。

凱麗：　兩百塊一定不夠花吧？現在一張電影票要80元。要是去星巴克喝一杯咖啡，就要30元。兩百塊一下子就沒了。

瑪麗婭：是啊，好在我暑假的時候去打工，掙了一點錢。要不然，200元一定不夠。你零用錢不夠的時候，怎麼辦？

凱麗：　我父母給了我一張銀行卡，在緊急情況下，我可以去拿錢。但是如果沒有緊急情況，我用錢用得多了，他們下個月就不給我那麼多錢了。比如，我這個月用了400元，那麼下個月，他們只給我200元。如果我用了600元，下個月他們就一分錢都不給我了。

瑪麗婭： 要是你非常想去看芭蕾舞，我可以借錢給你。等你有了錢，再還給我好了。

凱麗： 謝謝，我看我還是不去了。如果我這個月就花下個月的錢，那下個月就沒錢花了。

Unit 3.2 對話二

湯姆： 你今天看上去挺高興的，怎麼了？

大衛： 今天我姥姥給我寄來了50塊美元。

湯姆： 哇噻，你發財啦。今天是甚麼特別的日子？

大衛： 也不是甚麼特別的日子，我姥姥一高興就會給我們寄點小禮物，或者寄點錢甚麼的。她老說我一個人在上海上學，需要花錢的地方比較多，所以每過一兩個月就給我寄點錢。

湯姆： 你父母知道嗎？

大衛： 這是我跟姥姥之間的秘密。要是我父母知道了，一定就不會給我很多零用錢了。

湯姆： 你的零花錢夠用嗎？

大衛： 夠用，因為我從來不亂花錢。你呢？

湯姆： 我父母正在教我記帳呢。他們說，我每次花錢以後，都應該記下來。這樣我就知道我花了多少，還剩多少。要不然，我可能會亂花錢，錢花到哪兒自己都不知道。可是我覺得記帳挺麻煩的。再說，我一個月只有兩百塊，花到錢沒有了，就不花了。

大衛： 我覺得你父母說得對。我雖然沒有把每次花了多少錢都寫下來，但是在月初，我會計劃一下，這個月用50元買書，100元出去玩。如果說這個月書買得多了，那我就得少出去玩幾次。

湯姆： 真有你的。我得好好向你學習學習怎麼理財。

Unit 3.3 對話一

凱麗： 周末你們想去哪兒玩兒？

瑪麗婭：除了購物中心和幾個公園以外，上海沒有甚麼特別好玩的地方。

凱麗：聽說浙江有一些地方挺好玩的。比如安吉。

大衛：要是你們想去，我們可以坐旅游車去。

凱麗：坐旅游車比較貴。有沒有直接去那兒的公共汽車？

大衛：好像沒有。去安吉，我們先要坐火車，再換幾次公共汽車，我看一天都到不了那兒。

湯姆：去安吉最好自己開車。這樣，只要三小時左右就到了。

凱麗：開車？我們一不會開車，二沒有車。

大衛：就是，我們都沒學過開車。聽說美國的高中教學生怎麼開車，可是我們學校沒有這樣的課。

湯姆：我覺得每個高中都應該有駕駛課。會開車多方便啊！想去哪兒，就去哪兒。想甚麼時候去，就甚麼時候去。

瑪麗婭：可是我覺得在大城市裡，會不會開車都沒有關係，公共交通很方便。開車也有開車的問題。比如，交通很堵，停車也不容易。

湯姆：在上海，我們可以用公共交通，可是如果打算去郊游，自己開車還是挺不錯的。再說，開車給你帶來的那種自由的感覺，多好啊！

大衛：最好再開一輛很快的跑車，那感覺就更好了。

瑪麗婭：好了，別做夢了。這個周末去不去安吉？

凱麗：算了，還是以後再說吧。

Unit 3.3 對話二

瑪麗婭：美國的高中生甚麼時候可以開始學開車？

湯姆：十六歲左右。一般的高中都可以讓學生修駕駛者教育課和駕駛者培訓課。

瑪麗婭：是不是上完了課就可以開車了？

湯姆：不是的。他們還要參加路考。通過了路考，才可以開車。

瑪麗婭：也就是說，在美國十六歲就可以拿到駕照了，是嗎？

湯姆：對，如果你上完了課，路考也通過了，而且你父母同意你拿駕照的話，那麼你可以拿到一個臨時駕照。

瑪麗婭： 甚麼時候才可以拿到正式駕照呢？

湯姆： 十八歲。

瑪麗婭： 世界上不少國家都是要到了十八歲才可以開始開車。美國多不錯啊！十六歲就可以開車了。

湯姆： 你知道在中國，要到甚麼年齡才能拿到駕照嗎？

瑪麗婭： 也是十八歲。我哥哥快十八歲了，很想學開車，因為中國的學校沒有駕駛課，所以他正在找駕駛學校呢。

湯姆： 中國的駕駛學校收十八歲以下的學生嗎？我也很想學開車。

瑪麗婭： 好像不收。安東尼已經問過三四個駕駛學校了，他們都只培訓成年人。

湯姆： 如果你知道哪個學校收十八歲以下的學生，別忘了告訴我。我一定去報名。

瑪麗婭： 好的。

Unit 3.4 對話一

瑪麗婭： 大衛，昨天下課以後，你急急忙忙地離開了學校，去哪兒了？

大衛： 哦，我找到了一個兼職的工作，當法語家教。昨天去跟學生見面了。

瑪麗婭： 是嗎？你的學生上幾年級？

大衛： 她叫紅紅，今年六歲，在上幼兒園。不過她父母說，學外文越早越好。

瑪麗婭： 你每個星期要去幾次？

大衛： 兩次，每次一兩個小時。

瑪麗婭： 你要給她上課嗎？用甚麼課本？

大衛： 她父母說，我不用給紅紅上課，就是陪她玩，給她講講故事。這個工作很輕鬆。再說，從學校去她家也很方便。她家就住在學校對面的那個小區裡。我騎自行車過去，才三四分鐘。

瑪麗婭： 你怎麼想起來要當家教了？

大衛： 我本來也沒想到要去兼職。有一天，我在學校門口等公共汽車，紅紅和她媽媽也在等車，我們說了一會兒話。

紅紅的媽媽一聽我是法國人，就問我願意不願意給紅紅
當家教。我覺得當家教，一個星期也花不了多少時間，
還可以掙一點兒零花錢，就同意了。

瑪麗婭： 我覺得兼職挺不錯的。雖然中國的高中生一般都不打
工，可是在國外，高中生兼職是很平常的事。

大衛： 那你打算兼職嗎？

瑪麗婭： 如果有合適的工作，我也想去兼職。

Unit 3.4 對話二

(瑪麗婭給張經理打電話。)

瑪麗婭： 喂，請問張經理在嗎？

張經理： 我就是，請問您是哪位？

瑪麗婭： 我叫瑪麗婭。我的鄰居馬京生先生讓我打電話給您，請
問你們公司是不是正在招一名英文翻譯？我對這個工作
很有興趣。

張經理： 哦，馬京生告訴你了吧？這是一個臨時的工作。

瑪麗婭： 他告訴我了。他還說，你們需要把公司的網頁翻譯成英
文。

張經理： 是的，除了翻譯網頁以外，我有時候還需要一個翻譯幫
我看看英文電子郵件。你的英文怎麼樣？

瑪麗婭： 雖然我是在意大利出生的，可是我跟父母在美國和英國
住了幾年，我從小就說英文，英文還不錯。

張經理： 你不是中國人啊？你說中文說得那麼好，沒有一點外國
口音，我還以為你是中國人呢。我可不行，學了八九年
英文了，英文還是馬馬虎虎的，聽說讀寫都不好。我當
然很歡迎你來當翻譯，可是你知道，我的公司非常小，
只有三個人，我不可能給你全天的工作。

瑪麗婭： 沒關系。我現在是高中生，不能全天工作。我只想下課
以後，兼兼職。

張經理： 那太好了。你一個星期來工作四五個小時就行了。工作
時間很靈活，甚麼時候有空，就甚麼時候過來。不過，
你在上高中，出來打工會不會影響學習？

瑪麗婭： 一個星期工作四五個小時不會影響學習的。

張經理：那好。工資是一個小時二十元，月底發工資。

瑪麗婭：好，沒問題。這個星期五下午三點以後我有空，可以去
工作嗎？

張經理：當然可以。你知道我們公司的地址嗎？

瑪麗婭：知道，馬京生都已經告訴我了，你們公司就在他公司的
旁邊，是吧？

張經理：對，沒錯。那我們星期五下午見。

瑪麗婭：好的，再見。

Unit 3.5 對話一

湯姆：　最近我父母常常對我說，現在你長大了，可以做一些以
前不能做的事。但是你應該知道，做每件事都需要員責
任。比方說，如果我們給你零花錢，你應該計劃花在哪
兒，花多少，不能亂花。如果我們晚上讓你出去玩，你
應該知道甚麼時候必須回家…

凱麗：　哦，我懂了。他們的意思是，"世界上沒有免費的午
餐。"有時候我們好像得到了更多的自由，其實自由不
是免費的午餐，為了自由，我們要員更多的責任。比
如，如果我們可以開車了，就必須注意安全，別出事
故。

湯姆：　你怎麼那麼理解我父母的意思？你說的跟他們說的一
樣。

凱麗：　其實，我父母也常常跟我說這些。他們還特別關心我是
不是在談戀愛。他們說，談戀愛可以給一個人帶來很多
快樂，也可以帶來很多麻煩。他們讓我做每件事情，都
要想想後果。如果做一件事情，會帶來不好的後果，那
就不應該去做。

湯姆：　你父母很開通，還跟你說談戀愛的事。我媽媽可保守
了，總是跟我說，她和我爸爸是大學畢業以後才開始談
戀愛的。上高中不應該談戀愛，應該好好學習。還叫我
學習中國的高中生，說他們在高中的時候只關心高考，
只注意學習。要是我在高中就開始談戀愛，一定會影響
我的學習的。

凱麗：　我覺得不一定。兩個人也可以在學習上互相幫助啊。

湯姆：　我也是這麼跟我媽媽說的。可是我媽媽說，要是我非要談戀愛，就必須找一個學習好的女生，這樣我的學習就不會受到坏影響。

凱麗：　你媽媽真有意思。

Unit 3.5 對話二

大衛：　瑪麗婭，你找到兼職的工作了嗎？

瑪麗婭：找到了，現在我在幫一個小公司翻譯網頁，還幫公司的經理看看英文電子郵件。

大衛：　你喜歡那個工作嗎？

瑪麗婭：很喜歡。可是有時候覺得責任挺大的。這個公司的張經理是我鄰居的朋友。他一看我是外國人就說，太好了，我們請了個外國人來當翻譯，這樣我們公司的英文網頁一定是十全十美。他這麼一說，讓我覺得壓力很大。要是我沒做到十全十美，就都是我的責任了。

大衛：　你是說，翻譯完了以後，沒有人幫你看一看嗎？

瑪麗婭：是的。開始我把翻譯完了的東西帶回家，讓我爸爸幫我檢查一下。可是我爸爸為了讓我學會員責任，從來不替我看，老讓我自己檢查，自己改錯。我請安東尼幫我檢查，他就學我爸爸："瑪麗婭，你應該為自己做的事員責。"我真沒想到，兼職會有那麼多的責任。早知道這樣，我應該去找一個責任輕一點兒的工作。

大衛：　甚麼工作都要員責任。就拿我的工作來說吧，雖然聽上去只是陪紅紅玩玩，可是也有很多責任。要是她說中文，我就得提醒她說法文。跟她在一起，我要注意她的安全。那天她跟我出去玩兒，在路上亂跑，差一點被自行車撞到。嚇了我一跳。

瑪麗婭：看小孩的責任很重。

大衛：　不過，我們要看到好的一面。發了工資以後，我們花錢比以前自由多了吧？

瑪麗婭：你說得對。昨天我拿到了工資，我請你去喝一杯咖啡吧。

Unit 3.6 課文

一些中國的報紙報道說，因為中國的中學作業太多，所以有一半左右的中學生每天睡覺的時間不到七個小時。這不但影響了學生的健康，也影響了他們的學習。

　　廣東有一名中學生說："我現在每天晚上最早12點睡覺，早上6點30分起床。"他每天最多睡六七個小時，可是還是他們班睡覺睡得多的。他有一個同學，因為成績不太好，晚上常常睡不好覺，每晚只能睡三個小時，所以白天學習沒有精神。

　　另外一個中學生說，這學期他上五門課。只要每門課的老師一天給一個小時的作業，五門課就有五個小時的作業。寫得再快也要寫到晚上十一點。因為每天睡得很晚，等到下午上課的時候，他老想睡覺。

　　有一位學生家長說，雖然他的孩子在上小學六年級，但是每天晚上要六點半才到家。吃完晚飯七點開始做作業，一直做到十二點才能做完。第二天早上六點就必須起床了。這位家長很擔心孩子的身體健康。

　　還有一位學生家長說，他的孩子現在上高中一年級，但是已經每天做作業做到晚上十一點。前幾天，為了準備英文考試，每天要學習到十二點。因為睡覺睡得不夠，結果孩子病了。

　　中國的報紙說，為了學生的健康，學校應該少給學生一些作業。

Unit 3.6 對話

張奶奶：瑪麗婭，告訴你一個好消息，張爺爺的優盤找到了。

瑪麗婭：是嗎？是在哪兒找到的？是不是在黃黃的家？

張奶奶：不是的。那天我看到黃黃到三樓的白叔叔家去了，我就想，除了黃黃家以外，我還應該問問別的鄰居，黃黃有沒有把東西帶到他們家去。所以我就一家一家地去問。問到了六樓的王奶奶家，王奶奶說她一點兒都不懂電腦，不知道甚麼是優盤，但是她把黃黃帶到她家去的東西都放在一個盒子裡。她把盒子拿出來，讓我看看有沒有我要找的東西。結果我就在她那兒找到了優盤。

瑪麗婭：太好了。那黃黃是怎麼把優盤拿走的？

張奶奶：張爺爺的優盤上有一根繩子。貓常常很喜歡玩繩子，可能黃黃在玩繩子的時候，就把優盤帶走了。

瑪麗婭：謝天謝地，它把優盤帶到王奶奶家去了。要是帶到一個沒有人去的地方，我們怎麼找得到呢？

張奶奶：你說得對。

瑪麗婭：那個優盤沒壞吧？

張奶奶：沒有。張爺爺拿到優盤以後，馬上放到電腦上去看，一點都沒壞，張爺爺寫的小說都在那兒。他非常高興，現在每天從早到晚都在寫，我想很快就能寫完了。

瑪麗婭：太好了！

張奶奶：所以我們要謝謝你和大衛。要不是你們想到可能是黃黃，我們可能還找不到那個優盤呢。

瑪麗婭：要謝的話，應該謝謝大衛。他這個偵探當得挺不錯的。

Unit 4.1 對話

大衛：下個星期五學校要開運動會，體育老師讓我們班負責準備運動器材。

凱麗：開運動會需要很多運動器材吧。難道那麼多器材都由我們班準備嗎？

大衛：是的。別的班有別的班的工作，有的要準備比賽場地，有的要負責運動員休息室。

凱麗：今年的運動會是不是只有田徑和體操比賽？

大衛：不，還有球類比賽。我聽瑪麗婭說，要把班上的同學分成三個小組，每個小組準備一種比賽器材。

凱麗：瑪麗婭的主意不錯，這樣每個小組都有工作重點，不容易丟三落四。

大衛：我比較有力氣，應該去體操組，因為體操器材都比較重。

凱麗：你知道這次一共有多少個球類比賽項目嗎？

大衛：有籃球、排球、羽毛球、乒乓球和網球。

凱麗：哦，那我們除了準備球和球拍以外，別的就不用準備了吧？

大衛：我們還要在教室樓的前邊放四張乒乓桌。

凱麗：四張乒乓桌？放得下嗎？

大衛： 開運動會那天，教室樓前不能停自行車，應該放得下。
你看，這是運動會的介紹。星期五要同時舉行各種球類
比賽，乒乓球比賽在教室樓前邊舉行，羽毛球在體育
館，籃球在籃球場，排球在圖書館後邊。

凱麗： 這麼多比賽同時舉行，到時候一定會很熱鬧。

Unit 4.1 課文

上海國際學校春季運動會

各位家長、各位老師、各位同學：大家好！

　　歡迎您來參加上海國際學校春季運動會。今年的運動會有
40多個比賽項目，有200多名師生要參加比賽。下面是今天比賽的
場地和時間：

　　　　田徑比賽 (男女團體和個人)
　　　　　　時間：上午8點半到下午3點　　地點：學校操場

　　　　體操比賽 (男女團體和個人)
　　　　　　時間：上午8點半到11點半　　地點：學校體育館

　　　　球類比賽 (男女團體和個人)
　　　　　　時間：下午1點到4點　　　　地點：乒乓球(教室樓前邊)
　　　　　　　　　　　　　　　　　　　　　籃球(籃球場)
　　　　　　　　　　　　　　　　　　　　　羽毛球 (體育館)
　　　　　　　　　　　　　　　　　　　　　排球 (圖書館後邊)

　　為了方便大家，學生餐廳全天供應茶水和點心，11:45到
1:15供應午飯。另外，教室樓的一樓有運動員休息室，二樓有家長
和師生休息室。如果您需要其他服務，請跟服務人員聯系－他們
都戴著藍色的棒球帽。

　　祝運動員得到好成績！祝運動會舉辦成功！

春季運動會組織小組
3月30日

Unit 4.2 對話一

明英： 學校馬上要舉辦國際文化日了，我們漢語班要介紹中國
文化。中國文化有許多方面，我們應該介紹哪一方面
呢？

湯姆： 這個問題提得好。我參加過不少國際文化活動，可是有些活動太一般了，總是聽聽報告，看看外國電影，或者大家唱唱歌，跳跳舞。我們班的活動應該有點兒新意。

凱麗： 比方說…

湯姆： 比方說我們可以用不同的活動來介紹文化的一個方面。中國人不是特別喜歡"食文化"嗎？我們為甚麼不介紹一下"食文化"呢？

大衛： 甚麼是"十"文化，十種文化嗎？

湯姆： 不，"食"是"食品"的食，就是關於吃的東西。

明英： 中國人是特別重視吃甚麼，怎麼吃。也重視食品和健康的關系。你打算怎麼介紹？

湯姆： 我們可以組織一個烹調表演。

大衛： 烹調表演算不上有甚麼新意。

湯姆： 烹調表演只是活動之一。我們可以好好計劃計劃，再加上一些別的活動。比方說，我們可以介紹中國各地的環境，說一說那個地方的食品有哪些特點。

明英： 好主意。我們需要先研究一下中國各地的菜有甚麼不同，然後我們可以分成幾個小組，讓每個小組做一個地方的菜，比如廣東菜、四川菜、上海菜等等。

瑪麗婭： 對，每個小組還可以介紹那個地區的地理環境和气候，因為地理環境和气候都會影響農業出產，也決定了那個地區的飲食。

湯姆： 介紹完了以後，就舉行烹調比賽。每個小組不但要表演怎麼做菜，而且還要把做好的菜讓觀眾嘗一嘗。最後我們請觀眾投票選舉哪個小組的菜做得最好吃。

大衛： 行，我們就這麼做。

Unit 4.2 對話二

瑪麗婭： 丁老師說，國際文化日那天只有我們班要舉行烹調表演，所以我們可以用學生餐廳的廚房。我們可以先去廚房看一下，那裡有沒有我們需要的東西。

（在廚房裡。）

明英： 你們看，這兒有盤子、杯子和刀叉，那兒還有很多筷子。不過，好像沒有餐巾紙，我們應該準備一些餐巾紙。

大衛： 我看做飯的鍋子夠了，可是這兒只有一個大炒菜鍋，我們有四個烹調小組，還需要三個。

凱麗： 廚房的炒菜鍋又大又重，做菜不方便，我們還是去借四個小一點兒的炒菜鍋吧。

明英： 好，我正在寫我們需要的東西："餐巾紙、四個炒菜鍋"，還需要甚麼別的嗎？

大衛： 我們組還需要一個蒸籠。

湯姆： 你是不是在廣東組？廣東人做點心常常需要蒸籠。我們組要做烤肉，所以最好有一個烤箱。

瑪麗婭： 那兒有兩個大烤箱。

湯姆： 哪兒？

瑪麗婭： 就在微波爐的旁邊。

明英： 湯姆，你們小組要做哪個地區的菜？怎麼要做烤肉？我在中國飯店很少吃到烤肉。

湯姆： 我們組決定要做中國新疆少數民族的飯菜。那裡的少數民族做的烤肉好吃極了。哎，你們上海組要做甚麼菜？

明英： 因為上海好吃的菜很多，每次討論，大家都七嘴八舌，我們到現在還沒做出決定。

Unit 4.3 對話一

凱麗： 昨天下午我沒找到你，你去哪兒了？

瑪麗婭： 我們歷史課的學生去校外考察了。這幾天我們正在學習上海歷史，所以白老師帶我們去外灘了。

凱麗： 外灘有甚麼特別的歷史嗎？

瑪麗婭： 白老師說，1844年英國人開始用外灘作為碼頭，還開了不少公司，外灘就開始發展了。到了1848年，在黃浦江邊造了一條大馬路，這條馬路的名字叫 The Bund。

凱麗： 原來是這樣，怪不得外國人常常把外灘叫作 The Bund。

瑪麗婭： 從十九世紀中開始，上海的外國公司和外國銀行越來越多，外灘地區成了上海的金融和商業中心，在那裡造了很多商業大樓。

凱麗： 你是說外灘那些大樓都是十九世紀造的嗎？

瑪麗婭： 不，外灘是從十九世紀開始發展的，可是多數的大樓都是在二十年代或者三十年代造的。

凱麗： 你知道外灘一共有多少大樓嗎？

瑪麗婭： 白老師說，在外灘和外灘附近的馬路上，一共有五六十座大樓，有英國式、法國式、西班牙式、希臘式等等。現在這些大樓都是上海政府要保護的歷史建築。

凱麗： 現在誰在用這些大樓？

瑪麗婭： 有些大樓是政府的辦公樓。還有一些大樓裡有公司、銀行、飯店、商店。

凱麗： 對了，外灘還有黃浦公園。黃浦公園是甚麼時候建立的？

瑪麗婭： 黃浦公園是上海最老的一個公園，是1868年建立的。

凱麗： 歷史課的社會考察聽上去很有意思，讓你學到了那麼多外灘的歷史。

瑪麗婭： 要是你想了解外灘的歷史，黃浦公園裡有一個外灘歷史紀念館，裡邊有很多歷史照片，介紹了外灘和上海的發展歷史。

凱麗： 是嗎？下次去外灘，我一定要去那個紀念館看一看。

Unit 4.3 對話二

張先生： 歡迎上海國際學校的師生來東海國際社區參觀。我是東海國際社區的負責人，姓張。

同學們： 張先生好！

張先生： 大家好。我先給你們介紹一下社區的情況。東海國際社區是1995年建立的。在這以前，這裡都是菜地。

湯姆： 菜地？這裡以前沒有建築嗎？

張先生： 對，這些大樓和馬路都是1995年以後造的。大家知道，從九十年代開始，上海經濟發展得很快，建立了許多新公司和新工廠。我們這個地區現在有100多個公司和工廠。為了方便，在這兒工作的人都希望能住得離公司和工廠近一些，所以就建立了東海國際社區。

大衛：　為甚麼叫國際社區呢？是不是有很多外國人住在這兒？

張先生：對，現在有二十多個國家六百多家居民住在東海國際社區。我們社區的生活環境非常好，綠化多，空氣好，購物交通服務都很方便。

瑪麗婭：剛才我們在社區門口看到很多白色的面包車，上面寫著東海國際社區。為甚麼你們有那麼多車子？

張先生：那是我們社區的班車。每十分鐘有一班車去地鐵站。居民只要坐上了地鐵，二十分鐘就能到人民廣場。另外每二十分鐘有一班車去附近的超市，方便居民買東西。

凱麗：　除了這些高樓以外，那兒的那些小房子也是你們社區的嗎？

張先生：是的。我們不但有公寓樓，還有別墅。我們可以過去看一下，這些別墅有的是西班牙式的，有的是法國式的。

湯姆：　住在這兒的居民買東西方便嗎？

張先生：超市離這兒坐車要十分鐘。但是如果居民只需要一般的服務，我們有一個東海社區服務中心，那兒有商店、銀行、郵局、飯店等等。我們看完了別墅，可以去服務中心參觀一下。好，請大家跟我來。

Unit 4.4 課文

通知

同學們：

　　這個周末，漢語班的老師和同學要去南京參加華東地區的"中學生漢語演講大賽"。演講大賽將在南京大學舉行，有三千多名學生要參加今年的比賽。

　　為了方便大家，學校已經為我們訂好了一輛大客車，送我們直接去南京大學。大客車定於星期五下午三點出發，七點左右到達南京。到南京以後，我們將住在"南京明日大酒店"。以下是我們在南京的行程安排：

星期六	7點	在明日大酒店吃早飯
	8點	出發去南京大學
	9點–17點	參加中學生漢語演講大賽
	18點	參觀南京夫子廟，吃晚飯，逛夜市
	21點	回飯店
星期日	7點	在明日大酒店吃早飯
	8點	出發去鍾山風景區
	9點–15點	參觀鍾山風景區
	19點	回到上海國際學校

這個周末南京的天气是晴天，最高气溫15–17度，最低气溫7–10度。請大家根据天气情況，準備合適的衣服。

班長：瑪麗婭
三月二十日

Unit 4.4 對話

瑪麗婭：這個周末我們要去南京，你的行李都準備好了嗎？

凱麗：　準備好了。你看，我就只帶這個背包。

瑪麗婭：這個背包那麼小，放得下很多東西嗎？

凱麗：　我們一共才去兩天，不用帶很多東西。

瑪麗婭：我看我得帶一個拉桿箱，不然我的東西放不下。

凱麗：　拉桿箱？你要帶很多東西嗎？

瑪麗婭：也不太多，兩套衣服、兩雙鞋子、帽子、太陽眼鏡、幾本書、筆記本、漢語詞典、一些吃的東西。我還打算把筆記本電腦、MP3播放機、手機和游戲機都帶去。對了，我還要帶一些洗漱用品。

凱麗：　這個機那個機的，你帶這些去幹甚麼？

瑪麗婭： 有了電腦，晚上可以上網；有了手機，可以打電話發短信；有了MP3和游戲機，在去南京的路上可以玩兒。我覺得這些東西都會用到。

凱麗： 那你為甚麼要帶兩雙鞋子呢?

瑪麗婭： 我穿一雙球鞋，可是還要帶一雙皮鞋，因為去參加演講比賽的時候需要穿得漂亮一點兒。另外我還要帶一雙拖鞋，在房間裡可以穿。

凱麗： 我看你沒必要帶拖鞋，中國的飯店不但有洗漱用品，而且還有拖鞋。

瑪麗婭： 我知道，可是飯店的牙刷、牙膏、梳子、拖鞋都是一次性的。我自己帶這些東西，不是比較環保嗎?

凱麗： 好吧，那你就帶一個大箱子吧。

Unit 4.5 課文

家長開放日活動介紹

各位家長：

歡迎您前來參加上海國際學校的家長開放日。為了讓您更好地了解學校的教學情況，我校今天五月六日(星期五)上午8:30到下午3:30舉辦家長開放日。以下是開放日的活動安排：

1. 全校教師的課程都對家長開放，家長可以去各個班級聽課。

2. 家長可以在8:30, 10:30，或12:30去學校大禮堂聽校長介紹我校的教學情況。

3. 初三家長可以在9:30–10:30去教學樓三樓的大教室。初三的教師要報告我校初中畢業考試和高中招生的情況，并聽取家長對學校工作的意見和建議。

4. 高三家長可以在9:30–10:30去學校禮堂。高三的教師要報告高考信息，回答家長關於高考的問題，并聽取家長對學校工作的意見和建議。

5. 學校體育館全天有學生書畫、作文、科學實驗展覽。

6. 下午2:00在學校大禮堂有學生表演。

7. 學校圖書館全天有教師教案、論文的展覽。

8. 學生食堂、宿舍、體育館、圖書館、電子閱覽室、電腦房、活動中心全天對家長開放。

　　非常感謝您參加家長開放日的各種活動，請多提意見和
建議。

上海國際學校
五月六日

Unit 4.5 對話

瑪麗婭： 這個星期五是我們學校的家長開放日。那天，有不少學
　　　　生家長要來我們學校聽課，聽報告，參觀，看展覽。

湯姆： 我們那天還上課嗎？

瑪麗婭： 上午要上課。那天所有的課都對家長開放，家長可以隨
　　　　便到哪個教室去聽課。

大衛： 除了聽課以外，家長還可以參加別的活動嗎？

瑪麗婭： 星期五學校有報告、展覽、參觀、表演甚麼的。我們上
　　　　完課以後，還需要跟家長座談。家長們不但想從老師那
　　　　兒了解學校的教學情況，也想聽聽我們學生的看法。

凱麗： 我們樂隊跟戲劇社和合唱團的同學還要表演節目。我要
　　　　去彈鋼琴。

瑪麗婭： 那天下午我們會很忙，有些同學要去表演，有些要去開
　　　　座談會，還有一些要在學校的各個地方接待家長。同
　　　　時，我們班還參加了在體育館舉辦的書畫、作文、和科
　　　　學實驗展覽，需要一些同學去做講解員。

大衛： 大家是不是可以自願報名參加各種活動？

瑪麗婭： 自願報名最好，這樣每個人都可以做自己感興趣的事。
　　　　大衛，你想做甚麼？

大衛： 我去參加座談會吧。

瑪麗婭： 太好了，我們班的座談會就由你負責吧，想參加座談會
　　　　的同學可以去你那裡報名。誰負責展覽的講解工作呢？
　　　　湯姆，你能負責嗎？

湯姆： 對不起，我已經有安排了，要去電腦房幫助老師接待家
　　　　長。

凱麗： 明英這幾天一直在準備書畫展覽，我看就由她負責吧。

瑪麗婭： 好，那就這樣吧。

Unit 4.6 課文

這是大衛寫的博客：

今天我們學校舉行了國際文化日活動。全校的老師和同學都參加了。我們國際學校有來自三十多個國家和地區的學生和老師，國際文化日是我們了解各國文化的大好機會。

每個外語班的同學都準備了一些活動來介紹他們正在學習的語言和文化。有些外語是幾個國家的語言，這個班的同學就選其中一個國家的情況來介紹。比如，美國、英國、新西蘭、澳大利亞都說英文，去年英語班介紹了美國，今年就主要介紹澳大利亞。我們漢語班的同學介紹了中國文化，還有日語班、德語班、法語班、西班牙語班、阿拉伯語班都介紹了不同國家的情況。

我覺得我們漢語班的活動很有意思，也特別受大家的歡迎。今天我們重點介紹的是中國的"食文化"。以前我只知道中國菜的味道不太一樣。有的中國菜有點兒辣，有的有點兒甜。這次我們班的同學先介紹了各地的農業出產、地理環境和气候對飲食的影響，然後我們分成四個小組做了四個地方的菜。我們做了廣東菜、新疆菜、上海菜、和山東菜。我在山東組，我們做了包子和餃子。廣東組做了很多點心，上海組做了上海有名的"小籠包子"，新疆組做了烤肉。我們把做好的菜讓觀眾嘗一嘗，然後請他們投票選舉出最好吃的菜。結果新疆組得了38票，山東組得了36票，上海組和廣東組都得了33票。新疆組贏了。雖然我們組沒有贏，但是我還是覺得我們組做的餃子是最好吃的，比餃子店做的要好吃多了。

Unit 4.6 對話

大衛： 今天我上網的時候看到，網上有一個國際數學競賽。全世界有幾十万的中小學生都打算參加這個競賽。

凱麗： 是嗎？這是一個甚麼樣的數學競賽？為甚麼有那麼多人要參加？

大衛： 這個競賽叫"國際網上數學競賽"，是2007年由澳大利亞一家教育網站開始舉辦的。來自一百個左右國家的中小學生已經參加過這個競賽，做了幾千万個數學題。這個數學競賽主要是比賽口算的能力。

湯姆： 你是說，學生不能用紙和筆來做數學題嗎？

大衛： 對。

凱麗： 這聽上去有點兒難。

大衛： 不一定，因為這個教育網站會根據學生的年齡把他們分到不同的比賽組。要是你是小學生，就做小學的數學題。是中學生，就做中學的數學題。

凱麗： 哦，是這樣。

明英： 要是我想參加，怎麼報名？要交報名費嗎？

大衛： 不需要。這個網上數學競賽是免費的。想參加競賽的中小學生，可以直接上網報名。

凱麗： 那競賽的時候，是許多人一起比賽嗎？

大衛： 我也不太清楚，網上說，這個網站會讓兩個或者更多的學生一起在網上比賽口算的能力，看誰算得又快又準確。這個數學競賽常常有幾千個學生同時在網上參加。如果一個學生算得又快又好，就可以多得分。

明英： 這個競賽是用英文講解的嗎？如果用英文，許多中國的中小學生就可能不會去參加吧？

大衛： 競賽是用英文的。但是我覺得，現在中國中小學生的英文越來越好，可能參加的人也會越來越多。對了，我看到說，這兩年，北京、上海、天津一些國際學校的學生已經開始參加競賽了。

凱麗： 是嗎？那我們也上網去看看。

生词索引
Vocabulary Index (Chinese–English)

This list contains vocabulary found in each lesson's New Words and Extend Your Knowledge (EYK) sections. Words from Extend Your Knowledge are shown in color because they are supplementary and not required for students to memorize. For proper nouns, see the Proper Nouns Index.

Simplified	Traditional	Pinyin	Part of Speech	English	Lesson
A					
阿姨		āyí	n.	aunt (mother's sister), *way to address an adult woman*	2.1
爱情	愛情	àiqíng	n.	love between lovers	2.1 EYK
安静	安静	ānjìng	adj./n.	quiet, peaceful; peacefulness	2.3
B					
八九不离十	八九不離十	bā jiǔ bù lí shí	s.p.	pretty close, about right	3.1
芭蕾舞		bāléiwǔ	n.	ballet	3.2
把		bǎ	part.	*a structural particle word*	1.1
白领	白領	báilǐng	n.	white collar (worker)	3.1
班会	班會	bānhuì	n.	class meeting	1.5
班级	班級	bānjí	n.	class	4.5
班委		bānwěi	n.	class council	1.5 EYK

Simplified	Traditional	Pinyin	Part of Speech	English	Lesson
班长	班長	bānzhǎng	n.	class president	1.2
搬家		bānjiā	v.o.	move, move house	1.1
半职		bànzhí	n.	part-time job	3.4 EYK
半决赛	半決賽	bànjuésài	n.	semifinals	4.1 EYK
保护	保護	bǎohù	n./v.	protection; protect	4.3
保守		bǎoshǒu	adj.	conservative	3.5
报道	報道	bàodào	n./v.	(news) report; report	3.6
抱怨		bàoyuàn	n./v.	complaint; complain	1.5
刨子		bàozǐ	n.	peeler	4.2 EYK
背包		bèibāo	n.	backpack	4.4
背书	背書	bèishū	v.o.	recite a lesson from memory	1.3
本来	本來	běnlái	adv.	originally, at first	3.4
变得	變得	biàndé	v.c.	change into	1.2
变化	變化	biànhuà	n./v.	change; change	2.5
遍		biàn	m.w.	*time (frequency) of taking an action*	1.1
辩论队	辯論隊	biànlùn duì	n.	debate club	1.4 EYK
比方说	比方說	bǐfāngshuō	s.p.	for example, for instance	1.4
比如		bǐrú	s.p.	for example, for instance	3.2
笔记本	筆記本	bǐjìběn	n.	notebook	4.4
必修课	必修課	bìxiūkè	n.	required course	1.3
表		biǎo	n.	form	1.3
别墅		biéshù	n.	villa, single family house	4.3
冰箱		bīngxiāng	n.	refrigerator	4.2 EYK
博客		bókè	n.	web log, blog	4.6
不得了		bùdéliǎo	adv.	extremely	2.1
不过	不過	bùguò	conj.	but (informal)	1.5

Simplified	Traditional	Pinyin	Part of Speech	English	Lesson
不一定		bùyīdìng	adv.	not necessarily	4.6
布艺	布藝	bùyì	n.	arts and crafts made of fabrics	4.5 EYK

C

财务委员	財務委員	cáiwù wěiyuán	n.	treasurer	1.5 EYK
菜刀		càidāo	n.	cutting/chopping knife	4.2 EYK
菜地		càidì	n.	vegetable plot	4.3
餐巾纸	餐巾紙	cānjīnzhǐ	n.	paper napkin	4.2
餐饮业	餐飲業	cānyǐnyè	n.	restaurant industry	4.3 EYK
茶壶	茶壺	cháhú	n.	teapot	4.2 EYK
场地	場地	chǎngdì	n.	area, space, place	4.1
超车	超車	chāochē	v.o.	pass a car	3.3 EYK
炒菜锅	炒菜鍋	chǎocàiguō	n.	wok, frying pan	4.2
车道	車道	chēdào	n.	car lane	3.3 EYK
成功		chénggōng	n./v.	success; succeed	1.2
成年人		chéngniánrén	n.	adult	3.3
诚实	誠實	chéngshí	adj.	honest	1.2 EYK
迟到	遲到	chídào	v.	arrive late	3.1 EYK
出产	出產	chūchǎn	n./v.	product; produce	4.2
出生		chūshēng	v.	to be born	1.1
出生率		chūshēnglǜ	n.	birthrate	2.2 EYK
初赛	初賽	chūsài	n.	preliminary	4.1 EYK
初中		chūzhōng	n.	junior middle school	1.1 EYK
储蓄	儲蓄	chǔxù	n./v.	saving; save	3.2 EYK
传统	傳統	chuántǒng	n./adj.	tradition; traditional	2.5
床		chuáng	n.	bed	2.3
次修		cìxiū	n.	minor, secondary field of study	1.3 EYK
刺绣	刺繡	cìxiù	n.	embroidery	4.5 EYK
从来	從來	cónglái	adv.	always, all along	1.3
存钱	存錢	cúnqián	v.o.	deposit money	3.2 EYK

Simplified	Traditional	Pinyin	Part of Speech	English	Lesson
D					
打交道		dǎjiāodào	v.o.	interact with	1.2
大鼻子		dàbízǐ	n.	big nose (foreigner) (slang)	2.4 EYK
大方		dàfāng	adj.	generous	1.2 EYK
大学教育储蓄计划	大學教育儲蓄計劃	dàxuéjiàoyù chǔxùjìhuà	n.	college savings plan	3.2 EYK
大专	大專	dàzhuān	n.	junior college	1.1 EYK
代		dài	n.	generation	2.5
单亲	單親	dānqīn	n.	single parent	2.5
单身	單身	dānshēn	adj.	unmarried, single	2.5
耽误	耽誤	dānwù	v.	delay	3.1 EYK
当	當	dāng	v.	serve as, work as	1.2
导师	導師	dǎoshī	n.	academic adviser (in colleges)	1.3 EYK
倒车	倒車	dàochē	v.o.	back up the car	3.3 EYK
得		dé	v.	get, obtain	4.6
得分		défēn	n.	scores	4.1 EYK
等等		děngděng	pron.	etc., and so on	2.3
地理		dìlǐ	n.	geography	1.3
地区	地區	dìqū	n.	region, area	1.3
第一名		dìyīmíng	n.	first, the first place	2.2
电吹风	電吹風	diànchuīfēng	n.	hair dryer	4.4 EYK
电子	電子	diànzǐ	n.	electronics	3.1
掉头	掉頭	diàotóu	v.o.	make a U turn	3.3 EYK
订婚	訂婚	dìnghūn	v.o.	engaged, engagement	2.1 EYK
丢		diū	v.	lose, be missing	1.6
丢三落四		diū sān là sì	s.p.	forgetful, miss this or that	4.1
懂事		dǒngshì	v.o.	sensible, thoughtful (to describe a child)	2.2

Simplified	Traditional	Pinyin	Part of Speech	English	Lesson
独立	獨立	dúlì	adj./n.	independent; independence	2.2
独生子女	獨生子女	dúshēngzǐnǚ	n.	only child	2.2
多半		duōbàn	n.	majority, most part	2.6
多么	多麼	duōme	adv.	such, how, what	1.1
多数	多數	duōshù	n./adj.	majority; most	2.1
F					
发	發	fā	v.	distribute, issue, give out	3.4
发展	發展	fāzhǎn	n./v.	development; develop	2.4
反正		fǎnzhèng	adv.	anyway, in any case, anyhow	2.2
方法		fāngfǎ	n.	method, means	1.5
防晒霜	防曬霜	fángshàishuāng	n.	sunscreen	4.4 EYK
房地产业	房地產業	fángdìchǎnyè	n.	real estate industry	4.3 EYK
放心		fàngxīn	v.o.	feel relieved, rest assured	2.2
肥皂		féizào	n.	soap	4.4 EYK
分		fēn	v.	divide, separate	4.1
粉领	粉領	fěnlǐng	n.	pink collar (service job)	3.4 EYK
枫糖浆	楓糖漿	fēng tángjiāng	n.	maple syrup	2.4
服务业	服務業	fúwùyè	n.	service industry	4.3 EYK
负责	員責	fùzé	adj.	responsible	1.2 EYK
副修		fùxiū	n.	minor, secondary field of study	1.3 EYK
G					
改		gǎi	v.	correct, change, revise	3.5
感觉	感覺	gǎnjué	n.	feeling	3.3

Simplified	Traditional	Pinyin	Part of Speech	English	Lesson
刚	剛	gāng	adv.	just, just now, just about to	1.3
高鼻子		gāobízi	n.	high nose (foreigner) (slang)	2.4 EYK
高科技产业	高科技產業	gāokējìchǎnyè	n.	high-tech industry	4.3 EYK
个人	個人	gèrén	n.	individual	4.1
个体户	個體戶	gètǐhù	n.	self-employed	3.4 EYK
各		gè	adj.	various, each, every	1.4
根		gēn	m.w.	*for long and thin objects*	3.6
根据	根據	gēnjù	prep.	according to, on the basis of	4.4
工厂	工廠	gōngchǎng	n.	factory	4.3
工业	工業	gōngyè	n.	industry	4.3 EYK
公路		gōnglù	n.	highway	3.3 EYK
公寓		gōngyù	n.	apartment	4.3
供应	供應	gōngyìng	n./v.	supply; supply	4.1
股票		gǔpiào	n.	stock	3.2 EYK
怪		guài	v.	blame	2.2
关灯	關燈	guāndēng	v.o.	turn off light	2.2
关于	關於	guānyú	prep.	about, with regard to	1.5
冠军	冠軍	guànjūn	n.	champion, first place	4.1 EYK
管		guǎn	v.	manage, control, be in charge of	2.2
锅子	鍋子	guōzǐ	n.	pan, pot	4.2
国际学生俱乐部	國際學生俱樂部	guójì xuéshēng jùlèbù	n.	international students club	1.4 EYK
国家队	國家隊	guójiāduì	n.	national (athletic) team	1.4
国外	國外	guówài	n.	abroad, overseas	2.4
过时	過時	guòshí	adj.	outdated	3.5 EYK

Simplified	Traditional	Pinyin	Part of Speech	English	Lesson
H					
汉语俱乐部	漢語俱樂部	Hànyǔ jùlèbù	n.	Chinese club	1.4 EYK
合唱团	合唱團	héchàngtuán	n.	chorus, choir	2.1, 1.4 EYK
合同工		hétónggōng	n.	contract worker	3.4 EYK
后父	後父	hòufù	n.	stepfather	2.5 EYK
后父/继父的孩子	後父/繼父的孩子	hòufù de háizǐ	n.	stepfather's children from previous marriage(s)	2.5 EYK
后果	後果	hòuguǒ	n.	result, consequence	3.5
后母	後母	hòumǔ	n.	stepmother	2.5 EYK
后母/继母的孩子	後母/繼母的孩子	hòumǔ de háizǐ	n.	stepmother's children from previous marriage(s)	2.5 EYK
候补人名单	候補人名單	hòubǔrén míngdān	n.	waiting list	1.3 EYK
互相		hùxiāng	adv.	mutually, each other	1.1
护发素	護發素	hùfàsù	n.	conditioner	4.4 EYK
花		huā	v.	spend	1.5
话剧	話劇	huàjù	n.	modern drama, stage play	1.4
话题	話題	huàtí	n.	topic	1.5
环保	環保	huánbǎo	n.	environmental protection	4.4
环境	環境	huánjìng	n.	environment	1.3
换车道	換車道	huànchēdào	v.o.	change lanes	3.3 EYK
皇帝		huángdì	n.	emperor	2.2
婚礼	婚禮	hūnlǐ	n.	wedding	2.1 EYK
J					
机器人	機器人	jīqìrén	n.	robot	1.4
激进	激進	jījìn	adj.	radical	3.5 EYK

Simplified	Traditional	Pinyin	Part of Speech	English	Lesson
及时	及時	jíshí	adv.	in time, timely	3.1 EYK
急忙		jímáng	adv.	in a hurry, hastily	3.4
极端	極端	jíduān	adj.	extreme	3.5 EYK
计划生育	計劃生育	jìhuàshēngyù	n.	family planning	2.2 EYK
记下来	記下來	jìxiàlai	v.c.	write it down, keep a record	3.2
记帐	記帳	jìzhàng	v.o.	keep accounts, keep books	3.2
纪念馆	紀念館	jìniànguǎn	n.	memorial museum, memorial hall	4.3
技校		jìxiào	n.	vocational school	1.1 EYK
季军	季軍	jìjūn	n.	third place	4.1 EYK
寄		jì	v.	mail	3.2
继父	繼父	jìfù	n.	stepfather	2.5
继母	繼母	jìmǔ	n.	stepmother	2.5
加课	加課	jiākè	v.o.	add a class	1.3
加上		jiāshàng	v.	add	4.2
加油		jiāyóu	v.o.	add fuel, come on, make a greater effort	1.2
家教		jiājiào	n.	tutor	3.4
家长	家長	jiāzhǎng	n.	parent	3.6
驾驶	駕駛	jiàshǐ	v.	drive	3.3
驾驶者	駕駛者	jiàshǐzhě	n.	driver	3.3
驾照	駕照	jiàzhào	abbr.	driver's license	3.3
兼职	兼職	jiānzhí	v.o.	get a part-time job	3.4
剪刀		jiǎndāo	n.	scissors	4.2 EYK
剪纸	剪紙	jiǎnzhǐ	n.	paper cutout	4.5 EYK
建立		jiànlì	v.	establish, set up	2.5
建筑	建築	jiànzhù	n./v.	architecture; build	4.3
建筑业	建築業	jiànzhùyè	n.	construction industry	4.3 EYK

Simplified	Traditional	Pinyin	Part of Speech	English	Lesson
将来	將来	jiānglái	adv./n.	in the future; future	1.1
讲	講	jiǎng	v.	tell	1.3
讲民主	講民主	jiǎng mínzhǔ	v.o.	pay attention to democracy	3.1
讲解	講解	jiǎngjiě	v.	explain, interpret	4.5
讲解员	講解員	jiǎngjiěyuán	n.	guide (for exhibition)	4.5
讲座	講座	jiǎngzuò	n.	lecture	1.5
郊游	郊遊	jiāoyóu	v.	go on an excursion	3.3
教案		jiào'àn	n.	lesson plan	4.5
教授		jiàoshòu	n.	professor	1.1
教务处	教務處	jiàowùchù	n.	academic affairs office	1.3
接待		jiēdài	n./v.	reception; receive	4.5
结婚	結婚	jiéhūn	v.	marry, get married	2.1
介绍人	介紹人	jièshàorén	n.	matchmaker	2.1 EYK
借读	借讀	jièdú	v.	study at a school on a temporary basis	1.1
金领	金領	jīnlǐng	n.	gold collar (corporate executive)	3.4 EYK
金牌		jīnpái	n.	gold medal	4.1 EYK
金融		jīnróng	n.	finance	4.3
紧	緊	jǐn	adj.	tight, close	3.1
紧急	緊急	jǐnjí	adj.	urgent, emergent	3.2
进步	進步	jìnbù	n./v.	progress; advance	1.1
进退两难	進退兩難	jìntuìliǎngnán	s.p.	be in a dilemma, difficult to proceed or to draw back	1.3
精神		jīngshén	n.	spirit, mind, energy	3.6
景泰蓝	景泰藍	jǐngtàilán	n.	cloisonné enamel	4.5 EYK
竞赛	競賽	jìngsài	n.	competition, contest	4.6
竞选	競選	jìngxuǎn	v.	campaign for, run for	1.2
竞争	競爭	jìngzhēng	n./v.	competition; compete	2.3

Simplified	Traditional	Pinyin	Part of Speech	English	Lesson
镜子	鏡子	jìngzǐ	n.	mirror	4.4 EYK
酒席		jiǔxí	n.	banquet	2.1
舅舅		jiùjiù	n.	uncle (mother's brother)	2.1
举行	舉行	jǔxíng	n.	hold, stage	4.2
俱乐部	俱樂部	jùlèbù	n.	club	1.4
剧团	劇團	jùtuán	n.	theatrical company, troupe	3.2
剧院	劇院	jùyuàn	n.	theatre, opera house	3.2
决赛	決賽	juésài	n.	finals	4.1 EYK
爵士乐队	爵士樂隊	juéshì yuèduì	n.	jazz band	1.4 EYK

K

Simplified	Traditional	Pinyin	Part of Speech	English	Lesson
咖啡壶	咖啡壺	kāfēihú	n.	coffeepot	4.2 EYK
开放	開放	kāifàng	adj./v.	open, open-minded; open	4.5
开罐刀	開罐刀	kāiguàndāo	n.	can opener	4.2 EYK
开明	開明	kāimíng	adj.	open-minded	1.2 EYK, 3.5 EYK
开通	開通	kāitōng	adj.	open-minded, liberal	3.5
开玩笑	開玩笑	kāiwánxiào	v.o.	joke, make a joke	1.1
开学	開學	kāixué	v.o.	semester begins	1.6
看法		kànfǎ	n.	opinion, idea	4.5
考察		kǎochá	n./v.	investigation; investigate	4.3
烤肉		kǎoròu	n./v.	barbecue(d) meat, roast(ed) meat	4.2
烤箱		kǎoxiāng	n.	oven (for baking, roasting)	4.2
科学兴趣小组	科學興趣小組	kēxué xìngqù xiǎozǔ	n.	science club	1.4 EYK

Simplified	Traditional	Pinyin	Part of Speech	English	Lesson
客车	客車	kèchē	n.	bus (charter)	4.4
客气	客氣	kèqì	adj.	polite, courteous	1.2 EYK
课时	課時	kèshí	n.	class/course meeting hours	1.3 EYK
空气	空氣	kōngqì	n.	air	4.3
口		kǒu	m.w.	*for number of people in a family*	2.3
口算		kǒusuàn	v.	say the result aloud after solving a math problem in one's head	4.6
口音		kǒuyīn	n.	accent	2.4
哭		kū	v.	cry	2.3
跨国	跨國	kuàguó	adj.	multinational, transnational	2.4

L

Simplified	Traditional	Pinyin	Part of Speech	English	Lesson
拉杆箱	拉桿箱	lāgānxiāng	n.	wheeled luggage	4.4
啦啦队	啦啦隊	lālāduì	n.	cheerleading squad	1.4 EYK
蜡染	蠟染	làrǎn	n.	wax printing	4.5 EYK
来得及	來得及	lái de jí	v.c.	there is still time, in time for	3.1
来不及	來不及	láibùjí	s.p.	not enough time	3.1 EYK
来自	來自	láizì	v.	come from	2.4
蓝领	藍領	lánlǐng	n.	blue collar (manual work)	3.4 EYK
篮子	籃子	lánzǐ	n.	basket	4.2 EYK
劳动委员	勞動委員	láodòng wěiyuán	n.	work/project chair	1.5 EYK
老		lǎo	adv.	always	3.1
老外		lǎowài	n.	foreigner (*slang*)	2.4 EYK
姥爷	姥爺	lǎoyé	n.	maternal grandfather	2.1

Simplified	Traditional	Pinyin	Part of Speech	English	Lesson
冷门课	冷門課	lěngménkè	n.	unpopular class, a class not in popular demand	1.3 EYK
理财	理財	lǐcái	v.o.	manage finance, manage money	3.2
离婚	離婚	líhūn	v.o.	divorce	2.5
力气	力氣	lìqi	n.	strength	4.1
了		liǎo	part.	*used in potential complements*	1.3
了解		liǎojiě	n./v.	understanding; understand	1.3
临时	臨時	línshí	adj.	temporary	3.3
临时工	臨時工	línshígōng	n.	temporary worker	3.4 EYK
灵活	靈活	línghuó	adj.	flexible, agile	3.4, 1.2 EYK
零工		línggōng	n.	odd jobs	3.4 EYK
零花钱	零花錢	línghuāqián	n.	pocket money, allowance	2.3
零用钱	零用錢	língyòngqián	n.	pocket money	3.2
领导	領導	lǐngdǎo	n./v.	leader, leadership; lead	1.2
另外		lìngwài	adv.	in addition, moreover, besides	2.5
炉子	爐子	lúzǐ	n.	oven (stovetop)	4.2 EYK
路边	路邊	lùbiān	n.	road side	3.3 EYK
路考		lùkǎo	n./v.	road test, driving test; take a road test	3.3
录像	錄像	lùxiàng	n./v.	video; record on video	2.1
乱	亂	luàn	adv.	recklessly, randomly	3.2
论文	論文	lùnwén	n.	research paper, thesis	4.5
旅游车	旅遊車	lǚyóuchē	n.	tour bus	3.3
旅游业	旅遊業	lǚyóuyè	n.	tourism industry	4.3 EYK

Simplified	Traditional	Pinyin	Part of Speech	English	Lesson
律师	律師	lǜshī	n.	lawyer	2.5
绿化	綠化	lǜhuà	n./v.	greenbelt; make area green with plants	4.3

M

Simplified	Traditional	Pinyin	Part of Speech	English	Lesson
码头	碼頭	mǎtóu	n.	dock	4.3
满	滿	mǎn	adj.	full	1.3
美术社	美術社	měishù shè	n.	fine arts club	1.4 EYK
秘密		mìmì	n.	secret	1.6
棉签	棉籤	miánqiān	n.	cotton swab	4.4 EYK
棉球		miánqiú	n.	cotton ball	4.4 EYK
免费	免費	miǎnfèi	adj.	free, free of charge	3.5
面包车	麵包車	miànbāochē	n.	van	4.3
面霜		miànshuāng	n.	facial cream	4.4 EYK
面纸	面紙	miànzhǐ	n.	facial tissue	4.4 EYK
木雕		mùdiāo	n.	wood carving	4.5 EYK

N

Simplified	Traditional	Pinyin	Part of Speech	English	Lesson
奶油		nǎiyóu	n.	cream	2.4
男朋友		nánpéngyǒu	n.	boyfriend	2.1 EYK
男子个人赛	男子個人賽	nánzǐgèrénsài	n.	men's individual competition	4.1 EYK
男子团体赛	男子團體賽	nánzǐtuántǐsài	n.	men's team competition	4.1 EYK
难道	難道	nándào	adv.	can it be that… (used in a question for emphasis)	2.2
难忘	難忘	nánwàng	adj.	unforgettable	1.2
能干	能幹	nénggàn	adj.	capable, competent	1.2
泥人		nírén	n.	clay figurine	4.5 EYK

Simplified	Traditional	Pinyin	Part of Speech	English	Lesson
年代		niándài	n.	decade of a century, years, time	4.3
年龄		niánlíng	n.	age	2.1
年级	年級	niánjí	n.	grade, year (in school)	3.4
年轻	年輕	niánqīng	adj.	young	2.5
农村	農村	nóngcūn	n.	countryside, rural area	2.6
农业	農業	nóngyè	n.	agriculture	4.2
努力		nǔlì	adj./v.	hard-working; work hard	1.2
女朋友		nǔpéngyǒu	n.	girlfriend	2.1 EYK
女子个人赛	女子個人賽	nǔzǐgèrénsài	n.	women's individual competition	4.1 EYK
女子团体赛	女子團體賽	nǔzǐtuántǐsài	n.	women's team competition	4.1 EYK

P

Simplified	Traditional	Pinyin	Part of Speech	English	Lesson
怕		pà	v.	fear, worry	2.2
排名		páimíng	n.	ranking	4.1 EYK
排球		páiqiú	n.	volleyball	4.1
跑车	跑車	pǎochē	n.	sports car	3.3
培训	培訓	péixùn	n./v.	training; train	3.3
皮鞋		píxié	n.	leather shoes	4.4
票价	票價	piàojià	n.	ticket price	3.2
乒乓球		pīngpāngqiú	n.	table tennis, ping-pong	4.1

Q

Simplified	Traditional	Pinyin	Part of Speech	English	Lesson
七嘴八舌		qīzuǐbāshé	s.p.	all talking at once	4.2
妻子		qīzǐ	n.	wife	2.6
其实	其實	qíshí	adv.	actually, in reality, in fact	3.5
起动	起動	qǐdòng	v.	start the car	3.3 EYK

Simplified	Traditional	Pinyin	Part of Speech	English	Lesson
气候	氣候	qìhòu	n.	climate	4.2
器材		qìcái	n.	equipment	4.1
签名	簽名	qiānmíng	n./v.	signature; sign	1.3 EYK
前夫		qiánfū	n.	ex-husband	2.5 EYK
前六名		qiánliùmíng	n.	the top six	4.1 EYK
前妻		qiánqī	n.	ex-wife	2.5 EYK
前卫	前衛	qiánwèi	adj.	forward-thinking	3.5 EYK
亲姐妹	親姊妹	qīnjiěmèi	n.	sisters of the same parents	2.5 EYK
亲戚	親戚	qīnqi	n.	relatives	2.1
亲兄弟	親兄弟	qīnxiōngdì	n.	brothers of the same parents	2.5 EYK
青少年		qīngshàonián	n.	teenager	3.1
轻工业	輕工業	qīnggōngyè	n.	light industry	4.3 EYK
轻松	輕鬆	qīngsōng	adj.	relaxing, relaxed, light	1.4
球类	球類	qiúlèi	n.	category of ball games	4.1
球拍		qiúpāi	n.	racket, bat	4.1
球鞋		qiúxié	n.	sports shoes	4.4
取钱	取錢	qǔqián	v.o.	withdraw money	3.2 EYK
取消		qǔxiāo	n./v.	cancellation; cancel	1.3 EYK
全		quán	adj./adv.	entire; all, complete	4.5
全职		quánzhí	n.	full-time job	3.4 EYK
全家福		quánjiāfú	n.	photograph of the whole family	2.3
全天		quántiān	n.	all day, full time	3.4

R

热门课	熱門課	rèménkè	n.	popular class, a class in popular demand	1.3 EYK
热闹	熱鬧	rènao	adj.	lively, full of noise and excitement	2.1

Simplified	Traditional	Pinyin	Part of Speech	English	Lesson
热情	熱情	rèqíng	adj.	warm	1.2 EYK
热心	熱心	rèxīn	adj.	warmhearted	1.2 EYK
人口		rénkǒu	n.	population	2.2 EYK
认真	認真	rènzhēn	adj./adv.	conscientious(ly), serious(ly)	1.5, 1.2 EYK

S

Simplified	Traditional	Pinyin	Part of Speech	English	Lesson
商业	商業	shāngyè	n.	commerce, business	4.3
少生		shǎoshēng	n.	fewer births	2.2 EYK
社		shè	n.	organization	1.4
社区	社區	shèqū	n.	community	1.2
社团	社團	shètuán	n.	club, organization	1.4
摄影兴趣小组	攝影興趣小組	shèyǐng xìngqù xiǎozǔ	n.	photography club	1.4 EYK
绳子	繩子	shéngzǐ	n.	rope, string	3.6
生父		shēngfù	n.	birth father	2.5 EYK
生活委员	生活委員	shēnghuó wěiyuán	n.	logistics chair	1.5 EYK
生母		shēngmǔ	n.	birth mother	2.5 EYK
剩		shèng	v.	remain, be left over	3.2
诗歌社	詩歌社	shīgē shè	n.	poetry club	1.4 EYK
石雕		shídiāo	n.	stone carving	4.5 EYK
时代	時代	shídài	n.	time, era	3.1
实验	實驗	shíyàn	n./v.	experiment	4.5
食		shí	n./v.	food; eat	4.2
食品		shípǐn	n.	food, food item	4.2
式		shì	n.	style, type	4.3
世纪	世紀	shìjì	n.	century	4.3
适时	適時	shìshí	adv.	timely	3.1 EYK
收		shōu	v.	accept, admit, receive	3.3
手工业	手工業	shǒugōngyè	n.	handicraft industry	4.3 EYK

Simplified	Traditional	Pinyin	Part of Speech	English	Lesson
守旧	守舊	shǒujiù	v.	sticks to the old ways	3.5 EYK
首		shǒu	m.w.	*for songs and poems*	2.1
受		shòu	v.	receive, bear, endure	1.2
受到		shòudào	v.	be subject to	3.5
书法	書法	shūfǎ	n.	Chinese calligraphy	4.5 EYK
书画	書畫	shūhuà	n.	calligraphy and painting	4.5
梳子		shūzǐ	n.	comb	4.4
数	數	shǔ	v.	count	2.3
漱口液		shùkǒuyè	n.	mouthwash	4.4 EYK
水壶	水壺	shuǐhú	n.	water kettle	4.2 EYK
水墨画	水墨畫	shuǐmòhuà	n.	ink painting	4.5 EYK
算		suàn	v.	be counted as, be considered as	2.4
算了		suàn le	s.p.	forget it, leave it at that	3.3
虽然	雖然	suīrán	conj.	although, though	2.3
随和	隨和	suíhé	adj.	amiable, easygoing	1.2 EYK
孙女	孫女	sūnnǚ	n.	granddaughter	2.5
孙子	孫子	sūnzǐ	n.	grandson	2.5
所有		suǒyǒu	adj.	(including) all	4.5

T

Simplified	Traditional	Pinyin	Part of Speech	English	Lesson
谈		tán	v.	speak, talk, discuss	1.5
谈恋爱	談戀愛	tán liàn'ài	v.o.	date	2.1
讨论	討論	tǎolùn	n./v.	discussion; discuss	1.5
特点	特點	tèdiǎn	n.	special feature	4.2
提前		tíqián	v./adv.	arrive ahead of time; ahead of time	3.1 EYK
提醒		tíxǐng	v.	remind	3.5
提早		tízǎo	v./adv.	arrive ahead of time; ahead of time	3.1 EYK

Simplified	Traditional	Pinyin	Part of Speech	English	Lesson
体操	體操	tǐcāo	n.	gymnastics	4.1
体育委员	體育委員	tǐyù wěiyuán	n.	sports chair	1.5 EYK
剃须刀	剃須刀	tìxūdāo	n.	razor	4.4 EYK
剃须膏	剃須膏	tìxūgāo	n.	shaving cream	4.4 EYK
田径	田徑	tiánjìng	n.	track and field	4.1
甜点	甜點	tiándiǎn	n.	dessert	2.4
甜言蜜语	甜言蜜語	tiányánmìyǔ	s.p.	sweet words, speak sweet words	1.1
填写	填寫	tiánxiě	v.	fill in (a form)	1.3
听取	聽取	tīngqǔ	v.	listen to	4.5
听上去	聽上去	tīngshàngqu	s.p.	sound, sound like	1.4
停车	停車	tíngchē	v.o.	park (a car)	3.3
通过	通過	tōngguò	v./prep.	pass; through, by means of	3.3
同		tóng	adj.	same	2.5
同时	同時	tóngshí	adv.	simultaneously, at the same time	4.1
同意		tóngyì	n./v.	agreement; agree	2.4
铜牌	銅牌	tóngpái	n.	bronze medal	4.1 EYK
投（票）		tóu (piào)	v.	cast (a vote)	1.2
投资	投資	tóuzī	n./v.	investment; invest	3.2 EYK
图片	圖片	túpiàn	n.	picture	1.6
团体	團體	tuántǐ	n.	group, team	4.1
推迟	推遲	tuīchí	v.	postpone	3.1 EYK
退出		tuìchū	v.c.	withdraw (from)	1.4
退课	退課	tuìkè	v.o.	drop a class	1.3
拖鞋		tuōxié	n.	slippers	4.4

W

外国客人	外國客人	wàiguókèrén	n.	foreign guest (foreigner)	2.4 EYK

Simplified	Traditional	Pinyin	Part of Speech	English	Lesson
外国朋友	外國朋友	wàiguópéngyǒu	n.	foreign friend (foreigner)	2.4 EYK
外国人	外國人	wàiguórén	n.	foreigner	2.4
外国人	外國人	wàiguórén	n.	foreigner	2.4 EYK
外联委员	外聯委員	wàilián wěiyuán	n.	public relations chair	1.5 EYK
外向		wàixiàng	adj.	extroverted	1.4
晚到		wǎndào	v.	arrive late	3.1 EYK
晚婚		wǎnhūn	n.	later marriage	2.2 EYK
晚生		wǎnshēng	n.	later childbirth	2.2 EYK
万无一失	萬無一失	wàn wú yī shī	s.p.	not a chance of an error, perfectly safe	3.1
网页	網頁	wǎngyè	n.	web page	3.4
微波炉	微波爐	wēibōlú	n.	microwave oven	4.2
为人处事	為人處世	wéirénchǔshì	s.p.	the way to conduct oneself and deal with others	1.2
卫生委员	衛生委員	wèishēng wěiyuán	n.	health chair	1.5 EYK
卫生纸	衛生紙	wèishēngzhǐ	n.	toilet paper	4.4 EYK
未婚		wèihūn	adj.	unmarried, single	2.1 EYK
温和		wēnhé	adj.	moderate	3.5 EYK
文学社	文學社	wénxué shè	n.	literary arts club	1.4 EYK
文娱委员	文娛委員	wényù wěiyuán	n.	recreational activities chair	1.5 EYK
午餐		wǔcān	n.	lunch	3.5

X

西方人		Xīfāngrén	n.	Westerner	2.4 EYK
希望		xīwàng	n./v.	hope; hope	1.1
洗发液	洗發液	xǐfàyè	n.	shampoo	4.4 EYK
洗手液		xǐshǒuyè	n.	hand soap	4.4 EYK

Simplified	Traditional	Pinyin	Part of Speech	English	Lesson
洗漱		xǐshù	v.	wash one's face and rinse one's mouth	4.4
洗碗机	洗碗機	xǐwǎnjī	n.	dishwasher	4.2 EYK
戏剧	戲劇	xìjù	n.	drama, theater, play	1.4
吓一跳	嚇一跳	xiàyītiào	v.o.	be startled, be frightened	3.5
先生		xiānsheng	n.	Mr. (title), teacher, husband	3.4
现金	現金	xiànjīn	n.	cash	3.2 EYK
现金卡	現金卡	xiànjīnkǎ	n.	debit card	3.2 EYK
香肠	香腸	xiāngcháng	n.	sausage	2.4
香水		xiāngshuǐ	n.	perfume	4.4 EYK
想起来	想起來	xiǎngqǐlai	v.c.	think of, remember, recall	3.4
项目	項目	xiàngmù	n.	item, (sports) event	4.1
消息		xiāoxí	n.	news	3.6
小区	小區	xiǎoqū	n.	complex, residential area	3.4
小组	小組	xiǎozǔ	n.	small group	1.4
校外		xiàowài	n.	out of school, off campus	4.3
新意		xīnyì	n.	novel ideas, fresh ideas	4.2
信		xìn	v.	believe	1.5
信		xìn	n.	letter	2.1
信用卡		xìnyòngkǎ	n.	credit card	3.2 EYK
行程		xíngchéng	n.	itinerary	4.4
幸运	幸運	xìngyùn	adj./n.	fortunate, lucky; fortune, luck	1.1
休息室		xiūxīshì	n.	lounge, break room	4.1
选	選	xuǎn	v.	elect, select	1.2
选举	選舉	xuǎnjǔ	n./v.	election; elect	4.2

Simplified	Traditional	Pinyin	Part of Speech	English	Lesson
选修课	選修課	xuǎnxiūkè	n.	elective course	1.3
学分	學分	xuéfēn	n.	units of credit	1.3 EYK
学生报社	學生報社	xuéshēng bàoshè	n.	student newspaper	1.4 EYK
学生辅导员	學生輔導員	xuéshēng fǔdǎoyuán	n.	academic counselor (in secondary schools)	1.3 EYK
学习委员	學習委員	xuéxí wěiyuán	n.	academic chair	1.5 EYK

Y

Simplified	Traditional	Pinyin	Part of Speech	English	Lesson
压力	壓力	yālì	n.	pressure, stress	1.5
牙膏		yágāo	n.	toothpaste	4.4
牙签	牙籤	yáqiān	n.	toothpick	4.4 EYK
牙刷		yáshuā	n.	toothbrush	4.4
牙线	牙線	yáxiàn	n.	dental floss	4.4 EYK
亚军	亞軍	yàjūn	n.	second place	4.1 EYK
呀		ya	aux.w.	a variant of 啊	1.5
严	嚴	yán	adj.	strict, rigorous, stern	2.2
研究		yánjiū	n./v.	research; do research	1.1
演		yǎn	v.	act (in a play/movie)	1.4
演讲	演講	yǎnjiǎng	n./v.	speech, lecture; give a speech	1.2
演员	演員	yǎnyuán	n.	actor (in a play/movie)	1.4
眼镜	眼鏡	yǎnjìng	n.	eyeglasses, spectacles	1.6
洋人		yángrén	n.	Westerners	2.4 EYK
要不然		yàobùrán	conj.	otherwise, or, or else	3.2
夜市		yèshì	n.	night market	4.4
夜总会	夜總會	yèzǒnghuì	n.	nightclub	3.1
一心一意		yī xīn yī yì	s.p.	wholeheartedly, devote wholly to	2.1
一言中的		yī yán zhòng dì	s.p.	right on target, right to the point	1.5

Simplified	Traditional	Pinyin	Part of Speech	English	Lesson
一次性		yīcìxìng	adj./n.	disposable; one time	4.4
一面		yīmiàn	n.	one side	3.5
一直		yīzhí	adv.	always, continuously	1.1
医药业	醫藥業	yīyàoyè	n.	pharmaceutical industry	4.3 EYK
移民		yímín	n./v.	immigrant, immigration; immigrate	2.4
已婚		yǐhūn	adj.	married	2.1 EYK
以为	以為	yǐwéi	v.	assume, think, believe	3.4
以下		yǐxià	prep.	below, under	4.4
异	異	yì	adj.	different	2.5
意见	意見	yìjiàn	n.	opinion, view, idea	2.3
银行卡	銀行卡	yínhángkǎ	n.	bank card	3.2 EYK
银牌	銀牌	yínpái	n.	silver medal	4.1 EYK
赢		yíng	v.	win	4.6
影响	影響	yǐngxiǎng	n./v.	influence; affect	3.4
勇敢		yǒnggǎn	adj.	brave	1.2 EYK
优点	優點	yōudiǎn	n.	merit, strong point, virtue	1.2
优生	優生	yōushēng	n.	healthier childbirth	2.2 EYK
优育	優育	yōuyù	n.	better childrearing	2.2 EYK
幽默		yōumò	adj.	humorous	1.2 EYK
由		yóu	prep.	by	3.1
友好		yǒuhǎo	adj.	friendly	1.6, 1.2 EYK
于	於	yú	prep.	in, at (a time, place)	4.4
羽毛球		yǔmáoqiú	n.	badminton	4.1
玉雕		yùdiāo	n.	jade carving	4.5 EYK
娱乐业	娛樂業	yùlèyè	n.	entertainment industry	4.3 EYK

Simplified	Traditional	Pinyin	Part of Speech	English	Lesson
愿意	願意	yuànyì	o.v.	be willing to	3.4
约会	約會	yuēhuì	n.	appointment, meeting	2.1 EYK
月初		yuèchū	n.	beginning of a month	3.2
月底		yuèdǐ	n.	end of a month	3.2
阅览室	閱覽室	yuèlǎnshì	n.	reading room	4.5
越		yuè	adv.	more	1.5
越来越	越來越	yuèláiyuè	adv.	more and more	2.4
运动会	運動會	yùndònghuì	n.	sports meet	4.1
运动员	運動員	yùndòngyuán	n.	athlete	1.4

Z

再婚		zàihūn	v.o.	remarry	2.5
早到		zǎodào	v.	arrive early	3.1 EYK
早退		zǎotuì	v.	leave early	3.1 EYK
造		zào	v.	build	4.3
责任	責任	zérèn	n.	responsibility	3.5
增长	增長	zēngzhǎng	n./v.	increase; increase	2.2 EYK
展览	展覽	zhǎnlǎn	n./v.	exhibition; exhibit	4.5
长大	長大	zhǎngdà	v.c.	grow up	3.5
账户	帳戶	zhànghù	n.	account	3.2 EYK
招		zhāo	v.	recruit, enroll	3.4
招生		zhāoshēng	v.o.	admit students	4.5
照顾	照顧	zhàogù	v.	care for, look after	1.6
这样	這樣	zhèyàng	adv.	in this way, like this	2.1
砧板		zhēnbǎn	n.	cutting board	4.2 EYK
蒸笼	蒸籠	zhēnglóng	n.	steamer	4.2
正式		zhèngshì	adj.	official, formal	3.3
正直		zhèngzhí	adj.	honest, fair and just	1.2 EYK
挣	掙	zhèng	v.	earn (money)	3.2
之一		zhī yī	s.p.	one of . . .	4.2

Simplified	Traditional	Pinyin	Part of Speech	English	Lesson
之间	之間	zhījiān	prep.	between	3.2
支票		zhīpiào	n.	check	3.2 EYK
直爽		zhíshuǎng	adj.	candid, straightforward	1.2 EYK
直线	直線	zhíxiàn	n.	straight line	3.3 EYK
只有…才…		zhǐyǒu … cái …	conj.	only … then …	1.2
中庸		zhōngyōng	adj.	middle of the road, moderate	3.5 EYK
钟点工	鍾點工	zhōngdiǎngōng	n.	hourly worker	3.4 EYK
重点	重點	zhòngdiǎn	n.	emphasis, focal point	4.1
重工业	重工業	zhònggōngyè	n.	heavy industry	4.3 EYK
重视	重視	zhòngshì	v.	take something seriously, value	4.2
重要		zhòngyào	adj.	important, essential	1.2
周年	週年	zhōunián	n.	anniversary	2.1
主修		zhǔxiū	n.	major, major field of study	1.3 EYK
主意		zhǔyì	n.	idea	4.1
注册	註冊	zhùcè	n./v.	registration; register for a class	1.3 EYK
注册表	註冊表	zhùcèbiǎo	n.	registration form	1.3 EYK
专业	專業	zhuānyè	n.	major, major field of study	1.3 EYK
转弯 / 拐弯	轉彎 / 拐彎	zhuǎnwān/ guǎiwān	v.	make a turn	3.3 EYK
转学	轉學	zhuǎnxué	v.o.	transfer to another school	1.1
篆刻		zhuànkè	n.	seal cutting	4.5 EYK
追		zhuī	v.	chase after, catch up with	2.3

Simplified	Traditional	Pinyin	Part of Speech	English	Lesson
准确	準確	zhǔnquè	adj./n.	accurate; accuracy	4.6
准时	準時	zhǔnshí	adv.	on time	3.1 EYK
桌(子)		zhuō(zi)	n.	table	2.3
自信		zìxìn	adj.	self-confident	1.2 EYK
自由		zìyóu	adj./n.	free; freedom	1.4
自由职业	自由職業	zìyóuzhíyè	n.	freelance	3.4 EYK
自愿	自願	zìyuàn	v.	volunteer	4.5
祖祖辈辈	祖祖輩輩	zǔzǔbèibèi	n.	for generations, from generation to generation	2.4
最近		zuìjìn	adj./adv.	recent; recently	2.5
作文		zuòwén	n.	composition	4.5
座		zuò	m.w.	*for mountains, large buildings*	4.3
座谈	座談	zuòtán	v.	discuss freely	4.5
座谈会	座談會	zuòtánhuì	n.	free discussion	4.5
做客		zuòkè	v.o.	be a guest, be a visitor	2.2
做梦	作夢	zuòmèng	v.o.	dream	3.3

生词索引
Vocabulary Index
(English–Chinese)

This list contains vocabulary found in each lesson's New Words and Extend Your Knowledge (EYK) sections. Words from Extend Your Knowledge are shown in color because they are supplementary and not required for students to memorize. For proper nouns, see the Proper Nouns Index.

English	Simplified	Traditional	Pinyin	Part of Speech	Lesson
A					
about, with regard to	关于	關於	guānyú	prep.	1.5
abroad, overseas	国外	國外	guówài	n.	2.4
academic adviser (in colleges)	导师	導師	dǎoshī	n.	1.3 EYK
academic affairs office	教务处	教務處	jiàowùchù	n.	1.3
academic chair	学习委员	學習委員	xuéxí wěiyuán	n.	1.5 EYK
academic counselor (in secondary schools)	学生辅导员	學生輔導員	xuéshēng fǔdǎoyuán	n.	1.3 EYK
accent	口音		kǒuyīn	n.	2.4
accept, admit, receive	收		shōu	v.	3.3
according to, on the basis of	根据	根據	gēnjù	prep.	4.4
account	账户	帳戶	zhànghù	n.	3.2 EYK
accurate; accuracy	准确	準確	zhǔnquè	adj./n.	4.6

English	Simplified	Traditional	Pinyin	Part of Speech	Lesson
act (in a play/movie)	演		yǎn	v.	1.4
actor (in a play/ movie)	演员	演員	yǎnyuán	n.	1.4
actually, in reality, in fact	其实	其實	qíshí	adv.	3.5
add	加上		jiāshàng	v.	4.2
add a class	加课	加課	jiākè	v.o.	1.3
add fuel, come on, make a greater effort	加油		jiāyóu	v.o.	1.2
admit students	招生		zhāoshēng	v.o.	4.5
adult	成年人		chéngniánrén	n.	3.3
age	年龄		niánlíng	n.	2.1
agreement; agree	同意		tóngyì	n./v.	2.4
agriculture	农业	農業	nóngyè	n.	4.2
air	空气	空氣	kōngqì	n.	4.3
(including) all	所有		suǒyǒu	adj.	4.5
all day, full time	全天		quántiān	n.	3.4
all talking at once	七嘴八舌		qīzuǐbāshé	s.p.	4.2
although, though	虽然	雖然	suīrán	cónj.	2.3
always	老		lǎo	adv.	3.1
always, all along	从来	從來	cónglái	adv.	1.3
always, continuously	一直		yīzhí	adv.	1.1
amiable, easygoing	随和	隨和	suíhé	adj.	1.2 EYK
anniversary	周年	週年	zhōunián	n.	2.1
anyway, in any case, anyhow	反正		fǎnzhèng	adv.	2.2
apartment	公寓		gōngyù	n.	4.3
appointment, meeting	约会	約會	yuēhuì	n.	2.1 EYK

English	Simplified	Traditional	Pinyin	Part of Speech	Lesson
architecture; build	建筑	建築	jiànzhù	n./v.	4.3
area, space, place	场地	場地	chǎngdì	n.	4.1
arrive ahead of time; ahead of time	提前		tíqián	v./adv.	3.1 EYK
arrive ahead of time; ahead of time	提早		tízǎo	v./adv.	3.1 EYK
arrive early	早到		zǎodào	v.	3.1 EYK
arrive late	迟到	遲到	chídào	v.	3.1 EYK
arrive late	晚到		wǎndào	v.	3.1 EYK
arts and crafts made of fabrics	布艺	布藝	bùyì	n.	4.5 EYK
assume, think, believe	以为	以為	yǐwéi	v.	3.4
athlete	运动员	運動員	yùndòngyuán	n.	1.4
aunt (mother's sister), *way to address an adult woman*	阿姨		āyí	n.	2.1
auxiliary word; a variant of 啊	呀		ya	aux.w.	1.5

B

English	Simplified	Traditional	Pinyin	Part of Speech	Lesson
back up the car	倒车	倒車	dàochē	v.o.	3.3 EYK
backpack	背包		bèibāo	n.	4.4
badminton	羽毛球		yǔmáoqiú	n.	4.1
ballet	芭蕾舞		bāléiwǔ	n.	3.2
bank card	银行卡	銀行卡	yínhángkǎ	n.	3.2 EYK
banquet	酒席		jiǔxí	n.	2.1
barbecue(d) meat, roast(ed) meat	烤肉		kǎoròu	n./v.	4.2

English	Simplified	Traditional	Pinyin	Part of Speech	Lesson
basket	篮子	籃子	lánzǐ	n.	4.2 EYK
be a guest, be a visitor	做客		zuòkè	v.o.	2.2
be counted as, be considered as	算		suàn	v.	2.4
be in a dilemma, difficult to proceed or to draw back	进退两难	進退兩難	jìntuìliǎngnán	s.p.	1.3
be startled, be frightened	吓一跳	嚇一跳	xiàyītiào	v.o.	3.5
be subject to	受到		shòudào	v.	3.5
be willing to	愿意	願意	yuànyì	o.v.	3.4
bed	床		chuáng	n.	2.3
beginning of a month	月初		yuèchū	n.	3.2
believe	信		xìn	v.	1.5
below, under	以下		yǐxià	prep.	4.4
better childrearing	优育	優育	yōuyù	n.	2.2 EYK
between	之间	之間	zhījiān	prep.	3.2
big nose (foreigner) (slang)	大鼻子		dàbízǐ	n.	2.4 EYK
birth father	生父		shēngfù	n.	2.5 EYK
birth mother	生母		shēngmǔ	n.	2.5 EYK
birthrate	出生率		chūshēnglǜ	n.	2.2 EYK
blame	怪		guài	v.	2.2
blue collar (manual work)	蓝领	藍領	lánlǐng	n.	3.4 EYK
boyfriend	男朋友		nánpéngyǒu	n.	2.1 EYK
brave	勇敢		yǒnggǎn	adj.	1.2 EYK
bronze medal	铜牌	銅牌	tóngpái	n.	4.1 EYK

English	Simplified	Traditional	Pinyin	Part of Speech	Lesson
brothers of the same parents	亲兄弟	親兄弟	qīnxiōngdì	n.	2.5 EYK
build	造		zào	v.	4.3
bus (charter)	客车	客車	kèchē	n.	4.4
but (informal)	不过	不過	bùguò	conj.	1.5
by	由		yóu	prep.	3.1

C

English	Simplified	Traditional	Pinyin	Part of Speech	Lesson
calligraphy and painting	书画	書畫	shūhuà	n.	4.5
campaign for, run for	竞选	競選	jìngxuǎn	v.	1.2
can it be that… (used in a question for emphasis)	难道	難道	nándào	adv.	2.2
can opener	开罐刀	開罐刀	kāiguàndāo	n.	4.2 EYK
cancellation; cancel	取消		qǔxiāo	n./v.	1.3 EYK
candid, straightforward	直爽		zhíshuǎng	adj.	1.2 EYK
capable, competent	能干	能幹	nénggàn	adj.	1.2
car lane	车道	車道	chēdào	n.	3.3 EYK
care for, look after	照顾	照顧	zhàogù	v.	1.6
cash	现金	現金	xiànjīn	n.	3.2 EYK
cast (a vote)	投（票）		tóu (piào)	v.	1.2
category of ball games	球类	球類	qiúlèi	n.	4.1
century	世纪	世紀	shìjì	n.	4.3
champion, first place	冠军	冠軍	guànjūn	n.	4.1 EYK
change into	变得	變得	biàndé	v.c.	1.2
change lanes	换车道	換車道	huànchēdào	v.o.	3.3 EYK
change; change	变化	變化	biànhuà	n./v.	2.5

English	Simplified	Traditional	Pinyin	Part of Speech	Lesson
chase after, catch up with	追		zhuī	v.	2.3
check	支票		zhīpiào	n.	3.2 EYK
cheerleading squad	啦啦队	啦啦隊	lālāduì	n.	1.4 EYK
Chinese calligraphy	书法	書法	shūfǎ	n.	4.5 EYK
Chinese club	汉语俱乐部	漢語俱樂部	Hànyǔ jùlèbù	n.	1.4 EYK
chorus, choir	合唱团	合唱團	héchàngtuán	n.	2.1, 1.4 EYK
class	班级	班级	bānjí	n.	4.5
class council	班委		bānwěi	n.	1.5 EYK
class meeting	班会	班會	bānhuì	n.	1.5
class president	班长	班長	bānzhǎng	n.	1.2
class/course meeting hours	课时	課時	kèshí	n.	1.3 EYK
clay figurine	泥人		nírén	n.	4.5 EYK
climate	气候	氣候	qìhòu	n.	4.2
cloisonné enamel	景泰蓝	景泰藍	jǐngtàilán	n.	4.5 EYK
club	俱乐部	俱樂部	jùlèbù	n.	1.4
club, organization	社团	社團	shètuán	n.	1.4
coffeepot	咖啡壶	咖啡壺	kāfēihú	n.	4.2 EYK
college savings plan	大学教育储蓄计划	大學教育儲蓄計劃	dàxuéjiàoyù chǔxùjìhuà	n.	3.2 EYK
comb	梳子		shūzǐ	n.	4.4
come from	来自	來自	láizì	v.	2.4
commerce, business	商业	商業	shāngyè	n.	4.3
community	社区	社區	shèqū	n.	1.2
competition, contest	竞赛	競賽	jìngsài	n.	4.6
competition; compete	竞争	競爭	jìngzhēng	n./v.	2.3
complaint; complain	抱怨		bàoyuàn	n./v.	1.5

English	Simplified	Traditional	Pinyin	Part of Speech	Lesson
complex, residential area	小区	小區	xiǎoqū	n.	3.4
composition	作文		zuòwén	n.	4.5
conditioner	护发素	護髮素	hùfàsù	n.	4.4 EYK
conscientious(ly), serious(ly)	认真	認真	rènzhēn	adj./adv.	1.5, 1.2 EYK
conservative	保守		bǎoshǒu	adj.	3.5
construction industry	建筑业	建築業	jiànzhùyè	n.	4.3 EYK
contract worker	合同工		hétónggōng	n.	3.4 EYK
correct, change, revise	改		gǎi	v.	3.5
cotton ball	棉球		miánqiú	n.	4.4 EYK
cotton swab	棉签	棉籤	miánqiān	n.	4.4 EYK
count	数	數	shǔ	v.	2.3
countryside, rural area	农村	農村	nóngcūn	n.	2.6
cream	奶油		nǎiyóu	n.	2.4
credit card	信用卡		xìnyòngkǎ	n.	3.2 EYK
cry	哭		kū	v.	2.3
cutting board	砧板		zhēnbǎn	n.	4.2 EYK
cutting/chopping knife	菜刀		càidāo	n.	4.2 EYK

D

English	Simplified	Traditional	Pinyin	Part of Speech	Lesson
date	谈恋爱	談戀愛	tán liàn'ài	v.o.	2.1
debate club	辩论队	辯論隊	biànlùn duì	n.	1.4 EYK
debit card	现金卡	現金卡	xiànjīnkǎ	n.	3.2 EYK
decade of a century, years, time	年代		niándài	n.	4.3

English	Simplified	Traditional	Pinyin	Part of Speech	Lesson
delay	耽误	耽誤	dānwù	v.	3.1 EYK
dental floss	牙线	牙線	yáxiàn	n.	4.4 EYK
deposit money	存钱	存錢	cúnqián	v.o.	3.2 EYK
dessert	甜点	甜點	tiándiǎn	n.	2.4
development; develop	发展	發展	fāzhǎn	n./v.	2.4
different	异	異	yì	adj.	2.5
discuss freely	座谈	座談	zuòtán	v.	4.5
discussion; discuss	讨论	討論	tǎolùn	n./v.	1.5
dishwasher	洗碗机	洗碗機	xǐwǎnjī	n.	4.2 EYK
disposable; one time	一次性		yīcìxìng	adj./n.	4.4
distribute, issue, give out	发	發	fā	v.	3.4
divide, separate	分		fēn	v.	4.1
divorce	离婚	離婚	líhūn	v.o.	2.5
dock	码头	碼頭	mǎtóu	n.	4.3
drama, theater, play	戏剧	戲劇	xìjù	n.	1.4
dream	做梦	作夢	zuòmèng	v.o.	3.3
drive	驾驶	駕駛	jiàshǐ	v.	3.3
driver	驾驶者	駕駛者	jiàshǐzhě	n.	3.3
driver's license	驾照	駕照	jiàzhào	abbr.	3.3
drop a class	退课	退課	tuìkè	v.o.	1.3

E

English	Simplified	Traditional	Pinyin	Part of Speech	Lesson
earn (money)	挣	掙	zhèng	v.	3.2
elect, select	选	選	xuǎn	v.	1.2
election; elect	选举	選舉	xuǎnjǔ	n./v.	4.2
elective course	选修课	選修課	xuǎnxiūkè	n.	1.3
electronics	电子	電子	diànzǐ	n.	3.1
embroidery	刺绣	刺繡	cìxiù	n.	4.5 EYK

English	Simplified	Traditional	Pinyin	Part of Speech	Lesson
emperor	皇帝		huángdì	n.	2.2
emphasis, focal point	重点	重點	zhòngdiǎn	n.	4.1
end of a month	月底		yuèdǐ	n.	3.2
engaged, engagement	订婚	訂婚	dìnghūn	v.o.	2.1 EYK
entertainment industry	娱乐业	娛樂業	yùlèyè	n.	4.3 EYK
entire; all, complete	全		quán	adj./adv.	4.5
environment	环境	環境	huánjìng	n.	1.3
environmental protection	环保	環保	huánbǎo	n.	4.4
equipment	器材		qìcái	n.	4.1
establish, set up	建立		jiànlì	v.	2.5
etc., and so on	等等		děngděng	pron.	2.3
exhibition; exhibit	展览	展覽	zhǎnlǎn	n./v.	4.5
ex-husband	前夫		qiánfū	n.	2.5 EYK
experiment	实验	實驗	shíyàn	n./v.	4.5
explain, interpret	讲解	講解	jiǎngjiě	v.	4.5
extreme	极端	極端	jíduān	adj.	3.5 EYK
extremely	不得了		bùdéliǎo	adv.	2.1
extroverted	外向		wàixiàng	adj.	1.4
ex-wife	前妻		qiánqī	n.	2.5 EYK
eyeglasses, spectacles	眼镜	眼鏡	yǎnjìng	n.	1.6

F

English	Simplified	Traditional	Pinyin	Part of Speech	Lesson
facial cream	面霜		miànshuāng	n.	4.4 EYK
facial tissue	面纸	面紙	miànzhǐ	n.	4.4 EYK
factory	工厂	工廠	gōngchǎng	n.	4.3
family planning	计划生育	計劃生育	jìhuàshēngyù	n.	2.2 EYK
fear, worry	怕		pà	v.	2.2
feel relieved, rest assured	放心		fàngxīn	v.o.	2.2

English	Simplified	Traditional	Pinyin	Part of Speech	Lesson
feeling	感觉	感覺	gǎnjué	n.	3.3
fewer births	少生		shǎoshēng	n.	2.2 EYK
fill in (a form)	填写	填寫	tiánxiě	v.	1.3
finals	决赛	決賽	juésài	n.	4.1 EYK
finance	金融		jīnróng	n.	4.3
fine arts club	美术社	美術社	měishù shè	n.	1.4 EYK
first, the first place	第一名		dìyīmíng	n.	2.2
flexible, agile	灵活	靈活	línghuó	adj.	3.4, 1.2 EYK
food, food item	食品		shípǐn	n.	4.2
food; eat	食		shí	n./v.	4.2
for example, for instance	比方说	比方說	bǐfāngshuō	s.p.	1.4
for example, for instance	比如		bǐrú	s.p.	3.2
for generations, from generation to generation	祖祖辈辈	祖祖輩輩	zǔzǔbèibèi	n.	2.4
foreign friend (foreigner)	外国朋友	外國朋友	wàiguópéngyǒu	n.	2.4 EYK
foreign guest (foreigner)	外国客人	外國客人	wàiguókèrén	n.	2.4 EYK
foreigner	外国人	外國人	wàiguórén	n.	2.4
foreigner	外国人	外國人	wàiguórén	n.	2.4 EYK
foreigner (slang)	老外		lǎowài	n.	2.4 EYK
forget it, leave it at that	算了		suàn le	s.p.	3.3
forgetful, miss this or that	丢三落四		diū sān là sì	s.p.	4.1
form	表		biǎo	n.	1.3

English	Simplified	Traditional	Pinyin	Part of Speech	Lesson
fortunate, lucky; fortune, luck	幸运	幸運	xìngyùn	adj./n.	1.1
forward-thinking	前卫	前衛	qiánwèi	adj.	3.5 EYK
free discussion	座谈会	座談會	zuòtánhuì	n.	4.5
free, free of charge	免费	免費	miǎnfèi	adj.	3.5
free; freedom	自由		zìyóu	adj./n.	1.4
freelance	自由职业	自由職業	zìyóuzhíyè	n.	3.4 EYK
friendly	友好		yǒuhǎo	adj.	1.6, 1.2 EYK
full	满	滿	mǎn	adj.	1.3
full-time job	全职		quánzhí	n.	3.4 EYK

G

English	Simplified	Traditional	Pinyin	Part of Speech	Lesson
generation	代		dài	n.	2.5
generous	大方		dàfāng	adj.	1.2 EYK
geography	地理		dìlǐ	n.	1.3
get a part-time job	兼职	兼職	jiānzhí	v.o.	3.4
get, obtain	得		dé	v.	4.6
girlfriend	女朋友		nǚpéngyǒu	n.	2.1 EYK
go on an excursion	郊游	郊遊	jiāoyóu	v.	3.3
gold collar (corporate executive)	金领	金領	jīnlǐng	n.	3.4 EYK
gold medal	金牌		jīnpái	n.	4.1 EYK
grade, year (in school)	年级	年級	niánjí	n.	3.4
granddaughter	孙女	孫女	sūnnǚ	n.	2.5
grandson	孙子	孫子	sūnzǐ	n.	2.5
greenbelt; make area green with plants	绿化	綠化	lǜhuà	n./v.	4.3

English	Simplified	Traditional	Pinyin	Part of Speech	Lesson
group, team	团体	團體	tuántǐ	n.	4.1
grow up	长大	長大	zhǎngdà	v.c.	3.5
guide (for exhibition)	讲解员	講解員	jiǎngjiěyuán	n.	4.5
gymnastics	体操	體操	tǐcāo	n.	4.1

H

English	Simplified	Traditional	Pinyin	Part of Speech	Lesson
hair dryer	电吹风	電吹風	diànchuīfēng	n.	4.4 EYK
hand soap	洗手液		xǐshǒuyè	n.	4.4 EYK
handicraft industry	手工业	手工業	shǒugōngyè	n.	4.3 EYK
hard-working; work hard	努力		nǔlì	adj./v.	1.2
health chair	卫生委员	衛生委員	wèishēng wěiyuán	n.	1.5 EYK
healthier childbirth	优生	優生	yōushēng	n.	2.2 EYK
heavy industry	重工业	重工業	zhònggōngyè	n.	4.3 EYK
high nose (foreigner) (slang)	高鼻子		gāobízǐ	n.	2.4 EYK
high-tech industry	高科技产业	高科技產業	gāokējìchǎnyè	n.	4.3 EYK
highway	公路		gōnglù	n.	3.3 EYK
hold, stage	举行	舉行	jǔxíng	n.	4.2
honest	诚实	誠實	chéngshí	adj.	1.2 EYK
honest, fair and just	正直		zhèngzhí	adj.	1.2 EYK
hope; hope	希望		xīwàng	n./v.	1.1
hourly worker	钟点工	鍾點工	zhōngdiǎngōng	n.	3.4 EYK
humorous	幽默		yōumò	adj.	1.2 EYK

I

English	Simplified	Traditional	Pinyin	Part of Speech	Lesson
idea	主意		zhǔyì	n.	4.1
immigrant, immigration; immigrate	移民		yímín	n./v.	2.4

English	Simplified	Traditional	Pinyin	Part of Speech	Lesson
important, essential	重要		zhòngyào	adj.	1.2
in a hurry, hastily	急忙		jímáng	adv.	3.4
in addition, moreover, besides	另外		lìngwài	adv.	2.5
in the future; future	将来	將來	jiānglái	adv./n.	1.1
in this way, like this	这样	這樣	zhèyàng	adv.	2.1
in time, timely	及时	及時	jíshí	adv.	3.1 EYK
in, at (a time, place)	于	於	yú	prep.	4.4
increase; increase	增长	增長	zēngzhǎng	n./v.	2.2 EYK
independent; independence	独立	獨立	dúlì	adj./n.	2.2
individual	个人	個人	gèrén	n.	4.1
industry	工业	工業	gōngyè	n.	4.3 EYK
influence; affect	影响	影響	yǐngxiǎng	n./v.	3.4
ink painting	水墨画	水墨畫	shuǐmòhuà	n.	4.5 EYK
interact with	打交道		dǎjiāodào	v.o.	1.2
international students club	国际学生俱乐部	國際學生俱樂部	guójì xuéshēng jùlèbù	n.	1.4 EYK
investigation; investigate	考察		kǎochá	n./v.	4.3
investment; invest	投资	投資	tóuzī	n./v.	3.2 EYK
item, (sports) event	项目	項目	xiàngmù	n.	4.1
itinerary	行程		xíngchéng	n.	4.4

J

English	Simplified	Traditional	Pinyin	Part of Speech	Lesson
jade carving	玉雕		yùdiāo	n.	4.5 EYK
jazz band	爵士乐队	爵士樂隊	juéshì yuèduì	n.	1.4 EYK
joke, make a joke	开玩笑	開玩笑	kāiwánxiào	v.o.	1.1
junior college	大专	大專	dàzhuān	n.	1.1 EYK
junior middle school	初中		chūzhōng	n.	1.1 EYK

English	Simplified	Traditional	Pinyin	Part of Speech	Lesson
just, just now, just about to	刚	剛	gāng	adv.	1.3

K

keep accounts, keep books	记帐	記帳	jìzhàng	v.o.	3.2

L

later childbirth	晚生		wǎnshēng	n.	2.2 EYK
later marriage	晚婚		wǎnhūn	n.	2.2 EYK
lawyer	律师	律師	lǜshī	n.	2.5
leader, leadership; lead	领导	領導	lǐngdǎo	n./v.	1.2
leather shoes	皮鞋		píxié	n.	4.4
leave early	早退		zǎotuì	v.	3.1 EYK
lecture	讲座	講座	jiǎngzuò	n.	1.5
lesson plan	教案		jiào'àn	n.	4.5
letter	信		xìn	n.	2.1
light industry	轻工业	輕工業	qīnggōngyè	n.	4.3 EYK
listen to	听取	聽取	tīngqǔ	v.	4.5
literary arts club	文学社	文學社	wénxué shè	n.	1.4 EYK
lively, full of noise and excitement	热闹	熱鬧	rènao	adj.	2.1
logistics chair	生活委员	生活委員	shēnghuó wěiyuán	n.	1.5 EYK
lose, be missing	丢		diū	v.	1.6
lounge, break room	休息室		xiūxīshì	n.	4.1
love between lovers	爱情	愛情	àiqíng	n.	2.1 EYK
lunch	午餐		wǔcān	n.	3.5

English	Simplified	Traditional	Pinyin	Part of Speech	Lesson
M					
mail	寄		jì	v.	3.2
major, major field of study	主修		zhǔxiū	n.	1.3 EYK
major, major field of study	专业	專業	zhuānyè	n.	1.3 EYK
majority, most part	多半		duōbàn	n.	2.6
majority; most	多数	多數	duōshù	n./adj.	2.1
make a turn	转弯/拐弯	轉彎/拐彎	zhuǎnwān/guǎiwān	v.	3.3 EYK
make a U turn	掉头	掉頭	diàotóu	v.o.	3.3 EYK
manage finance, manage money	理财	理財	lǐcái	v.o.	3.2
manage, control, be in charge of	管		guǎn	v.	2.2
maple syrup	枫糖浆	楓糖漿	fēng tángjiāng	n.	2.4
married	已婚		yǐhūn	adj.	2.1 EYK
marry, get married	结婚	結婚	jiéhūn	v.	2.1
matchmaker	介绍人	介紹人	jièshàorén	n.	2.1 EYK
maternal grandfather	姥爷	姥爺	lǎoyé	n.	2.1
measure word for long and thin objects	根		gēn	m.w.	3.6
measure word for mountains, large buildings	座		zuò	m.w.	4.3
measure word for number of people in a family	口		kǒu	m.w.	2.3
measure word for songs and poems	首		shǒu	m.w.	2.1

English	Simplified	Traditional	Pinyin	Part of Speech	Lesson
measure word for time (frequency) of taking an action	遍		biàn	m.w.	1.1
memorial museum, memorial hall	纪念馆	紀念館	jìniànguǎn	n.	4.3
men's individual competition	男子个人赛	男子個人賽	nánzǐ gèrénsài	n.	4.1 EYK
men's team competition	男子团体赛	男子團體賽	nánzǐ tuántǐsài	n.	4.1 EYK
merit, strong point, virtue	优点	優點	yōudiǎn	n.	1.2
method, means	方法		fāngfǎ	n.	1.5
microwave oven	微波炉	微波爐	wēibōlú	n.	4.2
middle of the road, moderate	中庸		zhōngyōng	adj.	3.5 EYK
minor, secondary field of study	次修		cìxiū	n.	1.3 EYK
minor, secondary field of study	副修		fùxiū	n.	1.3 EYK
mirror	镜子	鏡子	jìngzǐ	n.	4.4 EYK
mister, teacher, husband	先生		xiānsheng	n.	3.4
moderate	温和		wēnhé	adj.	3.5 EYK
modern drama, stage play	话剧	話劇	huàjù	n.	1.4
more	越		yuè	adv.	1.5
more and more	越来越	越來越	yuèláiyuè	adv.	2.4
mouthwash	漱口液		shùkǒuyè	n.	4.4 EYK
move, move house	搬家		bānjiā	v.o.	1.1
multinational, transnational	跨国	跨國	kuàguó	adj.	2.4

English	Simplified	Traditional	Pinyin	Part of Speech	Lesson
mutually, each other	互相		hùxiāng	adv.	1.1

N

English	Simplified	Traditional	Pinyin	Part of Speech	Lesson
national (athletic) team	国家队	國家隊	guójiāduì	n.	1.4
news	消息		xiāoxí	n.	3.6
night market	夜市		yèshì	n.	4.4
nightclub	夜总会	夜總會	yèzǒnghuì	n.	3.1
not a chance of an error, perfectly safe	万无一失	萬無一失	wàn wú yī shī	s.p.	3.1
not enough time	来不及	來不及	láibùjí	s.p.	3.1 EYK
not necessarily	不一定		bùyīdìng	adv.	4.6
notebook	笔记本	筆記本	bǐjìběn	n.	4.4
novel ideas, fresh ideas	新意		xīnyì	n.	4.2

O

English	Simplified	Traditional	Pinyin	Part of Speech	Lesson
odd jobs	零工		línggōng	n.	3.4 EYK
official, formal	正式		zhèngshì	adj.	3.3
on time	准时	準時	zhǔnshí	adv.	3.1 EYK
one of . . .	之一		zhī yī	s.p.	4.2
one side	一面		yīmiàn	n.	3.5
only . . . then . . .	只有…才…		zhǐyǒu . . . cái…	conj.	1.2
only child	独生子女	獨生子女	dúshēngzǐnǔ	n.	2.2
open, open-minded; open	开放	開放	kāifàng	adj./v.	4.5
open-minded	开明	開明	kāimíng	adj.	1.2 EYK, 3.5 EYK
open-minded, liberal	开通	開通	kāitōng	adj.	3.5
opinion, idea	看法		kànfǎ	n.	4.5

English	Simplified	Traditional	Pinyin	Part of Speech	Lesson
opinion, view, idea	意见	意見	yìjiàn	n.	2.3
organization	社		shè	n.	1.4
originally, at first	本来	本來	běnlái	adv.	3.4
otherwise, or, or else	要不然		yàobùrán	conj.	3.2
out of school, off campus	校外		xiàowài	n.	4.3
outdated	过时	過時	guòshí	adj.	3.5 EYK
oven (for baking, roasting)	烤箱		kǎoxiāng	n.	4.2
oven (stovetop)	炉子	爐子	lúzǐ	n.	4.2 EYK

P

English	Simplified	Traditional	Pinyin	Part of Speech	Lesson
pan, pot	锅子	鍋子	guōzǐ	n.	4.2
paper cutout	剪纸	剪紙	jiǎnzhǐ	n.	4.5 EYK
paper napkin	餐巾纸	餐巾紙	cānjīnzhǐ	n.	4.2
parent	家长	家長	jiāzhǎng	n.	3.6
park (a car)	停车	停車	tíngchē	v.o.	3.3
part-time job	半职		bànzhí	n.	3.4 EYK
particle used in potential complements	了		liǎo	part.	1.3
pass a car	超车	超車	chāochē	v.o.	3.3 EYK
pass; through, by means of	通过	通過	tōngguò	v./prep.	3.3
pay attention to democracy	讲民主	講民主	jiǎng mínzhǔ	v.o.	3.1
peeler	刨子		bàozǐ	n.	4.2 EYK
perfume	香水		xiāngshuǐ	n.	4.4 EYK
pharmaceutical industry	医药业	醫藥業	yīyàoyè	n.	4.3 EYK

English	Simplified	Traditional	Pinyin	Part of Speech	Lesson
photograph of the whole family	全家福		quánjiāfú	n.	2.3
photography club	摄影兴趣小组	攝影興趣小組	shèyǐng xìngqù xiǎozǔ	n.	1.4 EYK
picture	图片	圖片	túpiàn	n.	1.6
pink collar (service job)	粉领	粉領	fěnlǐng	n.	3.4 EYK
pocket money	零用钱	零用錢	língyòngqián	n.	3.2
pocket money, allowance	零花钱	零花錢	línghuāqián	n.	2.3
poetry club	诗歌社	詩歌社	shīgē shè	n.	1.4 EYK
polite, courteous	客气	客氣	kèqì	adj.	1.2 EYK
popular class, a class in popular demand	热门课	熱門課	rèménkè	n.	1.3 EYK
population	人口		rénkǒu	n.	2.2 EYK
postpone	推迟	推遲	tuīchí	v.	3.1 EYK
preliminary	初赛	初賽	chūsài	n.	4.1 EYK
pressure, stress	压力	壓力	yālì	n.	1.5
pretty close, about right	八九不离十	八九不離十	bā jiǔ bù lí shí	s.p.	3.1
product; produce	出产	出產	chūchǎn	n./v.	4.2
professor	教授		jiàoshòu	n.	1.1
progress; advance	进步	進步	jìnbù	n./v.	1.1
protection; protect	保护	保護	bǎohù	n./v.	4.3
public relations chair	外联委员	外聯委員	wàilián wěiyuán	n.	1.5 EYK

Q

English	Simplified	Traditional	Pinyin	Part of Speech	Lesson
quiet, peaceful; peacefulness	安静	安静	ānjìng	adj./n.	2.3

English	Simplified	Traditional	Pinyin	Part of Speech	Lesson
R					
racket, bat	球拍		qiúpāi	n.	4.1
radical	激进	激進	jījìn	adj.	3.5 EYK
ranking	排名		páimíng	n.	4.1 EYK
razor	剃须刀	剃須刀	tìxūdāo	n.	4.4 EYK
reading room	阅览室	閱覽室	yuèlǎnshì	n.	4.5
real estate industry	房地产业	房地產業	fángdìchǎnyè	n.	4.3 EYK
receive, bear, endure	受		shòu	v.	1.2
recent; recently	最近		zuìjìn	adj./adv.	2.5
reception; receive	接待		jiēdài	n./v.	4.5
recite a lesson from memory	背书	背書	bèishū	v.o.	1.3
recklessly, randomly	乱	亂	luàn	adv.	3.2
recreational activities chair	文娱委员	文娱委員	wényù wěiyuán	n.	1.5 EYK
recruit, enroll	招		zhāo	v.	3.4
refrigerator	冰箱		bīngxiāng	n.	4.2 EYK
region, area	地区	地區	dìqū	n.	1.3
registration form	注册表	註冊表	zhùcèbiǎo	n.	1.3 EYK
registration; register for a class	注册	註冊	zhùcè	n./v.	1.3 EYK
relatives	亲戚	親戚	qīnqi	n.	2.1
relaxing, relaxed, light	轻松	輕鬆	qīngsōng	adj.	1.4
remain, be left over	剩		shèng	v.	3.2
remarry	再婚		zàihūn	v.o.	2.5
remind	提醒		tíxǐng	v.	3.5
(news) report; report	报道	報道	bàodào	n./v.	3.6
required course	必修课	必修課	bìxiūkè	n.	1.3
research paper, thesis	论文	論文	lùnwén	n.	4.5

English	Simplified	Traditional	Pinyin	Part of Speech	Lesson
research; do research	研究		yánjiū	n./v.	1.1
responsibility	责任	責任	zérèn	n.	3.5
responsible	负责	負責	fùzé	adj.	1.2 EYK
restaurant industry	餐饮业	餐飲業	cānyǐnyè	n.	4.3 EYK
result, consequence	后果	後果	hòuguǒ	n.	3.5
right on target, right to the point	一言中的		yī yán zhòng dì	s.p.	1.5
road side	路边	路邊	lùbiān	n.	3.3 EYK
road test, driving test; take a road test	路考		lùkǎo	n./v.	3.3
robot	机器人	機器人	jīqìrén	n.	1.4
rope, string	绳子	繩子	shéngzǐ	n.	3.6

S

English	Simplified	Traditional	Pinyin	Part of Speech	Lesson
same	同		tóng	adj.	2.5
sausage	香肠	香腸	xiāngcháng	n.	2.4
saving; save	储蓄	儲蓄	chǔxù	n./v.	3.2 EYK
say the result aloud after solving a math problem in one's head	口算		kǒusuàn	v.	4.6
science club	科学兴趣小组	科學興趣小组	kēxué xìngqù xiǎozǔ	n.	1.4 EYK
scissors	剪刀		jiǎndāo	n.	4.2 EYK
scores	得分		défēn	n.	4.1 EYK
seal cutting	篆刻		zhuànkè	n.	4.5 EYK
second place	亚军	亞軍	yàjūn	n.	4.1 EYK
secret	秘密		mìmì	n.	1.6
self-confident	自信		zìxìn	adj.	1.2 EYK

English	Simplified	Traditional	Pinyin	Part of Speech	Lesson
self-employed	个体户	個體戶	gètǐhù	n.	3.4 EYK
semester begins	开学	開學	kāixué	v.o.	1.6
semifinals	半决赛	半決賽	bànjuésài	n.	4.1 EYK
sensible, thoughtful *(to describe a child)*	懂事		dǒngshì	v.o.	2.2
serve as, work as	当	當	dāng	v.	1.2
service industry	服务业	服務業	fúwùyè	n.	4.3 EYK
shampoo	洗发液	洗發液	xǐfàyè	n.	4.4 EYK
shaving cream	剃须膏	剃須膏	tìxūgāo	n.	4.4 EYK
signature; sign	签名	簽名	qiānmíng	n./v.	1.3 EYK
silver medal	银牌	銀牌	yínpái	n.	4.1 EYK
simultaneously, at the same time	同时	同時	tóngshí	adv.	4.1
single parent	单亲	單親	dānqīn	n.	2.5
sisters of the same parents	亲姐妹	親姊妹	qīnjiěmèi	n.	2.5 EYK
slippers	拖鞋		tuōxié	n.	4.4
small group	小组	小组	xiǎozǔ	n.	1.4
soap	肥皂		féizào	n.	4.4 EYK
sound, sound like	听上去	聽上去	tīngshàngqu	s.p.	1.4
speak, talk, discuss	谈		tán	v.	1.5
special feature	特点	特點	tèdiǎn	n.	4.2
speech, lecture; give a speech	演讲	演講	yǎnjiǎng	n./v.	1.2
spend	花		huā	v.	1.5
spirit, mind, energy	精神		jīngshén	n.	3.6
sports car	跑车	跑車	pǎochē	n.	3.3
sports chair	体育委员	體育委員	tǐyù wěiyuán	n.	1.5 EYK
sports meet	运动会	運動會	yùndònghuì	n.	4.1

English	Simplified	Traditional	Pinyin	Part of Speech	Lesson
sports shoes	球鞋		qiúxié	n.	4.4
start the car	起动	起動	qǐdòng	v.	3.3 EYK
steamer	蒸笼	蒸籠	zhēnglóng	n.	4.2
stepfather	后父	後父	hòufù	n.	2.5 EYK
stepfather	继父	繼父	jìfù	n.	2.5
stepfather's children from previous marriage(s)	后父/继父的孩子	後父/繼父的孩子	hòufù de háizǐ	n.	2.5 EYK
stepmother	后母	後母	hòumǔ	n.	2.5 EYK
stepmother	继母	繼母	jìmǔ	n.	2.5
stepmother's children from previous marriage(s)	后母/继母的孩子	後母/繼母的孩子	hòumǔ de háizǐ	n.	2.5 EYK
sticks to the old ways	守旧	守舊	shǒujiù	v.	3.5 EYK
stock	股票		gǔpiào	n.	3.2 EYK
stone carving	石雕		shídiāo	n.	4.5 EYK
straight line	直线	直線	zhíxiàn	n.	3.3 EYK
strength	力气	力氣	lìqi	n.	4:1
strict, rigorous, stern	严	嚴	yán	adj.	2.2
a structural particle word	把		bǎ	part.	1.1
student newspaper	学生报社	學生報社	xuéshēng bàoshè	n.	1.4 EYK
study at a school on a temporary basis	借读	借讀	jièdú	v.	1.1
style, type	式		shì	n.	4.3
success; succeed	成功		chénggōng	n./v.	1.2
such, how, what	多么	多麼	duōme	adv.	1.1
sunscreen	防晒霜	防曬霜	fángshàishuāng	n.	4.4 EYK
supply; supply	供应	供應	gōngyìng	n./v.	4.1
sweet words, speak sweet words	甜言蜜语	甜言蜜語	tiányánmìyǔ	s.p.	1.1

English	Simplified	Traditional	Pinyin	Part of Speech	Lesson
T					
table	桌（子）		zhuō(zǐ)	n.	2.3
table tennis, ping-pong	乒乓球		pīngpāngqiú	n.	4.1
take something seriously, value	重视	重視	zhòngshì	v.	4.2
teapot	茶壶	茶壺	cháhú	n.	4.2 EYK
teenager	青少年		qīngshàonián	n.	3.1
tell	讲	講	jiǎng	v.	1.3
temporary	临时	臨時	línshí	adj.	3.3
temporary worker	临时工	臨時工	línshígōng	n.	3.4 EYK
the top six	前六名		qiánliùmíng	n.	4.1 EYK
the way to conduct oneself and deal with others	为人处事	為人處世	wéirénchǔshì	s.p.	1.2
theatre, opera house	剧院	劇院	jùyuàn	n.	3.2
theatrical company, troupe	剧团	劇團	jùtuán	n.	3.2
there is still time, in time for	来得及	來得及	lái de jí	v.c.	3.1
think of, remember, recall	想起来	想起來	xiǎngqǐlai	v.c.	3.4
third place	季军	季軍	jìjūn	n.	4.1 EYK
ticket price	票价	票價	piàojià	n.	3.2
tight, close	紧	緊	jǐn	adj.	3.1
time, era	时代	時代	shídài	n.	3.1
timely	适时	適時	shìshí	adv.	3.1 EYK
to be born	出生		chūshēng	v.	1.1
toilet paper	卫生纸	衛生紙	wèishēngzhǐ	n.	4.4 EYK
toothbrush	牙刷		yáshuā	n.	4.4
toothpaste	牙膏		yágāo	n.	4.4

English	Simplified	Traditional	Pinyin	Part of Speech	Lesson
toothpick	牙签	牙籤	yáqiān	n.	4.4 EYK
topic	话题	話題	huàtí	n.	1.5
tour bus	旅游车	旅遊車	lǚyóuchē	n.	3.3
tourist industry	旅游业	旅遊業	lǚyóuyè	n.	4.3 EYK
track and field	田径	田徑	tiánjìng	n.	4.1
tradition; traditional	传统	傳統	chuántǒng	n./adj.	2.5
training; train	培训	培訓	péixùn	n./v.	3.3
transfer to another school	转学	轉學	zhuǎnxué	v.o.	1.1
treasurer	财务委员	財務委員	cáiwù wěiyuán	n.	1.5 EYK
turn off light	关灯	關燈	guāndēng	v.o.	2.2
tutor	家教		jiājiào	n.	3.4

U

English	Simplified	Traditional	Pinyin	Part of Speech	Lesson
uncle (mother's brother)	舅舅		jiùjiù	n.	2.1
understanding; understand	了解		liǎojiě	n./v.	1.3
unforgettable	难忘	難忘	nánwàng	adj.	1.2
units of credit	学分	學分	xuéfēn	n.	1.3 EYK
unmarried, single	单身	單身	dānshēn	adj.	2.5
unmarried, single	未婚		wèihūn	adj.	2.1 EYK
unpopular class, a class not in popular demand	冷门课	冷門課	lěngménkè	n.	1.3 EYK
urgent, emergent	紧急	緊急	jǐnjí	adj.	3.2

V

English	Simplified	Traditional	Pinyin	Part of Speech	Lesson
van	面包车	麵包車	miànbāochē	n.	4.3
various, each, every	各		gè	adj.	1.4

English	Simplified	Traditional	Pinyin	Part of Speech	Lesson
vegetable plot	菜地		càidì	n.	4.3
video; record on video	录像	錄像	lùxiàng	n./v.	2.1
villa, single family house	别墅		biéshù	n.	4.3
vocational school	技校		jìxiào	n.	1.1 EYK
volleyball	排球		páiqiú	n.	4.1
volunteer	自愿	自願	zìyuàn	v.	4.5

W

English	Simplified	Traditional	Pinyin	Part of Speech	Lesson
waiting list	候补人名单	候補人名單	hòubǔrén míngdān	n.	1.3 EYK
warm	热情	熱情	rèqíng	adj.	1.2 EYK
warmhearted	热心	熱心	rèxīn	adj.	1.2 EYK
wash one's face and rinse one's mouth	洗漱		xǐshù	v.	4.4
water kettle	水壶	水壺	shuǐhú	n.	4.2 EYK
wax printing	蜡染	蠟染	làrǎn	n.	4.5 EYK
web log, blog	博客		bókè	n.	4.6
web page	网页	網頁	wǎngyè	n.	3.4
wedding	婚礼	婚禮	hūnlǐ	n.	2.1 EYK
Westerner	西方人		Xīfāngrén	n.	2.4 EYK
Westerners	洋人		yángrén	n.	2.4 EYK
wheeled luggage	拉杆箱	拉桿箱	lāgānxiāng	n.	4.4
white collar (worker)	白领	白領	báilǐng	n.	3.1
wholeheartedly, devote wholly to	一心一意		yī xīn yī yì	s.p.	2.1
wife	妻子		qīzǐ	n.	2.6
win	赢		yíng	v.	4.6
withdraw (from)	退出		tuìchū	v.c.	1.4

English	Simplified	Traditional	Pinyin	Part of Speech	Lesson
withdraw money	取钱	取錢	qǔqián	v.o.	3.2 EYK
wok, frying pan	炒菜锅	炒菜鍋	chǎocàiguō	n.	4.2
women's individual competition	女子个人赛	女子個人賽	nǚzǐgèrénsài	n.	4.1 EYK
women's team competition	女子团体赛	女子團體賽	nǚzǐtuántǐsài	n.	4.1 EYK
wood carving	木雕		mùdiāo	n.	4.5 EYK
work/project chair	劳动委员	勞動委員	láodòng wěiyuán	n.	1.5 EYK
write it down, keep a record	记下来	記下來	jìxiàlai	v.c.	3.2

Y

English	Simplified	Traditional	Pinyin	Part of Speech	Lesson
young	年轻	年輕	niánqīng	adj.	2.5

专有名词索引
Proper Nouns Index

This list contains proper nouns from each lesson's New Words and Extend Your Knowledge sections.

Simplified	Traditional	Pinyin	English	Lesson
A				
阿拉伯		Ālābó	Arabic; Arab	4.6
安吉		Ānjí	a place in Zhejiang province	3.3
澳大利亚	澳大利亞	Àodàlìyà	Australia	4.6
B				
巴西		Bāxī	Brazil	1.2
F				
法国国庆日	法國國慶日	Fǎguó Guóqìngrì	Bastille Day	2.4
夫子庙	夫子廟	Fūzǐmiào	Confucius Temple	4.4
H				
华东	華東	Huádōng	East China	4.4
黄浦公园	黃浦公園	Huángpǔ Gōngyuán	Huangpu Park	4.3
黄浦江		Huángpǔjiāng	Huangpu River	4.3
L				
联合国	聯合國	Liánhéguó	United Nations	2.4
M				
明英		Míngyīng	a personal name	1.1

Simplified	Traditional	Pinyin	English	Lesson
N				
南非		Nánfēi	South Africa	1.2
S				
十月节	十月節	Shíyuèjié	Oktoberfest	2.4
T				
太极拳	太極拳	Tàijíquán	Taiji boxing (Chinese exercise)	1.5
天鹅湖	天鵝湖	Tiān'é Hú	Swan Lake	3.2
W				
外滩		Wàitān	The Bund	4.3
X				
希腊		Xīlà	Greece	4.3
新疆		Xīnjiāng	an autonomous region in China	4.2
新西兰	新西蘭	Xīnxīlán	New Zealand	4.6
Y				
意大利	義大利	Yìdàlì	Italy	1.2
Z				
浙江		Zhèjiāng	a province in China	3.3
钟山风景区	鍾山風景區	Zhōngshān fēngjǐngqū	Zhongshan Scenic Area	4.4

语言注释索引
Language Notes Index

321

Credits

Murray Thomas contributed the following drawings:

5, 17, 27, 37, 38, 39, 55, 57, 58, 62, 63, 85, 92, 101, 111, 114, 125, 127, 156, 162, 163, 165, 170, 171, 172, 179, 180, 181, 182

Yun Zhuang contributed the following photos:

16, 23, 36, 155, 178

Jiaying Howard contributed the following photos:

3, 48, 89, 94, 102, 109, 123, 124, 135, 136, 144, 148, 153, 164, 189, 190, 191, 192, 198, 200, 202

Lanting Xu contributed the following photos and drawing:

47, 75, 81, 82, 138, 146, 182, 188, 200, 207, 219

Jing Chai contributed the following photos:

48, 116, 130, 138, 144

Xuexue Zhuang contributed the following photos:

36, 78, 114

Chuan Zhuang contributed the following photos:

58, 65, 74, 93, 99, 107, 118, 213

洋洋兔动漫

208

About the Authors

Dr. Jiaying Howard is Dean of the Immersion School at a language institute in Monterey, California. Previously, she was Professor of Chinese and Director of the Chinese Studies Program at the Monterey Institute of International Studies. She has more than two decades of experience in teaching Chinese as a foreign language, curriculum development, and teacher training. She has published many articles and books, including several Chinese language textbooks.

Ms. Lanting Xu has been a Chinese language teacher at the Bellarmine College Preparatory in San Jose, California for ten years. She is an active member of the Chinese Language Teachers Association of California and served as an AP° Chinese Exam Scoring Leader. Ms. Xu has also taught at Harvard University, the Monterey Institute of International Studies, and Kenyon College.